THE WAY,
THE WALK,
AND
THE WARFARE
OF THE
BELIEVER

THE WAY,
THE WALK,
AND
THE WARFARE
OF THE
BELIEVER

by
Frederick K. C. Price, Ph.D.

FAITH ONE
PUBLISHING
LOS ANGELES, CALIFORNIA

Unless otherwise indicated, all Scripture quotations are taken from the *King James Version* of the Bible.

The Way, the Walk, and the Warfare of the Believer
ISBN 1-883798-06-X
Copyright © 1994 by
Frederick K.C. Price, Ph.D.
P.O. Box 90000
Los Angeles, CA 90009

Published by Faith One Publishing
7901 South Vermont Avenue
Los Angeles, California 90044

Contents

Introduction ix

1   The Believer's Standing in Grace (Ephesians 1) 1
    Part 1 — Ephesians 1:1-5 1
    Part 2 — Ephesians 1:6-23 16

2   The Believer's Position in Christ (Ephesians 2) ...51
    Part 1 — Ephesians 2:1-8 51
    Part 2 — Ephesians 2:9-22 95

3   The Believer's Ability in Christ (Ephesians 3) 113

4   The Believer's Walk in Christ (Ephesians 4 & 5)...165
    Part 1 — Ephesians 4:1-32 165
    Part 2 — Ephesians 5:1-33 224

5   The Warfare of the Believer (Ephesians 6) 291
    Part 1 — Ephesians 6:1-10 291
    Part 2 — Ephesians 6:11-12 328
    Part 3 — Ephesians 6:13-24 357

End Notes..405

Introduction

The Book of Ephesians was written by Paul during his sojourn in Rome, and it is the first of his prison epistles. There has been some question as to whom the book was originally addressed.

Frankly, to me it does not matter who the actual recipients of this letter to the Church at Ephesus were supposed to be, since the New Testament books are addressed to all Christians everywhere in whatever place and time they live.

However, I do concede the fact that the historical climate at the time they were written might be of some significance in understanding certain passages of any of the epistles. Nonetheless, I take the view that people do not basically change, and what was true of the Ephesians, Corinthians, Philippians, or Romans, when the epistles were written, is essentially true of Christians today.

This commentary is not a scholarly work per se, but rather it is a practical contemporary comment on the verses and Scriptures I believe a Christian can take and apply in order to live that victorious, overcoming life in Christ *now*.

Frederick K.C. Price
Pastor, Crenshaw Christian Center
Los Angeles, California

1

The Believer's Standing in Grace
(Ephesians 1:1-23)

Part 1 — Ephesians 1:1-5

This epistle (or letter) to the Ephesians was originally written to the church at Ephesus. However, the
spiritual principle is that whatever is good for the
church at Ephesus is good for the church at Los
Angeles, the church at London, or the church wherever,
because the Church (meaning everyone who accepts
Jesus Christ as Savior and Lord) was and is a part of the
Body of Christ. Consequently, the teachings that are in
these New Testament books, unless otherwise speci-
fied as relating to a particular time, to a particular
group of people, or to a particular location, apply to all
believers down through the ages, even to this present
day.

The four gospels — Matthew, Mark, Luke, and
John — give an account of the earthly life and ministry
of the Lord Jesus Christ. The Book of Acts gives us the
account of the beginning of the Age of the Holy Spirit or
the Age of the Church, starting from the Day of
Pentecost. The Book of the Revelation is the study of

the end of the ages. All the books between the Acts and the Revelation, from Romans to Jude, are the letters of instructions to the family of God, either to a particular church or to the Body of Christ as a whole, and so it is with the Book of Ephesians.

> **Paul, an apostle of Jesus Christ by the will of God, to the saints which are at Ephesus, and to the faithful in Christ Jesus.**
>
> **(Eph. 1:1)**

We are not at Ephesus, so it is obvious that this aspect of the salutation does not apply to Christians today.

To the Faithful in Christ Jesus

This statement, however, does have reference to the Body of Christ at any time or in any place. If this is not true, then Paul is saying that there is a difference between "the saints" and "the faithful."

As Christians, we are, of course, also known as "the saints." But I believe that the Apostle Paul used the word *faithful* in this verse because as believers down through history follow the instructions in these books of the Bible, we become *the faithful* in that sense. Therefore, we can determine that this book was written to Christians everywhere, at any time, following its original writing.

> **Grace be to you, and peace, from God our Father, and from the Lord Jesus Christ.**
>
> **(Eph. 1:2)**

Notice that Paul says, **"Grace** [that is, God's unmerited favor] **be to you, and peace"** — not from Paul, but **from God.** This means that the peace of God "which passes all understanding" is mine because it comes from God, and the Bible tells me He wants me to have it.

> **Blessed be the God and Father of our Lord Jesus Christ, who hath blessed us with all spiritual blessings in heavenly places in Christ.**
>
> **(Eph. 1:3)**

In the King James Version of the Bible, the word *hath* is an Old English word that means *has*, which designates (in relationship to time) that the action has already taken place.

Consequently, we must *now* (at this point in time) be blessed — not cursed, because it says that **God *has* blessed us!**

I heard someone say one time, "I'm blessed, I'm blessed, I'm blessed. I don't deserve it, but I'm blessed."

I cannot go along with that, because it is not biblical. If we do not deserve to be blessed, why would God bless us? Since the Bible says God has blessed us (meaning all Christians) with all spiritual blessings in heavenly places in Christ Jesus, we must be deserving of the blessing — not necessarily because of anything we personally have done, but because God has deemed it His will and privilege to put His blessings upon us.

Notice something else that this third verse makes very clear. We are not in the process of being blessed,

3

God is not thinking about blessing us. But Paul says, **"who hath** [or has] **blessed us."** That means we are already blessed!

Someone might say, "Well, that's wonderful that God has blessed me with all spiritual blessings in heavenly places, but, Brother Price, I need some blessings down here on Earth. I need a blessing like having my taxes paid. I need a blessing like having a roof over my head. I need a blessing like having an automobile that will run right so that I can get to and from work. I need a blessing like being able to provide clothing and shoes and food for my family. I need a blessing of having a body that is free from sickness, disease, and pain. It is wonderful that I have blessings up there in heavenly places, but what about here on Earth?"

One of the fallacies of the teachings of the traditional church is that it has put off all the blessings of God to "after while, by and by, over there, on the other side." But this is not what is meant in this verse.

To understand what is being said here, we have to reason from the known to the unknown. In other words, we have to go from where we are to where we ought to be.

We have to understand that we are living in a physical, material, three-dimensional world that can be contacted with our physical senses. However, at the center and core of our being we are a spirit. You do not have a spirit — you are one! You have a soul, and you live inside a physical body.

With your spirit, you contact the realm of God who is a Spirit. With your body, through your five senses, you contact the physical and material universe around

4

you. And with your soul, which contains your desires, your will, your emotions, and your intellect, you contact the emotional and intellectual realm. Man can operate in three different worlds at the same time.

In John's gospel, chapter 4, beginning at verse 5, it says that when Jesus and His disciples went to the city of Sychar in Samaria, Jesus stopped at Jacob's well. He sent His disciples into the city to get some food. While the disciples were gone, a woman of Sychar came to the well to draw water. When she got to the well, Jesus engaged her in conversation. He said to her, "Give me some of your water."

She replied, "How is it that you, being a Jew, speak to me, a woman of Samaria?"

Jesus used this opportunity to witness to the woman about the Kingdom of God. He said to her, "If you had asked me, I would have given you living water [speaking of the salvation He would bring to those who would receive Him]."

And she said, "The well is deep and you have nothing to get water with. How are you going to get the water?"

In effect, Jesus answered her, "If you drink of the water that I give, you will never thirst again." The two of them continued in conversation, during which Jesus told her about her past.

She, being surprised at His knowledge concerning her, because she had never seen Him before, stated, "You must be a prophet, since you know all this about me."

Now with a different respect for Jesus, the woman said to Him: "The Jews say that in Jerusalem is the place to worship. But our forefathers tell us that here in the hills of Samaria is the place to worship."

Jesus said to her, **"Woman, believe me,..... the hour cometh and now is, when the true worshippers shall worship the Father in spirit and in truth:.... God is a Spirit: and they that worship him must worship him in spirit and in truth"** (John 4:23-24).

Genesis 1:26 tells us that when the Father, the Son, and the Holy Spirit were conferring about the creation of mankind, God said, **"Let us make man in our image, after our likeness: and let them have dominion over the fish of the sea, and over the fowl of the air, over the cattle, and over all the earth, and over every creeping thing that creepeth upon the earth."**

If God made us in *His* image, after *His* likeness, then we, too, must be *spirits*. Since we are spirits, then we also must have the capacity to operate in the spirit world where God is.

Genesis 1:1 says, **"In the beginning God created the heaven and the earth."** That means that God, who is a Spirit, created a physical world; consequently, spiritual things have to be more real than physical things, because it took a spiritual Being to create material things.

The reason Paul says, **"Who hath blessed us with all spiritual blessings,"** is because everything material and physical was, first of all, spiritual. In fact, I believe the reason most people have a problem operating in faith is because they have a problem understanding this concept. The majority of people are so conditioned to functioning in a physical world that they cannot conceive of something existing apart from the physical.

Geography, geology, and history tell us that the Earth is spherical, or round. It bulges a little at the equator, but basically it is a sphere. Now, in order for God to create this world and make it round instead of square, round instead of diamond-shaped, round instead of pear-shaped, He would have had to have a thought in His mind about what He wanted the Earth to look like when He finished creating it. Then, when He spoke the thought into existence, He literally projected what was in His mind into physical manifestation. Therefore, the round Earth is a product of the mind of Almighty God.

Everything that is physical was first of all spiritual. If we, as believers, can grasp this principle, we can then understand how to operate in faith, because we will be able to understand how things can supposedly come from nothing and be changed into something. It is not that they are actually coming from nothing, it is that they are coming from a world that cannot be seen with our physical eyes, even though it is a world more real than the world we really live in.

For example, on a summer day, you may be driving down a highway and as you look down the road, you may begin to see what looks like a body of water on the road ahead of you. You keep on driving and driving, but you never get to the water. The reason you do not get to it is because the water is not there. What you have seen is an optical illusion.

Perhaps you have looked out on the horizon on a summer evening and seen a huge orange ball — it was the moon. It looked so close that you felt as though you could reach out and touch it. That might have been around 7:00 p.m. Later on, around 11:00 or 12:00 midnight, if you looked out again, you would have seen that the moon had moved farther up in the sky. Then, it would have been blue-white in color, and it looked a lot smaller than it did when you saw it on the horizon.

Did the moon change its size? No! When you saw it on the horizon, the atmosphere served to refract your vision. Therefore, when you look at something through refracted vision, you are not really seeing the object as it really is.

The point I am making is that some things are not as they seem to be. They look like one thing, but they are really something else. Everything in this world was, first of all, in the mind of God, or in the mind of the creatures God made.

Here is a case in point. I have a brown pin-stripe suit. This suit did not just fall out of the sky and materialize in my closet. It is made a certain way, and it has a certain texture and shape to it. Someone had a thought in his mind about making this suit. Then, as the ideas came into this person's mind, he or she went to a table and put these thoughts onto paper, which became a pattern. The designer then put the pattern onto material, cut it out, sewed it together, and the finished product was a beautiful suit. All things start out in the mind of someone, just as this world and the universe were first in the mind of God before they were manifested physically.

Jesus is our reason for being blessed. Because of our association with Him, by having accepted and received Him as our personal Savior and Lord, we get the benefit of that union with Him, which is to be blessed!

God knows everything we need. He knows what we will need, and He knows what we will desire in our lifetimes. He has already created all of those things. He has them on deposit in the bank of heaven for our benefit; however, they are in a spiritual form. By our faith, we bring them out of the spiritual world into the physical world. They become houses, automobiles, clothes, and all the other things we need or may desire that are consistent with a godly life. All we have to do is to use our faith and call them into existence, according to the Word of God.

All Spiritual Blessings

I like that word *all*. We are not blessed with only some things so that we have to struggle for the rest of them and beat our brains out on the anvils of life, struggling, fighting, and fussing in our efforts to get them. No, praise God, they are already provided for us. Yes, they start out in the spirit world, but we can bring them into physical manifestation by using our faith.

I am blessed because the Word says I am blessed. I am blessed because the Father said I was blessed. I am blessed, and because I am blessed, *I expect the blessings to materialize.* So, I talk blessings, I think blessings, I speak blessings, and the blessings come!

When I talk about being blessed, some people have accused me of trying to make God do something. You cannot *make* Almighty God do anything! You do not have to make Him do anything, because He *will* do all that He says He will do in His Word. He is not like men who change their minds. He cannot lie, and He does not go back on His Word. If He says it, He will do it! However, we have to exercise our faith, which gives Him the opportunity to move on our behalf.

Do not think you are being humble when you say, "Well, I just don't deserve all these blessings." You are not being humble, you are being biblically and scripturally stupid! If Jesus is your Lord, you deserve the blessings God wants to bestow on you as His child.

> **According as he hath chosen us in him before the foundation of the world, that we should be holy and without blame before him in love.**
>
> **(Eph. 1:4)**

From that statement, you could get the idea that what is being said is that God has already predetermined who is going to be saved and who is going to be lost.

If God chose us in Christ, **"before the foundation of the world,"** before the world was ever made, it does not make any difference what I do, because God has either chosen me or He has not chosen me. That is what you could get out of this verse if you are not careful. The next verse adds fuel to this concept.

Having predestinated us unto the adoption of children by Jesus Christ to himself, according to the good pleasure of his will.

(Eph. 1:5)

When I first felt the call to the ministry, I started attending a ministerial class that was being conducted by the pastor of the church I was attending at the time. During one of these classes, we got into a discussion of the subject of predestination. His teaching was based on the dictionary meaning of the word *predestination*.

The word *predestination* means "predetermined" or "determined before the fact." The way this topic was taught left the impression that God chose certain people to be saved, and certain people to be lost, no matter what anyone did or did not do.

That was shattering to me, and I said, "Isn't that something? Suppose I live all my life as a Christian and preach the gospel and do all the things that are supposedly right and then I get to the end of life and find out that my name is not written in the Lamb's Book of Life." That would be awful, wouldn't it?

There is a doctrine called the doctrine of predestination. *Predestination*, in this context, does mean "predetermined." However, we need to understand what the Bible is saying so that we do not get confused and think that God has already made up His mind regarding who will be saved and who will be lost.

That is not what the word *predestination* means in the Bible. In fact, the word is only used three times in

11

the New Testament. Let us carefully examine and dissect this portion of Scripture to see what is actually being said here.

God has willed to make us His children. He has willed to adopt us into His family. A child who is up for adoption cannot demand that a certain man and woman adopt him or her. The child does not have anything to say about it. It is the adopting parents who make the decision as to whether they will adopt a particular child or not.

What Paul is telling us here is that it is God's good pleasure to adopt us into His family. That is what this word *predestination* means, according to the Bible. It does not have reference to the fact that God has predetermined that one person will be saved and another lost.

The part that is predetermined is not our salvation. God does not predestine anyone to be saved or lost. Because God has all knowledge, He knows who is going to receive Jesus and who is going to reject Him. But that does not make God responsible for anyone making that choice. The following illustration elaborates on this truth.

God created a man named Adam and He put him in the Garden of Eden. Gold told Adam that he could eat of all the trees of the Garden except the one in the middle. He said, "If you eat of that tree, you shall surely die." God then left Adam in control of the Garden.

Did God know that Adam was going to mess up, or did Adam's mess-up catch God by surprise? God knew Adam would sin! How did He know? Because He is omniscient, and He knows everything. Was it

God's fault that Adam ate from the tree? No, it was not His fault, even though God knew Adam was going to do it.

In His foreknowledge, God knows everyone who is going to accept Jesus and everyone who is going to reject Him. But that does not make God responsible for people's decisions.

For example, people who own the corner gas stations know that automobiles in today's society either take regular, unleaded, or premium gasolines. So they usually have at least three pumps, one for each of these gasolines. Now these owners do not know exactly who is coming into their gas stations to buy gasoline, but they know someone will because they possess the foreknowledge that automobiles use gasoline, and people driving cars need to buy gas.

They have the pumps ready, they have the attendants ready to serve, and the tanks are full. But the fact that they have gas in the tanks does not make them responsible for any particular person coming into their stations to buy gas.

By the same token, God knows who is and who is not going to accept Jesus, even though He is not responsible for anyone doing or not doing so. Based on that foreknowledge, He has determined or predestined that those who do accept Jesus are going to become His children by adoption, and that is the only thing that has been predetermined.

In Romans 8, there are two other verses that use the term *predestination,* and I believe it is very important to add this information to our store of Bible knowledge so that we can have a comprehensive understanding of what God is doing when it comes to this concept of *predestination.*

> **For whom he did foreknow, he also did predestinate to be conformed to the image of his Son, that he might be the firstborn among many brethren.**
>
> **(Rom. 8:29)**

The Word *foreknow* is the key. *Foreknow* means "to know in advance." That word is the catalyst for understanding the word *predestination.*

In other words, what God predestined is that when He gets finished with us, we are going to look like Jesus. He is not predestinating that we accept Jesus or reject Him.

We are going to look like Jesus. That is why we are called Christians. We are "little Christs." We ought to look like Jesus, we ought to act like Jesus, we ought to think like Jesus, we ought to talk like Jesus, and we ought to *live* like Jesus!

> **Moreover whom he did predestinate, them he also called: and whom he called, them he also justified [declared righteous]: and whom he justified, them he also glorified.**
>
> **(Rom. 8:30)**

We do not know who is going to accept or reject Jesus. But God has designed a method by which He can bring out into the open those who will accept Christ.

God knows what is in people's hearts; however, the folks who have accepted Christ need something to bring their acceptance out into the open so that they themselves will know they are the ones who have accepted Him.

How are they going to know who they are? God is going to call them, and when He calls them, they will respond. When they respond, they will know that they are the ones whom God has chosen and predetermined to look like Jesus, because they themselves are now aware of the fact that they have been called. God uses the preaching of the gospel to bring their calling to their attention.

To say it more simply, *God knew ahead of time those of us who would respond to Him, so He uses the method of the gospel to bring that response out of us.* This is deep material, and that is why I want us to look at verse 30 again:

> **Moreover whom he did predestinate, them he also called: and whom he called, them he also justified: and whom he justified, them he also glorified.**
>
> **(Rom. 8:30)**

God has chosen us to be His sons. It was not because He chose us that made us sons. It was the fact that we first accepted *His Son,* and as a result of that, He then chose us. But notice that He did it by virtue of the fact that He knew ahead of time who was going to accept His Son. It was not Him choosing us that made us chosen, it was because we accepted Jesus that He was then able to choose us!

Part 2 — Ephesians 1:6-23

> **To the praise of the glory of his grace, wherein he hath made us accepted in the beloved.**
>
> **(Eph. 1:6)**

Obviously, before that time, we were not accepted. In other words, God made the rules so that we could fit into them. We did not qualify on our own, but He so structured the game plan that the rules would allow us to be accepted by Him because of *His* grace (unmerited favor).

> **In whom we have redemption through his blood, the forgiveness of sins, according to the riches of his grace.**
>
> **(Eph. 1:7)**

"According to the riches of his grace" simply means that we did not have any demands we could make on God. He accepted us based on His unmerited favor.

We Have Redemption...

It does not say that we are going to get it, but it says that we *have* it.

Man's redemption is actually in two stages; however, God includes both stages under one covering — the Blood of Jesus.

The reason our redemption is in two parts is because it deals with two facets of our nature. The first part is spiritual, and it happens when we become born again, according to John 3:3.

This is the moment when you say, "I recognize that I am a sinner. I recognize that I am without hope in the world. And, Father, I recognize that you are the Lord of glory and that Jesus is your Son. I know that you sent Him to the Earth to redeem mankind, that He came in the flesh and died in the flesh, and that He rose from the dead and ascended into heaven. I accept Jesus' sacrifice and I accept Him as my Savior and Lord."

The moment you make that declaration, instantaneously you are transformed in your spirit. According to 2 Corinthians 5:17, you then become a new creature in Christ Jesus — that transformation takes care of the spirit part of your redemption.

But we are still living in physical bodies, in this physical world. And it is God's plan and purpose that just as we receive a new spirit when we become born again, there is a day coming when we will receive a new body — a glorified body, a body that is made like the body of the Lord Jesus Christ — a body that can operate in the Earth and that can operate in the heavens — a body that can operate in the physical and can operate in the spiritual — a body that is the kind of body all Christians are going to receive. Right now, we are waiting for our bodies to be changed. Right now, my body is just like it was the day before I accepted Christ as my personal Savior. Unfortunately, it is still subject to pain. It is still subject to sickness and disease. It is still subject to aging and getting out of shape. But, thank

God, I am going to get a new body! And so will you, if you are born again. When that takes place, the second part of our redemption will have been completed.

> **Wherein he hath abounded toward us in all wisdom and prudence; Having made known unto us the mystery of his will, according to his good pleasure which he hath purposed in himself.**
>
> **(Eph. 1:8-9)**

This is a strange statement, and yet it is filled with importance. It does not say He *is* in the process of making it known, and it does not say He will make it known. It says, **"having made known unto us...."**

How did God do that? He made known this mystery to us by His Word, which means by His Spirit.

The word *mystery* implies something that is hidden or unknown. In other words, a mystery is not something you can look at and grasp readily or easily.

The word *mystery*, however, does not apply to the children of the Kingdom; rather, it applies to those outside of the family of God. Those outside of Christ cannot know what the Bible means. It is a coded language to them. They can read the various translations, and they can etymologically understand the words on the page, but they do not know what message is being conveyed.

We can gather more information regarding this word *mystery* in the second chapter of 1 Corinthians, beginning at verse 7.

> But we speak the wisdom of God in a mystery, even the hidden wisdom, which God ordained before the world unto our glory: Which none of the princes of this world knew: for had they known it, they would not have crucified the Lord of glory. But as it is written, Eye hath not seen, nor ear heard, neither have entered into the heart of man, the things which God hath prepared for them that love him. But God hath revealed them unto us by his Spirit: for the Spirit searcheth all things, yea, the deep things of God.
>
> (1 Cor. 2:7-10)

With these supportive verses in mind, let us look at Ephesians 1:9 again:

> Having made known unto us the mystery of his will, according to his good pleasure which he hath purposed in himself.
>
> (Eph. 1:9)

God makes known the mystery to us by His Spirit. That is why it is so necessary to operate in the fullness of the Holy Spirit. The devil tries to keep the baptism with the Holy Spirit and the gifts of the Spirit out of the Church, because he knows when you get into the power of God, you get into the solution to the mysteries. If you are not able to function and operate in the Spirit of God, you are not going to know the mystery of the Word.

There are people who read the Bible, but remain in the dark. They go around quoting Scriptures, but they have no idea how these Scriptures relate to their lives.

But, thank God for the Spirit of God who helps us walk in the knowledge of the mysteries, so that we can know the plan and the purpose of our heavenly Father.

> **That in the dispensation of the fulness of times he might gather together in one** [that is talking about the Body of Christ] **all things in Christ, both which are in heaven, and which are on earth; even in him.**
>
> **(Eph. 1:10)**

Presently, some Christians are living on the Earth and some who have already died are in heaven. At the moment they breathed their last breath, their spirits and souls, like caged birds, took wings, as it were, and ascended to the lofty pinnacles of glory and sailed into the very presence of God.

In the Book of the Revelation, the Apostle John had a vision of heaven while he was on the Island of Patmos. He said, "I saw under the altar the souls of them...." He saw the spirits and the souls of them who had died. The spirit and the soul go hand in hand like wetness goes with water. We sometimes dissect them in order to teach on them, but the spirit and the soul go together.

Physical death is the termination of physical life. The bodies of the dead Christians who are in the grave are the ones referred to when we talk about the resurrection of the dead. There is coming a time when Jesus Christ will come back to this Earth to gather together those that are His. When He comes, He is going to bring with Him the souls and the spirits of those Christians who have departed from this Earth.

A great host, a mighty host, will be sent out of heaven like a great cloud. And the trumpet of God shall sound. You talk about a great day — that is going to be *the* day!

At the sound of the trumpet, the bodies of the dead in Christ shall rise. They shall come up out of the ground in their reconstituted bodies. Scientists tell us that there is something called the indestructibility of matter. They say that matter does not really cease to exist. It may change from a solid to a gaseous state, but whatever was a part of this Earth is still out there somewhere in the universe moving around in another form. And the "heavenly computers" are all programmed to keep track of every molecule and every cell. They know exactly where every molecule and cell is. Even if someone's body has been blown up into a million pieces, God knows where every piece is. When the trumpet sounds, every one of those microscopic pieces will be drawn together by the power of God.

If Jesus were to come today, we Christians who are still alive would not have to die. We would be translated in a moment of time. Then all that Paul talked about in verse 10 will come together.

> **In whom also we have obtained an inheritance,**
> **being predestinated according to the purpose of him**
> **who worketh all things after the counsel of his own will.**
> **(Eph. 1:11)**

An inheritance means someone has left you something after their death.

Christians are walking through Earth like paupers and beggars. We are not beggars! We are the family of God, and we have an inheritance!

> **That we should be to the praise of his glory, who first trusted in Christ.**
>
> **(Eph. 1:12)**

This means that the heavenly Father wants to receive praise and glory out of our lives. God wants to be proud of His children, just as any earthly parent would. He wants to be made happy by the achievements of His children, just as earthly parents do.

> **In whom ye also trusted, after that ye heard the word of truth, the gospel of your salvation: in whom also after that ye believed, ye were sealed with that holy Spirit of promise.**
>
> **(Eph. 1:13)**

There is a transaction in the context of Christianity where a born-again man or a born-again woman comes in contact with Jesus Christ as the Baptizer with the Holy Spirit. This particular transaction is for divine, supernatural enduement of power, and one must already be a Christian in order to qualify for this special gift of the Third Person of the Godhead, the Holy Spirit or the Holy Ghost.

There is also another transaction that is called being born again, or the new birth. Being born again, of course, is the first transaction, and then being filled with the Holy Spirit is secondary to it.

When I was born again, I was told by the particular denomination that I was affiliated with that I also was filled with the Holy Spirit at the same time.

The thirteenth verse of Ephesians 1, which talks about being **"sealed with that holy Spirit of promise,"** is not talking about being filled with the Spirit; it is talking about being born again, and it is necessary to understand this important distinction.

It is obvious that this is what is being talked about because it says that you, **"heard the word of truth, the gospel of your salvation: in whom also after that ye believed, ye were sealed...."** It did not say, "You were filled with," it said, "You were sealed."

There are various ways to seal something. You can take a jar and put a lid or a cover or a cap on it, and screw the cap down until it is tight enough so that no substance can escape. Then there is the kind of seal that involves a metal embosser placing an embossed impression on a document. When a document has such an embossed seal on it, it is considered to be a legal document, and it will stand up in any court in the land. I believe these are the two basic ways we use to indicate the word *sealing*, even though there are other ways of sealing things as well.

What does the Bible mean when it says that you are sealed by the Holy Spirit? I do not believe God puts a lid on us and screws it down so that we cannot get out. I believe the kind of sealing the Bible is talking about is like the legal embossing seal which indelibly stamps us with the seal of God, so that everyone in the universe knows that we now belong to Him. When this happens, we have His seal, with His name on us — the name of

23

Jesus, and we are sealed with that name. It is, however, the Holy Spirit who does the sealing; that is why it says we are **"sealed with that holy Spirit of promise."**

When Jesus was risen from the dead, He appeared to His disciples for approximately forty days, and He showed them infallible proofs that it was, in fact, He who had risen from the dead. He told them things concerning the Kingdom of God, and He commissioned them to go to the four corners of the Earth to continue the work He had begun. He told them not to leave Jerusalem until they had received the promise of the Father. In Acts 1:8, He said, **"But ye shall receive power [divine ability], after that the Holy Ghost is come upon you: and ye shall be witnesses unto me...."** That was the promise of the Holy Spirit that Jesus gave.

The Holy Spirit's purpose for coming is twofold. First of all, it is to re-create those who accept Jesus as Savior and Lord and to seal them as God's own children, and secondly to fill us with God's power. It is the same Holy Spirit, but He is functioning in two separate capacities.

In the story concerning the man Nicodemus, who came to Jesus by night, Jesus told him about his need to be born again. Nicodemus thought that Jesus was talking about physical birth, and he asked Jesus, "How can a man be born when he is old? Can he enter a second time into his mother's womb?" In the sixth verse of the third chapter of John, Jesus said:

> **That which is born of the flesh is flesh; and that which born of the Spirit is spirit.**
>
> **(John 3:6)**

Notice that the first word *Spirit* is capitalized as it ought to be, because it is referring to the Holy Spirit. The second word *spirit* is in the lower case, and that is as it ought to be, because it is referring to the spirit of man. So, the new birth is the rebirth of the human spirit. It is the Holy Spirit that makes it work. He is the one who causes this transaction to take place. By an act of his will, a person says "yes" to the claims of Christ, and I believe at that moment in time, that person is sealed with the seal of God, and he becomes God's own child.

Some of God's children do not know they have been sealed because they have not been taught who they are in Christ, but Satan and every demon in hell, and every angel in heaven, know who the children of God are. Once we find out who we are, and begin to live up to our privileges, when the devil sees us coming, he will start running like an old dog. He knows we have authority over him, because we are sealed in the name of Jesus by the Holy Spirit.

In the eighth chapter of Romans, we see something else about being sealed by the Holy Spirit which helps to clarify some misunderstandings about being filled with the Spirit.

> **There is therefore now no condemnation to them which are in Christ Jesus, who walk not after the flesh, but after the Spirit.**
>
> **(Rom. 8:1)**

The word *condemnation* there means *judgment*. What this verse is saying is that there is no more *judgment* concerning whether you are saved or lost, whether you are God's child or not, whether you are spiritually alive or spiritually dead. Once you accept Christ as your personal Savior, you pass out of judgment. You may not realize it, but when you come into the world, you come into it with a cloud of judgment on you already. The wrath of God is on you from your mother's womb.

The wrath of God is not going to come on you at the end of life, it is on the unbeliever *now*. But the moment you accept Christ, you come out from under the wrath of God — you come out from under the condemnation and the judgment.

The only judgment Christians will have to face is the Judgment Seat of Christ. Its purpose will be to see whether the works you have performed in the name of Jesus will stand up under the test of fire. If they do, then you will get a reward for your works. But this has nothing to do with your salvation.

Let us examine other Scriptures concerning the wrath of God. In the Gospel of John 3:30-36, John the Baptist is speaking. In reference to Christ, he says:

> He [referring to Jesus] **must increase, but I must decrease. He that cometh from above is above all: he that is of the earth is earthly, and speaketh of the earth: he that cometh from heaven is above all. And what he hath seen and heard, that he testifieth; and no man receiveth his testimony. He that hath received his testimony hath set to his seal that God is true. For he whom God hath sent speaketh the words of God: for God giveth not the Spirit by measure unto him. The Father loveth the Son, and hath given all things into his hand. He that believeth on the Son**

hath everlasting life: and he that believeth not the Son shall not see life; but *the wrath of God* abideth on him.

(John 3:30-36, italics mine)

Notice that this passage does not say, "He that believeth not, the wrath of God *shall abide* on him" — indicating a future-tense transaction. It says, **"...the wrath of God** *abideth*...," which implies that it was already there and because of the rejection of the Son, it is going to stay there.

Let us continue with our study concerning the wrath of God by looking at Romans 8:1-9.

There is therefore now no condemnation to them which are in Christ Jesus, who walk not after the flesh, but after the Spirit. For the law of the Spirit of life in Christ Jesus hath made me free from the law of sin and death. For what the law could not do, in that it was weak through the flesh, God sending his own Son in the likeness of sinful flesh, and for sin, condemned sin in the flesh: That the righteousness of the law might be fulfilled in us, who walk not after the flesh, but after the Spirit. For they that are after the flesh do mind the things of the flesh; but they that are after the Spirit the things of the Spirit. For to be carnally [or fleshly] minded is death; but to be spiritually minded is life and peace. Because the carnal mind is emnity against God: for it is not subject to the law of God, neither indeed can be. So then they that are in the flesh cannot please God. But ye are not in the flesh, but in the Spirit, if so be that the Spirit of God dwell in you. Now if any man have not the Spirit of Christ, he is none of his.

(Rom. 8:1-9)

27

This is where some people get confused. They read that verse and say, "Oh see, everybody is filled with the Spirit."

You do not find the words "filled with the Spirit" in that verse. Verse nine does not say anything about receiving the gift of the Holy Spirit. It does not say anything about being baptized with the Spirit. It simply says, **"...if any man have not the *Spirit of Christ*, he is none of his."**

When we are filled with the Holy Spirit, we are filled with the Spirit of God. This is talking about the Spirit of Christ. That means that the Holy Spirit's work, at this point, is to represent Jesus Christ.

The Bible says, **"Christ in you, the hope of glory"** (Col. 1:27). This is not talking about Jesus being in you physically. Jesus is, geographically and physically, seated at the right hand of the Majesty on high.

Jesus is not inside of me physically. But He is inside of me by His representative, the Spirit of God. Or, in this reference (Rom. 8:9), He is called the **"Spirit of Christ,"** because in this part of the salvation transaction, He is acting on behalf of Jesus. He is making Christ in us, the hope of glory.

Every born-again person has the Spirit of Christ in him. Just as the Bible says, **"If any man have not the Spirit of Christ, he is none of his."** This means if you do not have the Spirit of Christ, you have not been born again.

But every born-again person does have the Spirit of Christ, but that is not being *filled* with the Spirit. Being born of the Spirit is one thing, and being filled with the Spirit is something entirely different.

28

I want to cover the last part of the thirteenth verse of Ephesians 1 again because it ties right in with the fourteenth verse.

> ...ye were sealed with that holy Spirit of promise, Which is the earnest of our inheritance until the redemption of the purchased possession, unto the praise of his glory.
>
> (Eph. 1:13-14)

The sealing of the Holy Spirit is the promise, and it is the earnest of our inheritance. This means it is the down payment on our redemption.

Earlier, I said that our redemption is accomplished in two stages. Our redemption is not only spiritual — which we instantaneously receive at the new birth — but it is also physical. The day is coming when we are going to get the last installment on our redemptive package — the transformation of our physical bodies into a glorious body like that of Jesus Christ. Until then, we have the guarantee of the fact that this is going to happen, and that is the sealing of the Holy Spirit.

That sealing is your salvation — your being born again is the fact that you have a new nature. It is the fact that you have a new heart. It is the fact that Christ has come to take up residence in your spirit by and through the Spirit of God, and that is your down payment on the rest of the package deal. Because of that which has already happened, the door opens, enabling the last installment to be paid.

> **which is the earnest** [down payment] **of our inheritance until....**
>
> **(Eph. 1:14)**

Until implies that what is going on now is not yet finished. *Until* means there is something else coming. And what is that something else? It is the redemption of your physical body!

> **...the redemption of the purchased possession...**
>
> **(Eph. 1:9)**

The *possession* has been purchased, but the full redemption has not yet been manifested, referring to your physical body.

So, until Jesus comes back again, you have the responsibility to govern your body. If *you* do not do so, it will not be done. As I have said before, the problem is in the body. If you could get rid of your flesh, you would not have any problems.

Just think, if you did not have a body, you would never be sick or overweight. In fact, if you did not have a body, you would not be bound to one location. You could travel anywhere in the universe indiscriminately. You could even travel in time; you could go back thirty, forty, even fifty years — the only thing that would hinder you from doing so is your body.

Your body is a source of problems for many things in the Christian life. Your body is the place where sins take hold. I have never heard of a spirit committing fornication, but I have heard about a body doing so. I have never heard of a spirit making a mistake and getting pregnant outside of wedlock, but many bodies are having that problem today.

Thank God we are going to get new bodies! We are going to live throughout eternity in a body — a physical flesh-and-bone body. I did not say *blood*; I said *flesh and bone*. That is the kind of body Jesus has right now — no blood, but flesh and bone, because He shed His blood on behalf of all mankind. Someone might say, "I cannot believe that; how in the world can someone exist without blood?" By the power of God — that is how!

We do not know everything. All we have is the accumulated knowledge of those who preceded us. Our knowledge cannot go further than that. That is all we know, but that is not all there is to know. There are things that people are doing now, medically speaking, that they were not doing fifty years ago. Probably some of the doctors who lived in the earlier days would have said that these things were not possible to do.

The Bible says, **"In the beginning God created the heaven and the earth"** (Gen. 1:1). Where did God come from? What was He doing all those years before He created the Earth? Have you ever thought about that? I have! We cannot figure it out. You know why? Because we have *finite* knowledge. In order to understand God, we have to have *infinite* knowledge.

There are many things to which we may respond, "Well, I cannot believe that." The reason we cannot believe it is because our knowledge goes only so far, and we can only understand to the extent that our knowledge permits. As far as God's Word is concerned, we need to have the attitude, "God said it, and that settles it!"

I want to share some Scriptures that show us that our salvation comes in two packages. When your physical body is changed, that will be the totally finished redemptive package. Until then, you have a down payment on it; you have the earnest of it, the guarantee of it. What is that guarantee? It is the sealing of the Spirit.

> **For as many as are led by the Spirit of God, they are the sons of God. For ye have not received the spirit of bondage again to fear; but ye have received the Spirit of adoption, whereby we cry, Abba, Father. The Spirit itself [or actually himself] beareth witness with our spirit, that we are the children of God.**
>
> **(Rom. 8:14-16)**

The reason our spirits can do this for us is because of the sealing of the Holy Spirit. When we accepted Christ, we were sealed or baptized into the Body of Christ. We had the down payment given to us in our hearts, or spirits, and that was the fact that we were re-created and made new creatures in Christ Jesus.

> **And if children, then heirs; heirs of God, and joint-heirs with Christ; if so be that we suffer with him, that we may be also glorified together.**
>
> **(Rom. 8:17)**

The word *suffer*[1] does not imply sickness, nor does it mean going with your bills unpaid. The meaning of the Greek word here has to do with the fact that we as Christians are going to have to experience the same kind of persecution Jesus did, because we are identified with Him.

In the same way that Satan did not like Jesus when He walked the Earth, Satan does not like the children of the Kingdom, and he will try to put the same pressures on us that he put on Jesus through persecution. This pressure does not involve people being sick and poor, however. It means that people are not going to understand who you are any more than they understood who Jesus was. They will accuse you of being everything but a child of God, and they will try to stop you in every way they can. That is the kind of persecution the Bible says we will suffer.

> **For I reckon that the sufferings of this present time are not worthy to be compared with the glory which shall be revealed in us.**
>
> **(Rom. 8:18)**

Paul says it is a glory that **"...shall be revealed."** Apparently it has not yet been revealed or he would not have said, *"shall be revealed."*

> **For the earnest expectation of the creature** [that is, the animal kingdom] **waiteth for the manifestation of the sons of God.**
>
> **(Rom. 8:19)**

If the creatures are waiting for the manifestation of the sons of God, then it is obvious that the sons of God have not yet been manifested. For if the sons of God had already been manifested, then the creatures would not still be waiting.

That manifestation will happen when we get our brand-new bodies which will complete our redemptive package. That is what the creatures are waiting for!

> **For the creature was made subject to vanity, not willingly, but by reason of him who hath subjected the same in hope. Because the creature itself also shall be delivered** [they are not delivered yet, but *shall be* delivered] **from the bondage of corruption into the glorious liberty of the children of God.**
>
> **(Rom. 8:20-21)**

What does **"bondage of corruption"** mean? Corruption means death, corruption means decay, corruption means dying.

After a baby is born, we often say that he or she is growing up. Really, the baby is not growing up —he or she is *dying!* The moment the baby comes out of the mother's womb, he or she begins to die. Yes, the child has to grow up to die (all things being equal), but he or she *is* dying. We could say the child is corrupting, or wasting away. His or her body is going through a change, and so must we all, unless Jesus returns before we die.

Death is bondage! The Father God never intended for man to die. Death came as a result of Adam's transgression.

In reality, what is death? For one thing, it is a perversion of life; it is just the opposite of life. Because of Adam's sin, life was perverted, and it opened the door for death to come in and for the process of corruption to begin in our bodies.

In 2 Corinthians 4:16 we are told that the outward man is perishing, but the inward man is being renewed day by day. The outward man may be wasting away, but one of these days, death will be arrested by the coming of Jesus. And there will be no more corruption, no more dying.

Paul tells us that the creatures themselves will also be delivered. So apparently in the Kingdom that is coming, there will be some animals around.

> **For we know that the whole creation groaneth and travaileth in pain together until now.**
>
> **(Rom. 8:22)**

What kind of pain? The corruption pain — the pain of dying, the pain of wasting away.

> **And not only they, but ourselves also, which have the firstfruits [or down payment] of the Spirit, even we ourselves groan within ourselves, waiting for the adoption, to wit, the redemption of our body.**
>
> **(Rom. 8:23)**

What is the Firstfruits of the Spirit?

The very fact that it says *firstfruits* implies second fruit, third fruit, fourth fruit, and so forth. If there is no other fruit coming, you do not say *first*, you just say *fruits*.

We are not going to get it. We already have it, because we have been born again. We have the sealing of the Spirit. We have Christ in us, the hope of glory. That is the down payment, that is the pledge, that is the earnest money. That is the firstfruits!

Waiting for the Adoption...

You do not wait unless something is about to happen. You do not wait if it is already done. So if you are waiting, that means that whatever you are waiting for has not yet happened. If it had already happened, you would not be waiting.

> **Wherefore I also, after I heard of your faith in the Lord Jesus, and love unto all the saints, Cease not to give thanks for you, making mention of you in my prayers.**
>
> **(Eph. 1:15)**

I pray for my congregation. I pray for the television ministry. I may not even know the names of the people, but I pray for them nonetheless.

Paul said that he "ceased not to give thanks" for the body of believers at Ephesus, and he stated that he mentioned them in his prayers. Then he prayed a specific thing.

This is something we need to be aware of concerning prayer. When we pray about something, we ought to pray specifically. Too many times people just glibly say something like, "Well, Lord, bless him and bless her." That does not mean a thing, and that kind of praying is not going to accomplish anything. We need to pray about specific things, for specific people. Yes, there are times when it is appropriate to pray general prayers, but whenever we pray for a particular person or a particular situation, we should be specific regarding whom or what we are praying about.

> **That the God of our Lord Jesus Christ, the Father of glory, may give unto you the spirit of wisdom and revelation in the knowledge of him.**
>
> **(Eph. 1:17)**

The knowledge we need to gain *is the knowledge of Him.* Thank God for all the other knowledge that is available to us today — and there is a profusion of it.

There are all kinds of schools and universities. In fact, you can even go to school by mail. There are all kinds of wonderful schools to help people become anything they want to be.

But the truly wise individual will gain the knowledge of God first. That is the ultimate knowledge we need to help us tie all other forms of knowledge together in order to make sense out of life. With all of our vaunted education and all of our intellectual excellence, mankind has yet to begin to correct the social ills affecting humanity. We have more poverty, more famine, more murders, more strife, more prejudice, more wars, more hate, more starvation than we have ever had in the history of the world. At the same time, we have more education and more knowledge than ever before. Obviously, the accumulated knowledge of mankind has not solved these massive problems.

Human knowledge has not solved prejudice. It has not solved the problem of babies being born with congenital defects. It has not solved the problems related to murder and rape and lying and cheating and all the rest of mankind's ills.

That ought to tell us that human knowledge alone is not sufficient knowledge for mankind. We also have to get the knowledge of God.

I am not saying we should not take advantage of secular knowledge. We ought to get all the knowledge and education we can, but with all our getting, we need to be sure to get understanding as well, and *that* you can get only from our heavenly Father, through His Word.

> **The eyes of your understanding being enlightened; that ye may know what is the hope of his calling, and what the riches** [not the poverty but the *riches*] **of the glory of his inheritance in the saints.**
>
> **(Eph. 1:18)**

Whether you know it or not, all Christians are saints. I am not talking about someone who has been made into a statue, sitting on some pedestal somewhere in a park or in some building or in front of some church somewhere.

All of us who have been born again are "the saints." There is no special group of saints other than the Body of Christ. God sees us in Christ because the Bible says that not only are we heirs of the Father, but we are joint-heirs with Christ.

That Ye May Know...

There are many people who say, "Well, you just never know about the things of God. The Lord works in a mysterious way, His wonders to perform. And we just have to float along in life and hope that maybe someday He might give us a revelation here and there. But one thing we know is that one of these days, over there on the other side, we will understand it all in the sweet by-and-by."

Thank God we can understand it in the now-and-now. We praise God for the "sweet by-and-by," but we are not in the by-and-by. We are in the now-and-now, and we need to be enlightened about the things of God *now*!

> And what is the exceeding greatness of his power to us-ward who believe, according to the working of his mighty power.
>
> (Eph. 1:19)

A few years back, some folks were talking about "power to the people." God has given power to the saints — to all believers — and that includes you, if you have been born again.

And What Is the Exceeding....

I like God's superlatives. Paul does not say, *"And what is the greatness of his power,"* but he says, *"What is the exceeding greatness of his power."* Everything God does, He does on a grand scale. Our God is an extravagant God! He is not wasteful — but He is extravagant. He embellishes everything He does in a grand style, and He does the same thing with His children. We are the saints, and we are God's children — if you have been born again! If you have, you ought to be winning in life.

Too many Christians are just struggling along and saying things like, "Well, I am just an old sinner, saved by grace. Pray for me that I will hold out steadfast to the end. I know that some day, over on the other side, I will make it through, but I am just so weak." That is a lie.

Look at what the Apostle Paul is saying here through the anointing of the Holy Ghost. He says, **"to us-ward who believe."** There is dynamic power available in and through us who believe. Power, in this context, means ability, but you have to put that power to work if it is going to do you any good.

> **Which he wrought in Christ, when he raised him from the dead, and set him at his own right hand in the heavenly places.**
>
> **(Eph. 1:20)**

In other words, the Lord wants us to know how much and how great this power to usward is. I wish that all Christians could get a glimpse of the magnitude of this power. It would change the complexion of the entire Body of Christ if they did so. The Church has operated too long in the "poverty syndrome."

When I say *poverty*, as in "poverty syndrome," I am not talking about material things only (i.e., money to pay your bills, automobiles, houses, clothing, and the necessary things of life). The word *poverty* also applies to the Christian's ability to make an impression on this world — poverty in our ability to demonstrate the power of Almighty God in our daily living.

Tremendous power is available to us. For too long, the Church has acted as though it had *no* power. "Well, we are just struggling, Brother Price, and we are trying to make it, but you know after all, we are just the Church." *Just the Church?* If only we could grasp who we really are in Christ!

God wants us to turn our attention to the Resurrection of Jesus. This is God's power and that is the power Paul is talking about in the twentieth verse of Ephesians 1.

It takes power to overcome corruption. It takes power to overcome death, and our heavenly Father has that kind of power. That same power has been given to the Body of Christ. What you do not know, you cannot use. When you are not aware of something being available to you, you will never be able to take advantage of it. Sometimes you may even know that something is available, but you do not know how to appropriate it in your life. Such unappropriated knowledge will not do you any good!

41

There is resurrection power in the Body of Christ. This power that is manifested to us was demonstrated by God when He raised Jesus from the dead.

It is important for you to talk to yourself by saying, *"I have the power of God in me. I have the same kind of resurrection power, the same kind of death-overcoming power, the same kind of power that Almighty God used when He raised Jesus from the dead. That power is there for me to use."*

The Body of Christ is going to have to rise up in that God-kind of power and start operating in it. For too long, Christians have just been floaters, floating along through life, in whatever way the wind blows; many just float along that way. No! Jesus never floated along with the wind. He was always deliberate when He did anything. He stepped where He was directed by the Spirit of the Father, and whenever the wind would blow, He would say, *"Peace, be still."*

I know some people will say, "Well, yes, Jesus did those things because He was Jesus. He was the Son of God." No, Jesus did those things because He was operating by the power of the Holy Spirit, and that same power has been made available to us today. It was demonstrated when God raised Jesus from the dead.

> **Far above all principality, and power, and might, and dominion, and every name that is named, not only in this world, but also in that which is to come.**
> **(Eph. 1:21)**

Oh, I like that! Notice what Paul says, **"far above"** — not a little above, not a mile above, but *far above*! Do you know how far *far* is?

Astronomers tell us that our sun is ninety-three million miles away. And Jesus is far above that!

Astronomers tell us that the star closest to our solar system is known as Alpha-Centauri. This star is four light-years away from the Earth. If you could attain the speed of light, which is approximately 186 thousand miles a second, you would have to travel that fast for four years to get to Alpha-Centauri. That is "far out." Jesus is farther out than that! He is farther than ninety-three million miles above; He is farther than four light-years above — He is *far above*!

The word *power* in this verse is actually the word *authority*, or *authorities*.

Jesus is **"far above...every name that is named."** Any name that has ever been named — Jesus Christ is not *just* above it, but *"far above"* it.

This is the reason why I could never waste my time studying other religions, because whatever the name is, be it Buddhism, Muhammadanism, Confucianism or Zoroastranism, the Bible says that Jesus is far above any name you can name and that the heavenly Father has exalted Him *"far above principality, and power and might, and dominion, and every name that is named."* He is number one — the top man.

I am not trying to give you a spiritual pep pill; I am trying to elevate your sights so that you know who you are in Christ. When you really get confident about this, and you really know that *the Man* is on your side, you will not take any garbage from the devil or any of his cohorts. You can stand in the eye of the storms of life and take the Word of God and change the circumstances around you. Instead of being a victim of the circumstance, you will be the master.

I do not know where people get these ideas from that we are supposed to be defeated and beat down. This is not what Jesus came to Earth for, to rescue a bunch of slaves and a group of people that were whipped and defeated. He came to let us know that He has made us the champions of this world. He came to let us know that we have been given dominion over this world.

The Bible says, **"The earth is the Lord's, and the fulness thereof..."** (Ps. 24:1). And we have to go to the world and practically get on our knees and beg them to let us build a church here or a church there. The ground belongs to God, but it is in the control of the world. *And it should not be that way!* Since the Earth is the Lord's, the gold and the silver belong to us through Him, and we ought to have it!

Not Only in This World, but also in That Which Is to Come

Did you know that there is another world coming? Do you think this vale of tears is the end? Do you think that life is meant to end up in a cemetery? Do you think God created us to be food for worms? NO! He created us to live. Sin brought death in, but Jesus whipped death for us. And now death is just a doorway. It is not the end. Not only that, but we are going to regain our bodies if we should die before Jesus returns. This is a real fact of life. It is not some kind of pill that is used to anesthetize us so that we are not aware of all of the pain of this life.

Paul said that Jesus Christ is the Head over all principality and power, and over every name that is named, not only in this world, but in the world to come. Well, if His name is above the world to come, then there must be a world coming. And in that world our dreams and aspirations will be fulfilled. But I have news for you, in the meantime, we are to dominate in this world — we are to be on the top and not on the bottom.

God told the nation of Israel, "You will be the head and not the tail, you will be blessed going out and blessed coming in, if you follow my Word." He told them, "You will have so much that your barns shall be overflowing. And you will be lending to many nations, and you will have no need to borrow." This is talking about Christians, too. Therefore, we ought to be the ones who are doing the lending and not the borrowing!

There is a world coming in which righteousness shall dwell, and there will be no more tears. There will be no more pain, no more agony, no more Satan and demons, no more sickness and disease, no more poverty and fear. Rather, we will be able to bask in the sunshine of God's great love, just as He originally intended for us to do.

I was listening to a message by Dr. Kenneth Hagin, a great man of faith and the Word. He was sharing about a vision he had received when the Lord appeared to him. In fact, it was the first vision Hagin had of Jesus; the vision came to him in 1950. He said that the

Lord took him up to heaven (in the spirit). He said he could look down and see his body on the platform where he had been kneeling in prayer.

Some folks will react to such a report with skepticism. They may say, "Well, what is this?" I encourage such people to read their Bibles. When he was on the Isle of Patmos, the Apostle John said, **"I was in the Spirit on the Lord's day"** (Rev. 1:10). John had been banished to a concentration camp on the Isle of Patmos because of his preaching the Word and the Kingdom of the Lord Jesus Christ.

John said that he was praying one minute and the next he was in heaven. He saw God and the angels and the heavenly throne room. The Bible says that Jesus Christ is **"the same yesterday, today, and forever"** (Heb. 13:8), so if He could do that for John, He can do it for Kenneth Hagin.

Hagin said that he and Jesus went up to heaven and he saw the City of God. He said to Jesus, "Is this the city that we read about in the Word of God?"

Jesus answered, *"Yes."*

Kenneth Hagin then asked, "Are those the mansions that we read about in the Word of God?"

Jesus replied, *"Yes, I will show you yours."*

Dr. Hagin said that it was as if he were looking through a telescope, and suddenly he saw a mansion up close. He went on to explain that he cannot truly describe the mansion because there is nothing in this life that is like it — nothing even looks remotely like it.

If you do not have a point of reference, how can you describe something that is unfamiliar to another person? If he were to say, "Well, it looks like the Empire State Building or the World Trade Center in New York, or the Capitol building in Washington, D.C.," immediately we would have some idea or reference point.

Could you imagine trying to describe to Orville and Wilbur Wright, right after they flew in their little plane, what a Boeing 747 jumbo jet looks like? What could you use to compare it with? Nothing, because there was nothing in their day to compare it with.

Can you imagine talking to Christopher Columbus, who came across the seas with his men on the Nina, the Pinta, and the Santa Maria? Can you imagine trying to tell him what the U.S. aircraft carrier *Enterprise* looks like?

Hagin said, "I have never seen a building like that mansion, and there is nothing in this world that I can compare it with."

It is over there in that other world, a world which we cannot even comprehend. Yes, there is another world coming. All we know is this life, and so we try to compare heavenly things with this life. Heaven is so far above anything you could ever dream; it is beyond the comprehension of the human mind.

Sometimes when I think about heaven, I want to go there right now. But then, when I think about what I have learned about faith in the last several years, I want to stay here. I want to stay here and take back what the devil has taken away. I want to help set the captives free: free from fear, free from sickness, free from disease, free from prejudice and hatred, and free from all of the rest of the things that have kept mankind in bondage.

Thank God, I discovered how to apply the Word. I want to stay around here for a hundred more years so I can help others find out how to operate in the Word. Eternity is forever. We do not have to worry about it — there is no rush to get to eternity.

What about *now*? This is where the captives are being held; this is where the blind are; this is where the sick are; this is where the poor are; this is where the scared are; and we need to be about our Father's business, setting them free.

> **And hath put all things under his feet, and gave him to be the head over all things to the church. Which is his body, the fulness of him that filleth all in all.**
> **(Eph. 1:22-23)**

Jesus Christ, the Son of God, has defeated the enemy, and He is the Head of the Church. The Father God told Him to sit on His right hand until His enemies were made His footstool.

The Bible tells us that we are His body. We are the Church. And when the Word says that God put all things under the feet of Jesus, that means they are under our feet as well, because He is the Head, and we are His body. That means we are on top. We may not be experiencing this in our individual lives, but that is our problem, not God's. He has made us more than conquerors. He has made us winners in every issue and encounter of life.

Christians have been schooled into a "poverty-way" of thinking and acting. The Church has taken a back seat on so many issues, because we thought this was where God wanted us. We thought that humility was being poor. We thought that humility was being sick without crying about it. We thought that humility meant that we should be the last in line and the last with everything. But this is not true. We ought to be on top. We need to start thinking that we are on top. We need to start visualizing ourselves as being on top. If we do all these things long enough, we will eventually rise to the top.

Possession is always preceded by confession. When you confess the Word of God as to who you are in Christ, it causes you to rise from the bottom to the top.

See yourself as a winner, and you will start winning. Talk winning, and you will win. You have to learn how to have God's viewpoint regarding yourself, and then you will be in a position to enjoy the fullness of that which has been provided for you as a believer in Christ Jesus.

I believe in winning. I do not believe in anything else. I do not believe the game is over until I win. We just play until I win. If it gets dark, we turn on the lights and keep on playing until I win. That is my attitude, and that is the biblical attitude. We are more than conquerors, *and conquerors are winners!*

2

The Believer's Position in Christ
(Ephesians 2:1-22)

Part 1 — Ephesians 2:1-8

> **And you hath he [referring to God] quickened,
> who were dead in trespasses and sins.**
>
> **(Eph. 2:1)**

The word *quickened*,[2] in New Testament Greek, literally means *to make alive*. It does not refer to *swift* or *fast*. You could accurately translate the verse like this:

> **And you has he made alive, who were dead.**

That's reasonable, is it not? God made us alive because we were dead, and the dead need life. Every person who has not accepted and confessed Jesus Christ as his personal Lord and Savior is spiritually dead to God.

You are not dead because you have done some bad thing; you are not dead because of acts that you have committed; you are dead because of what Adam did.

Adam was the representative of humankind, and what he did has passed down to all mankind — good or bad, we inherited Adam's sin nature. But thanks be to God that we can also inherit what Jesus has done. He has righted the wrong and has given mankind the opportunity to stand in the good graces of God as His children. However, it is up to each individual to receive Christ as his or her substitute, as his or her Savior, and as his or her Lord.

When the Bible says, "dead in sin," it does not mean dead in the sense of nonexistence. It means dead in the sense of being cut off and separated from God. Even though one still exists spiritually, one exists in a place apart from God. And God considers such a one as being *spiritually* dead.

> **Wherein in time past ye walked according to the course of this world, according to the prince of the power of the air, the spirit that now worketh in the children of disobedience.**
>
> **(Eph. 2:2)**

This world was created by the heavenly Father, and it was made for man. God put man in charge of this world. Adam was given dominion, control, rulership, and lordship over the earth-realm. He was even put in charge and in control of the animals.

When a person owns something, he has the right to do whatever he chooses with it. For example, if you have the title to an automobile, you could sign the title over to someone else and give the car away as a gift, or you could put the car up for sale. You own the car, and whatever you do with it is your responsibility.

Adam had the privilege of being, as it were, the god of this world. In effect, he owned the world. In other words, he held the title on the world. However, he committed an act of rebellion and gave the world to Satan who became, and is still, the god of this world. Satan is not the God of all the ages, but he is the ruler of this world system.

Satan is a spirit-creature. There are many people who do not believe in Satan, but that is their problem. The Bible says the devil is real, and you are deceived if you think he is not. You can call him any other name you want, but Almighty God, who is a lot smarter than we are, calls him the devil, or Satan. So there must be a devil who is called Satan, simply because God says there is.

This devil, by default, took over the rulership of this world. That is why things are so messed up.

I hope that you do not think, by any stretch of your imagination, that Almighty God has this world all messed up like it is. God is not the one who messed things up! It has been messed up by Satan, and then by man listening to the devil, instead of listening to God. Satan and mankind have turned this world topsy-turvy.

God is a God of order, and this world is out of order. This world is chaotic in so many different ways, but within the framework of God's plan and purpose, He is allowing Satan to run his course. When the fullness of time has come, God will step in and intervene in human history. Until then, in the natural, Satan has free course.

There is a sort of coexistence here in the earth-realm. There is the good, and there is the bad. There is the evil, and there is the righteous. There are the children of God, and there are the children of the devil. And we are all living on the Earth simply because that is what we were originally created for. We have physical bodies which are only good for living in this physical world.

The Prince of the Power of the Air

The word *prince*,[3] as it is used in the King James Version of the Bible, comes from a very interesting Greek word. It is literally the word *archon*, and it means *ruler*. The word *power*,[4] as it is used here, is the word *authority*. Therefore, what this verse is literally saying is: *according to the ruler of the authority of the air.* The air is filled with demonic forces, but at the same time, it is also filled with angelic forces.

Everyone, whether he or she is a Christian or not, has a guardian angel with him or her on the Earth. There are also demon forces who are trying to "gun us down."

Someone might respond to this by saying, "I can't believe that. You mean to tell me there is something out there that I cannot see? I'm not going to fall for that."

I have a question for such people. Have you ever heard of UHF television, VHF television, FM radio, and AM radio? Well, whether you know it or not, even though you cannot see the picture and even though you do not hear the program, while you are sitting where you are, running through your house or whatever building you are in, running through your body, through the area where you live and through everyone who is with you there are FM-radio waves, AM-radio waves, UHF and VHF-television transmissions running concurrently. The only reason you are not consciously aware of them is because they are in another dimension. However, with the proper kind of apparatus, which we call a television or radio (which are technically receivers), you tune in and receive the signals that are being transmitted on UHF, VHF, AM, and FM.

No, you cannot see the FM, AM, UHF, or VHF waves, but they are there nonetheless. And most people believe they are there, not because they have seen them, but because someone told them they could see pictures on the television set and hear sounds on the radio. Because they believed what someone told them, and have experienced the results, they consistently and regularly turn on their radios or their televisions and receive the benefits.

By the same token, this Earth is filled with twice as many creatures as there are among us in the physical dimension. However, these spiritual creatures exist in another dimension, a completely different realm.

Satan is the prince, or the ruler, of these demon forces who exist in this other realm, and he presides over them just as Almighty God and Jesus and the Holy Spirit preside over the Body of Christ — the Church.

> **The spirit that now worketh in the children of disobedience.**
>
> **(Eph. 2:2)**

I once heard someone say, "I went to that board meeting, and I tell you, the spirit of the meeting was just not right." That person was talking about something other than what Paul is talking about when he uses the word *spirit*. He is not talking about an atmosphere, some kind of a condition, such as the "spirit of the meeting" being up, or the "spirit of the meeting" being down.

This verse is talking about a *person* — not some kind of atmosphere at a meeting. It is not a psychological condition, but a creature — a spirit-creature.

Notice what this verse does *not* say. It does not say that spirit is working in the children of God, but in the children of disobedience. If that spirit is working in you, then you must be one of the children of disobedience. If so, all you need to do is start obeying the Word of God, and you will not be considered a child of disobedience any longer. That spirit should not be operating in the children of God.

Yes, we are in this world, and we will be influenced by some things around us. But we do not have to respond to everything we are influenced by, because we are in control.

> **Among whom also we all had our conversation in times past in the lusts of our flesh, fulfilling the desires of the flesh and of the mind; and were by nature the children of wrath, even as others.**
>
> **(Eph. 2:3)**

The word *conversation*, as it is used in this verse, does not only mean talking to someone verbally. It does include that meaning, but this word, in its original Greek understanding, has to do with your total lifestyle. *Conversation*[5] literally means your manner of life, and this would certainly include what you say, but even more important than that, it is talking about what you *do*. It is talking about the way you live — your manner of life.

Notice the word *had* in this verse. It is obvious that if we *had*, we do not have now, since *had* is a past-tense verb. Otherwise, this verse would say *we have*, which is a present-tense usage. This would refer to what we are doing *now*.

Had implies something that you used to do, but now you do not do it anymore. That means you are not telling lies, you are not in strife with anyone, you are not a backbiter, you are not a gossiper, and thank God you are not committing fornication (having sexual intercourse with someone you are not married to). And, praise the Lord, you are not an adulterer (having sexual intercourse with someone else's husband or wife). Thank God, you are not a God-robber (that is, stealing from God) by not paying your tithes and giving offerings. Paul said that is what we used to do before we were born again.

Fulfilling the Desires of the Flesh and of the Mind.

The natural man — the man outside of Christ — is governed by his body. Christians should not be governed by their flesh, but by their spirits. The Bible says, **For as many as are led by the Spirit of God, they are the sons** [children] **of God** (Rom. 8:14).

Notice the word *nature*; it is a very, very important word. It is the nature of man that makes man a sinner, not what he or she does.

The nature of a dog causes it to bark. The nature of a cat causes it to meow. The nature of a cow causes it to moo, and the nature of a pig causes it to oink. You have never heard a dog oink, and you have never heard a cow bark. It is not within the natural instincts of the dog or cow to do so.

Man's nature, outside of Christ, is to sin. He is a sinner by nature, not by his deeds. His deeds simply are indicators of his nature, just as barking is an indicator of being a dog.

Many people think you are a sinner because of what you do. What you do does not make you a sinner. Usually people (those outside of Christ) sin because that is what sinners do; they need a new nature. And that is what Jesus is all about. He came to give us a new nature. A nature that is like God's nature. A nature that is like the nature of Jesus Christ, so that the life of God and the life of Christ may be exemplified and manifested through our lives.

The nature of a person has to be transformed. This is not just a reformation of the individual or a changing of his or her actions. You can change your actions all you want, but if you do not change your nature, you will eventually revert to the same actions you started with.

There is a story about a man who had a pig that he liked. This pig was always found in the muck and mire and the filth and the slime and slop, because he was a pig. The owner of the pig got tired of seeing the pig that way, and he said, "Now, listen, I am getting tired of this pig acting like this. This is my favorite pig, and I am going to do something about him." So he went into his bathroom, got some bubble bath, and filled the bathtub with water. Then he sprayed cologne all around the bathroom. He even got his thermometer out and measured the temperature of the water to make sure it was just right.

After he got everything ready, he went outside and brought his filthy, dirty pig into the house. He put the pig in the bathtub, washed him, combed him down, brushed his hair, and sprayed him with cologne and put a red ribbon around his neck. Boy, that pig was looking good!

He took the pig into his parlor and set him in front of the fireplace, on a nice soft, thick rug. He proceeded to stand back and admire his handiwork, then he said, "Now, that is the way a pig ought to look."

Afterwards, he went back to the bathroom to clean things up, and to drain the bathtub. When he was all finished, he went back to the parlor to admire his new creation — his reformed pig. When he got to the parlor, he saw the rug, but no pig. He wondered, "What in the world has happened to my pig?" He looked behind the sofa, no pig. He looked under the coffee table and behind the television, no pig. Next, he noticed that the window was open, then he heard some noises coming from the outside, "slop, slop, oink, oink, oink." When he went to the window and looked out, he saw the pig back in the muck and mire, with the red ribbon and all!

Now why was that pig back in the muck and mire? Because he was a pig. The man had done nothing but dressed up the outside of his prize porker. The pig is a pig by nature, and it is his nature to wallow in muck and mire. You have to change the inside of the pig in order to affect the outside.

It is the same with mankind. You can send a man to school and give him a Ph.D.; you can dress him up in a three-piece suit; you can put a pair of expensive shoes on him; you can take him to the beauty parlor and get his nails done and get his hair styled; and you can put a diamond ring on his finger and a gold watch on his wrist. But unless he has accepted Jesus as his Lord and Savior, he is still a sinner and his nature is to sin. Yes, you can dress him up on the outside, but if you have not changed his nature, he is still going to lie, cheat, commit fornication, adultery, get drunk, use drugs, and do anything else that gratifies his sinful nature. This happens because he is a sinner by nature, not by the way he wears his clothes.

> **But God, who is rich in mercy, for his great love wherewith he loved us, Even when we were dead in sins, hath quickened us [made us alive] together with Christ, (by grace ye are saved;).**
>
> **(Eph. 2:4-5)**

That is a very strange statement.

Made Us Alive Together With Christ.

This statement implies that at some point in time Jesus must have been dead spiritually. Because if He were not, how could we be made alive together with Him? If He were already alive, then He would not have to be made alive, and if He were already alive, we could not be made alive like Him.

I need to clarify what I have just said because there are some people who will say I am teaching false doctrine here. But we have to go by what the Word says.

Even When We Were Dead in Sins.

Let us place emphasis on the word *were*. The word *were* is in the past tense. The implication is that once we were dead, but we are not dead now.

This is one of the least understood concepts in all the Scriptures. When people misunderstand what you say, they immediately go on the defensive and think what you are saying is that somehow Jesus committed some sin. But He did not. Jesus never did sin. The Bible says that He was **"in all points tempted like as we are, yet without sin"** (Heb. 4:15). He never violated the Word, the will, the plan, and the purpose of the heavenly Father.

Near the termination of Jesus' earthly ministry, He took His disciples to a place called the Garden of Gethsemane. Judas had left the group with the intent of betraying Jesus. When he had gone, Jesus took the rest of the apostles to the Garden. Then he said something to them that is recorded in the Matthew 26, beginning at verse 30, and continuing through verse 39:

> **And when they had sung an hymn, they went out into the mount of Olives.**
>
> **(Matt. 26:30)**

This took place just after the institution of the Lord's Supper in the Upper Room.

> **Then saith Jesus unto them, All ye shall be offended because of me this night: for it is written, I will smite the shepherd, and the sheep of the flock shall be scattered abroad.**
>
> **(Matt. 26:31)**

What did Jesus mean by the word *smite*? He meant that the shepherd was going to be killed, and the sheep would be scattered. He told the apostles that they would be offended because of Him. Jesus is the Shepherd of the sheep. He said,**"I am the good shepherd"** (John 10:11). Jesus said (in Matt. 26:31) that He was going to "smite" the shepherd of the sheep. In other words, He said He was going to kill the shepherd. What is Jesus actually talking about in this verse?

He is talking about our redemption. He is talking about our salvation; he is talking about our freedom; He is talking about righting the wrong that Adam did so many years before.

I Will Smite.

"I will...." Notice He did not say, "God will." He said, "I will."

> But after I am risen again, I will go before you
> into Galilee. Peter answered and said unto him,
> Though all men shall be offended because of thee,
> yet will I never be offended. Jesus said unto him,
> Verily I say unto thee, That this night, before the cock
> crow, thou shalt deny me thrice. Peter said unto him,
> Though I should die with thee, yet will I not deny
> thee. Likewise also said all the disciples. Then
> cometh Jesus with them unto a place called
> Gethsemane, and saith unto the disciples, Sit ye here,
> while I go and pray yonder. And he took with him
> Peter and the sons of Zebedee, and began to be sor-
> rowful and very heavy.
>
> (Matt. 26:32-37)

Jesus was sorrowful? The Son of God, the Rose of
Sharon, the Lily of the Valley, the Bright and Morning
Star, Emmanuel (God with us), the Mighty God, the
Everlasting Father, the Prince of Peace? Sorrowful?

If you read the life of Jesus, you will find He was
never truly sorrowful. He was never depressed. He
was on top of every situation and every circumstance of
His life. Suddenly, after three and a half years of a
public ministry that involved the raising of the dead,
opening the eyes of the blind, walking on the water,
turning the water into wine, performing miracles that
had never been seen or heard of before, the Bible says
He was **"sorrowful and very heavy."**

> Then saith he unto them, My soul is exceeding
> sorrowful, even unto death: tarry ye here, and watch
> with me. And he went a little farther, and fell on His
> face, and prayed, saying, O my Father, if it be pos-
> sible, let this cup pass from me: nevertheless not as I
> will, but as thou wilt.
>
> (Matt. 26:38-39)

What was that cup? It represented the sin of mankind. That cup represented the dregs of deprivation and alienation and condemnation and sin; that is what that cup contained. This cup was symbolic of what Jesus was going to have to drink in order to become the Redeemer of mankind.

Whatever you drink becomes a part of you. When you drink it, it goes down your throat, into your stomach, and is assimilated into the rest of your body. What you eat and what you drink become a part of you.

The cup was a symbol for sin. It was a symbol of spiritual death, and Jesus said to the Father, "Father, if there is any other way to redeem mankind, let us use that way."

Jesus was going to have to become sin. And in order to become sin and to take our place and receive our punishment so we would not have to receive it, He would have to be cut off from the life of God. He would have to be cut off from the fellowship of the Father.

In the Gospel of John 1:1, we read: **"In the beginning was the Word, and the Word was with God, and the Word was God."** Jesus (the Word) had never known anything but constant, perpetual, beautiful, sweet, harmonious fellowship with the Father. He had never been cut off from the love of the Father. He had never been separated from the fellowship of the Father. But in order to be mankind's substitute, He was going to have to become sin, which necessitated Him being separated and cut off from God.

All of those thoughts were running through Jesus' mind in the Garden, and He rebelled against the thought of separation from God. He did not rebel against the will and purpose of God — but He rebelled from the standpoint of not wanting to be consciously separated from His Father.

Yet, He was committed to do the will of God. He had told God, "Prepare me a body and I will go down and redeem mankind." Now, He was at the crossroads. He was at the point where He was going to have to make that decision. And all that was in Him — spirit, soul, and body — cried out and said, "Father, if there is any other way we can redeem mankind without my having to be separated from you, then let *us* find that other way. Not my will, but thine be done." Jesus prayed that prayer three times, and finally when He was satisfied there was no other way, He said, **"Not my will, but thy will be done."**

Jesus came into the world to redeem us, to set us free. The only way He could do that was to become what we were. He had to become our scapegoat.

The word *scapegoat* is a biblical term. When God set up the institution of sacrifices and offerings for the nation of Israel, there was a time when the high priest would go and lay his hands on the head of a goat. He was symbolically transferring all the sins of the children of Israel onto the goat. Then they would turn the goat loose and send him out into the wilderness. When they did this, it was as if they had gotten rid of the sins of the people. The scapegoat took the place of the people. Jesus became our scapegoat.

When He was in the Garden, the reason He said, **"I will smite the shepherd"** is because in order to redeem us, He would have to die spiritually. He would have to be identified with us in our sin so that we could have the privilege of being identified with Him in our redemption.

Jesus died that we might live. He died that we might be pardoned. We should have died — not physical death, not dying on Calvary, not dying on the cross, but the real death, which is the death of the spirit. We should have been placed into hell for eternity. But because of Jesus' great love for mankind and His grace, He came into this world to save it. He who knew no sin became sin for us. He did not commit any sin, but He became our sin offering.

Somewhere between the Garden and Calvary, I do not know exactly when, and I will not quibble about it, Jesus Christ died spiritually. That is what He meant when He said, "I will smite the shepherd."

He had to do this by an act of His will. He had to voluntarily give His life so that we might live. He became our substitute — our scapegoat — because He loved us so much.

Some Christians are sitting around pouting and crying and feeling sorry for themselves. They say, "Nobody loves me. Nobody is concerned about me." Jesus loves them. He gave His life for them.

Calvary is not the place where our redemption was bought and paid for. That was just a doorway for the beginning of our salvation. Some Christians go around, singing, "I should have been crucified." I do not know why! All their death would have accomplished is a dead person, and that would not have done anyone any good — not them, the human race, or anybody else.

It just so happened that crucifixion was the form of capital punishment that was used in the times of Jesus. If Jesus had died in California today, they would have put Him in the gas chamber. If He had died in Florida, they would have put Him in the electric chair, or in England, they would have hanged Him on the gallows. But crucifixion and Calvary were only the doorways through which physical death came.

The reason why the Virgin Birth is so important is because through this means Jesus came into this world with a spirit that was in communion and in contact with God. He did not inherit Adam's sin nature. He inherited His physical body from Mary, His mother, but He got His spiritual nature directly from the heavenly Father. Technically, Jesus Christ could have lived on this Earth and never faced death. Death had no claim on Him. Death had no authority over Him, because He was not under Satan's law. The devil could not do a thing to Jesus. He tried to kill Him in every way he could, but he could not do so because he did not have any authority over Jesus.

Before Adam sinned, there was no physical death in the earth-realm. When he sinned, he committed high treason against God, instantly died spiritually, and began to die physically. Physical death is the outward manifestation of spiritual death; however, Jesus, when He came into this world did not come into this world with a sin nature. Therefore, death had no claim on Him. They tried to kill Him on occasion, but they could not.

Jesus was in perfect communion and fellowship with the Father, and because physical death had no claim on Him, He had to voluntarily give up His own life. He forfeited His life because He loved us.

When Jesus physically died, His spirit and soul were able to leave His body, descend into the under-world (hell or Hades), and serve the sentence we should have served throughout eternity.

When Jesus went to serve our sentence, He served only three days and three nights because the physical body, at least in that part of the world at that particular time, would begin to decompose on the fourth day. The Bible states by prophecy, more than 500 years before Jesus' birth, that God would not suffer (or allow or permit) His Holy One (talking about Jesus) to see cor-ruption.

In other words, God had promised His Son that His body would never experience corruption. So Jesus had to come back into His body before four days had transpired. Otherwise, decomposition would have begun to set in. The three days and three nights Jesus spent in hell were compressed by God into eternity — He counted it as though Jesus served out eternity for us.

When divine justice was satisfied, Almighty God said, "It is enough." Jesus rose from the dead, picked up His now-transformed and glorified body, went back to heaven, and opened the door for makind to become free from Satan's authority by acceptance of Jesus as personal Lord and Savior.

When Jesus satisfied the demands of divine justice, and when God said, "It is enough," the price for mankind's redemption was paid in full. At that time,

Jesus became the first born-again man. He was not born again because He had sinned, but He was born again because He had died spiritually by virtue of a willful commitment of himself to be made sin for us.

One man took upon himself the sin of everyone that ever lived or ever will live. One solitary figure accepted the degradation, the punishment, the damnation, and hell for all of us.

When I was younger, I got involved with some other boys in an activity we called "joy riding." We had stolen someone's car and we were put in jail for it. I was considered an adult as far as the law was concerned, but I was only eighteen at the time. The sentence was reduced because it was my first offense, so they put me on probation for three years until I was twenty-one. It was on my record that I had been convicted of a felony. It was agreed that when I made restitution (I had to pay a certain amount of money) and went on probation for a while, my record would be cleared, and the judge would stamp my record as having been pardoned. The old record would be wiped out.

I was never so glad as I was when that day came. They had taken my driver's license from me; consequently, some of my activities had been seriously curtailed. But when that pardon came, everything was reinstated. This meant that everything became like it was before I committed the crime.

When Jesus went into hell and served our sentence for three days and three nights, God took our records out of the files of heaven and stamped them *pardoned,* and set us free. That is great news! That is a happy time — a true reason to celebrate!

I was one of the smart alecks, just like some of our young people today are. They think they are going to keep getting away with things just because they haven't been caught. I knew I was not supposed to drive because my license had been suspended, but I went ahead and drove anyway. I was "smart," and no one was going to catch me. But I did get caught, and the law put me in jail. After they put me in jail, I found myself looking through those jail bars, counting the days of my sentence on the wall of my cell, dreaming of the moment when I would get out. On the morning of my release, I got my clothes together and I hit the cement outside the jailhouse running, and I said, "I will never, never, but never, come back here again!" That was a happy time. I was free at last, and I was happy.

When I think of what Jesus did for me, I praise God. He set me free. He set you free — and anyone else who receives Him as Lord and Savior has been set free. Hallelujah!

Let's look at 2 Corinthians 5. This passage helps us to see the truth of this teaching. It is so very important to understand Ephesians 2:5, so that you can understand where you are, and who you are, and why you are in Christ Jesus. This is a legal transaction that is documented in heaven, taken down by the heavenly recorder on God's great computers for all time and eternity.

> **Therefore if any man be in Christ, he is a new creature** [or creation]**: old things are passed away; behold, all things are become new. And all things**

> are of God, who hath reconciled us to himself by Jesus Christ, and hath given to us the ministry of reconciliation.
>
> (2 Cor. 5:17-18)

We have not been given the ministry of condemnation. We do not need to go around, nor should we go around, condemning people and putting them in bondage. But we do need to go and tell them the good news, so that they can be free. We need to tell them about reconciliation — not about condemnation and judgment — and we need to tell them about the love of God.

> To wit, that God was in Christ, reconciling the world unto himself, not imputing [or counting] their trespasses unto them; and hath committed unto us the word of reconciliation. Now then we are ambassadors for Christ, as though God did beseech you by us: we pray you in Christ's stead, be ye reconciled to God. For he [God] hath made him [Christ] to be sin for us, who knew no sin; that we might be made the righteousness of God in Him.
>
> (2 Cor. 5:19-21)

Jesus did not do anything that was sinful; but it says He was "made to be sin" for us. Why? So that we could be exonerated from the penalty of sin, so that we could be set free in Him.

We do not have any righteousness of our own. We have no right to appear in the presence of God by and of ourselves. Just as we had no righteousness, Jesus had no sin. But because He was made to be sin for us, we are made to be the righteousness of God in Him.

In order for Jesus to have completed our redemption, He had to be born again, and He became the first man who was born again. When Jesus was born again, God saw us as being born again.

Look at the first chapter of Colossians, and we will see virtually the same thing, but I think it will perhaps make it somewhat clearer to us. It is so very important to understand our great redemption and our salvation and what price Jesus paid to achieve them, and what it cost Almighty God to redeem us.

> **Giving thanks unto the Father, which hath made us meet [or able] to be partakers of the inheritance of the saints in light: Who hath delivered us from the power [or dominion] of darkness, and hath translated us into the kingdom of his dear Son: In whom we have redemption through his blood, even the forgiveness of sins: Who is the image of the invisible God, the firstborn of every creature.**
>
> **(Col. 1:12-18)**

It is obvious that Paul is not talking about being the firstborn physically because Jesus Christ was not the firstborn physically. There were millions of people who were born before He was. This is not talking about physical birth; it is talking about spiritual rebirth, because Jesus was the first one who was born from the dead — from spiritual death into spiritual life.

72

The word *firstborn* implies *secondborn, thirdborn, fourthborn,* ad infinitum. You do not use the word *firstborn* unless there are other siblings involved. I have a son, and I have to say he is my secondborn son. He is the only son I have right now, but he is my secondborn son, because we had another son who was born earlier who was killed at a very young age in an automobile accident.

If you have only one son, you do not say, "This is my firstborn son." You say, "This is my only son." But when you say firstborn, you automatically separate the child you are referring to from the second, third, fourth children, etc.

The fact that Paul uses the word *firstborn* implies secondborn, thirdborn, ten millionth-born, etc. And, praise God, I am included somewhere in that number, and so are you if you are born again.

> **For by him were all things created, that are in heaven, and that are in earth, visible and invisible, whether they be thrones, or dominions, or principalities, or powers: all things were created by him, and for him. And he is before all things, and by him all things consist. And he is the head of the body, the church: who is the beginning, the firstborn from the dead; that in all things he might have the preeminence.**
>
> **(Col. 1:16-18)**

Jesus is the firstborn from the dead. We know this is not talking about physical death because we know that when Jesus walked the Earth, He raised the widow of Nain's son from the dead. He raised Jairus's twelve-year-old daughter from the dead, and He also raised

Lazarus from the dead. It is talking about spiritual death. The moment we accept Christ as our Savior and Lord, we are counted as having been raised up and born again with Him.

> **Even when we were dead** [this is talking about us] **in sins,** [that is spiritual death] **hath quickened** [made alive] **us together with Christ, (by grace ye are saved;).**
>
> (Eph. 2:5)

God sees us in Christ. So all we have to do is to accept what has already been bought and paid for. And we do that by faith. By accepting Jesus as our Savior and Lord, by repenting of our past life, by turning away from the government of self and the government of Satan, and turning to the government of God through the Lord Jesus Christ, then what Christ has done by becoming sin for us is credited to our account. His sacrifice sets us free, and we become children of God through Him.

> **And hath raised us up together, and made us sit together in heavenly places in Christ Jesus.**
>
> (Eph. 2:6)

The Church traditionally has failed to understand who we really are in Christ Jesus. We have had such a distorted view of ourselves as Christians, that we have done everything we could to cause God to shed many tears because of our ignorance of who we are. Yet, His Word clearly declares who we are. God does not see you as you. He sees you in Christ. He looks at you through Jesus, and when He looks at you through Jesus, you look real good.

We have been defeated in life because we have had a false image of who we really are. We have listened to the devil's lie through "religion and tradition" about what we do not have and what we cannot do. And we have believed the devil's lies, instead of going to the Word and finding out what God has to say about us.

We have been going around thinking we were being humble by saying, "Well, dear brothers and sisters, I want you all to pray for me. I just don't know whether I will be able to make it or not. I have been on the King's highway for many a year now, and I am just an old sinner saved by grace. I am just so unworthy. You all pray for me that I will just make it in, that I will hold steadfast to the end. I am just an old sinner saved by grace, but I am trying to make heaven my home."

That is the biggest lie you ever told! You thought you were being humble and did not know you were being ignorant when you talked about being "just a sinner saved by grace." Friend, if you were saved by grace, you are not a sinner anymore. You are a child of the King. But you are going to have to see yourself that way. You are going to have to get the same estimate of yourself that God has of you. You are somebody because of "Christ in you, the hope of glory" (Col. 1:27).

We need to see ourselves as the righteousness of God in Christ. In fact, if you start doing that, it will help you with your problems. It will help you with all that garbage about being sick and always making mistakes, and always having to come back and whine and cry every week about some dumb sin that you committed. The only reason you do that is because you have gone down to the level of the pig I referred to earlier. Your nature was changed when you received Christ, and you are no longer what you used to be.

The Bible says that you are the righteousness of God in Christ. (See Phil. 3:9.) The Bible tells us to be holy because He is holy. (See 1 Pet. 1:15.) The Bible says that you have been created in the image of God. (See Gen. 1:26.) And the Bible declares that you are more than a conqueror through Him that loved you. (See Rom. 8:37.) We need to see ourselves as holy, as His righteousness, as being created in His image, and as more than conquerors. The Church needs to rise up and see itself as the Body of Christ, instead of as some ragtag, Mickey Mouse, poor-mouthing, bingo-game playing, rummage-sale holding, chicken-dinner-selling church.

The way many Christians and churches see themselves is a disgrace before God. God wants us to see ourselves as the head, not the tail. We are above, not beneath. All too often, the Church has gotten the signals mixed up. We say, "We are the light of the world," but too many Christians seem to think He meant we were to be tail lights. God, however, wants us to be the headlight! We ought to be leading, but we cannot lead until we find out who we really are, until we get a true estimate of ourselves, and until we stop poor-mouthing and crying all the time.

God raised us up together with Christ, out of spiritual death. We have to look at Jesus and find out how God sees us. Whatever He says about Jesus, that is what He says about me and every other Christian.

The Bible says, He **"hath raised us up together, and made us sit together in heavenly places"** (Eph. 2:6). How do we sit in the heavenly places? In Christ! Notice what Ephesians 1:19-20 tells us:

> **And what is the exceeding greatness of his power to us-ward who believe, according to the working of his mighty power,** [The power is toward us — so the whole thing is for our benefit.] **Which he wrought in Christ, when he raised him from the dead, and set him at his own right hand in the heavenly places.**

Let's now return to Ephesians 2:6:

> **And hath raised up up together, and made us sit together in heavenly places.**

Compare this truth with Ephesians 1:20:

> **Which he wrought in Christ, when he raised him from the dead, and set him at his own right hand in the heavenly places.**

When God raised Jesus from the dead, He was physically raised from the dead. He took Him up to heaven and set Him at His own right hand. God, in the spirit, sees us seated there with Jesus, with the same benefits, with the same authority, with the same dominion, with the same power, with the same covenant, with the same Father, and with the same Holy Spirit.

> **Far above all principality, and power, and might, and dominion, and every name that is named, not only in this world, but also in that which is to come: And hath put all things under his feet, and gave him to be the head over all things to the church. Which is his body, the fulness of him that filleth all in all.**
> **(Eph. 1:21-23)**

Since God put all things under the feet of Christ, who is the Head, and we are the body (and the feet are located at the bottom of the body, not stuck to the head), that means that all things are under our feet. That puts us on top of everything, every circumstance, and every condition in life. That makes us winners, not losers. But you are going to have to see that by the Word and begin to take your rightful place!

We have to get God's vision. **"Where there is no vision, the people perish"** (Prov. 29:18), and that is what is happening to a multitude of Christians. They are perishing because they do not have the vision of the Word of God — the vision of the fact that they are unconquerable. Do you realize that you are unconquerable? The only person who can defeat you is *you*. The devil cannot do it, the demons cannot do it, no one can do it — just you!

> **That in the ages to come he might shew the exceeding riches of his grace in his kindness toward us through Christ Jesus.**
> **(Eph. 2:7)**

We need to realize how sweet God is. It says, "his kindness." Some people, even some Christians, are stiff-necked, hardhearted, pious-thinking know-it-alls. They talk about, "I am so great," as though they had done anything by themselves. They are dependent not only on God, but they are dependent on fifty million people everyday just for survival. They think they are such hot stuff: "I don't need the Church; I don't need Jesus; I don't need God; I can do it on my own."

We cannot do anything on our own. We are depending on someone else for just about everything we do. You did not make that automobile you drive; someone else's blood, sweat, and tears developed that automobile. You did not produce the gasoline that runs your car. In most cases, you did not produce or grow the food you eat every day. You did not build the house you live in. You do not provide the electricity you need to live by. You did not make the clothes you wear. We are all depending on someone else for our comforts and needs, and all of us, including those so-called atheists, are dependent upon God.

Thank God that because of His kindness and because of His tender mercy, and because of His love for us, we can become the children of God.

I do not care what some philosopher said about religion being the opiate of the people. No, I will tell you what the opiate of the people is — it is Satan and sin! And they are destroying and killing mankind. Jesus said, **"I have come that they might have life, and that they might have it more abundantly"** (John 10:10). When you learn how to live in terms of the Word of God, you will experience that abundant life!

> **For by grace are ye saved through faith; and that not of yourselves: it is the gift of God.**
>
> **(Eph. 2:8)**

In verse 8, we have a very profound statement concerning salvation:

> **For by grace are ye saved through faith...**

Grace, in its simplest definition, means God's unmerited favor. It is simply God granting to us something we do not deserve, something we have not earned, or something we cannot claim as being ours. Grace is something that is given to us without our having to do anything to receive it.

Saved Through Faith...

Faith is the key to salvation. Faith is the key to activating God's grace. Faith is the key that brings a man, woman, boy, or girl into a right and proper relationship with Almighty God through Jesus Christ.

There is a fallacy that has been promulgated through the years which fosters the idea that God is the "Father of all mankind." This doctrine stems from a philosophy that is based on "the Fatherhood of God and the brotherhood of man." The Bible promotes no such doctrine. You are not my brother unless we are in the same family. The fact that we are all God's creation does not make us all God's children.

The Bible says God created the mountains, the Earth, and the vegetation. But the vegetation is not a child of God, and the mountains are not His children.

Just because God created you does not make you His child. In order to become His child, you have to be adopted into His family. That is what Paul is talking about in Ephesians 2:8 when he says, **"For by grace are ye saved...."**

You may think you do not need to be saved. According to God, you do, because according to God, you are spiritually dead. You are cut off from Him and you cannot become a member of His family unless you have accepted His method of salvation, which is Jesus Christ. It does not make any difference whether you like it or not, that is just the way it is.

When I was a boy, I used to play baseball with my friends in the streets. There was always some guy in the crowd who was a bit better off financially than the majority of us. Invariably, he would be the one who owned the ball and bat. Usually he was also the one who could not play worth a dime. But he owned the bat and ball, so we had to let him play if we wanted to play baseball. I especially remember one boy who was like this. If he wanted to pitch, we had to let him, because it was his game. If things did not go his way, he would get upset and start crying. He would grab his ball and bat and go home. If we wanted to play with his ball and bat, we had to let him play the game his way.

In a somewhat similar vein, we need to remember that this is God's "game!" It is His ball and bat. And if you want to be on the team, you are going to have to play by His rules!

Because this business concerning salvation is so very important, I want to cover some other Scriptures to establish the fact that we (speaking of all mankind now) are not automatically the children of God just because we are born into the world.

Some people are going to be disappointed in the end, because they think that they can play the game by their own rules, and God has to accept anything they do as long as it is in a category they label as "good deeds." The Scriptures show us, however, that this is not the way the song is written.

The organized church, through its pastors and ministers, is supposed to tell the people the truth. They are *not* supposed to tell people only what they want to hear — they are supposed to tell them what they need to know.

You need to know that you are either in the family of God or you are not. You need to know that you are either saved or you are lost. You need to know that you have been born again, or you have not been born again. There is no middle ground — there is no neutral territory.

There was a man sent from God, whose name was John. [This is talking about John the Baptist.] **The same came for a witness, to bear witness of the Light, that all men through him might believe. He was not that Light, but was sent to bear witness of that Light. That was the true Light** [referring to Jesus], **which lighteth every man that cometh into the world.**

(John 1:6-9)

Notice that the Apostle John says, **"that was the true Light."** The only time you use the word *true* is when you want to distinguish it from the *false*. The very fact that he says "true light" implies that there is some "false light." There are many people today who are following that false light.

You ought to know whether what you are believing is true or not. If you do not know this, you have no business believing it. If you think it is true, then you ought to prove it.

When you find out that it is true, then hold on to it, and if you find out that it is not true, then get rid of it. It is just that simple.

There is a true light and there is a false light. And if you have to ask, "Well, how do you know what is true?" Then you do not have the true, because if you had it, you would not have to ask that question.

> **He was in the world, and the world was made by him, and the world knew him not. He came unto his own** [meaning the nation of Israel]**, and his own received him not. But as many as received him, to them gave he power** [the authority, the right, or the privilege] **to become the sons of God, even to them that believe on his name.**
>
> **(John 1:10-12)**

Now, the word *become* implies that whatever you become, you were not that before you became that, or you would not have to *become* that.

If God had to give us the power ("us" meaning those who received Jesus by this faith we are talking about in the second chapter of Ephesians), or the authority or the right or the privilege to become the sons of God, then it is obvious that before He gave us that right, we must not have been sons already. This lets us know that everyone is not automatically a child of God, but only those who receive Him are given this authority, this right, or this privilege.

If you have not received Jesus as Savior and Lord, guess what? You are not a child of God, and as simply as I can say it, you are going to hell.

Now do not get uptight with me. I did not write the Bible. The Holy Spirit wrote it through anointed men of God. And if you do not like it, you can change it. In fact, you are the only one who can. All you have to do is to receive Jesus, then you are automatically a child of the King.

How do you receive Him? By faith. How do you receive any truth that you cannot actually physically see or touch? By faith.

We see, then, that when it says (in the eighth verse of the second chapter of Ephesians), **"For by grace are ye saved through faith,"** this is talking about those who have received Christ. That is what salvation is all about — it is about receiving Christ. It is more than just believing in Him. There are many people who say, "Well, I believe in Jesus." What do you believe about Him? "Well, I believe that He lived." Wonderful. "I believe that He came 2,000 years ago to the Earth." Marvelous. "I believe that He died on the cross." Great. "I believe that He went into the grave for three days and three nights." Stupendous. "I believe that He rose from the dead. I believe that He went back to heaven. I believe that He is coming again." Yes, but have you accepted Him as your personal Savior and Lord? "No." Then you are going to hell, and you are going to miss out on the Kingdom of God.

And that not of yourselves: it is the gift of God....
(Eph. 2:8)

Paul is saying that Jesus himself is a gift to us, and when we receive Him as Lord and Savior, we receive salvation. You do not have to pay for this gift. There is nothing you can do to earn it, and you cannot be good enough to receive it on your own merit. Many people do not understand this fact. They think, "Well, I am not so bad. I don't get drunk, I don't smoke, I don't use drugs, I don't gamble. I don't carouse around. It is true I don't go to church, and I have not accepted Jesus as my Savior and Lord, but I am just as good as some of those people who do go to church."

But, friend, that is not what gets you saved. It is not a matter of doing this or not doing that or doing the other. If you slid out of your mother's womb into the arms of a nurse in the delivery room, and she immediately took you and placed you in the nursery, and you stayed there for the rest of your life without ever going outside, and you never did or thought anything bad, at the end of your lifetime, you would still go to hell.

Someone might say, "Why, I can't believe that, that does not make any sense." The only reason you cannot believe this is because you are missing the whole thing. You think that salvation is a matter of what a person does, but it is not. Salvation is the gift of God. When a gift is involved, there is nothing you can do to merit the gift. If you do anything to earn it, it ceases to be a gift, and it becomes a wage or something you have merited. The only thing you can do with a gift is either to accept it or reject it.

Not only is salvation a gift, but the faith by which or through which you get the salvation is also a gift. In other words, God has to give you that faith.

How does God give it to you? He gives it to you by the preaching of the Word.

> **So then faith cometh by hearing, and hearing by the Word of God.**
>
> **(Rom. 10:17)**

That is why ministers must preach the Word. I know some have thought that preachers preach in order to entertain, and there are some who do this. I have seen some who put on a pretty good show. However, the purpose of the verbal proclamation of God's Word is so that faith can come, so that people can receive knowledge concerning salvation.

The most needful thing that a man, woman, boy, or girl has need of is salvation. I do not know how salvation works, but there is something about verbally speaking God's Word that brings faith. That is the way God has designed the system.

Have you noticed that God has designed the system in the vegetable kingdom so that vegetables come forth by the planting of seeds? He has designed the system so that the trees and plants grow as a result of seeds being planted. He has also designed the system relative to His Word so that faith — His faith, which is a gift — will come when His Word is planted in the human heart (spirit).

That is the reason why it is necessary for you to be careful about what you hear, because what you hear will affect your faith, either in a positive or a negative way. That is the reason why many Christians do not have any more faith than they do, because they are listening to a bunch of noise and there is no faith coming from that. Then they often wonder why after they have heard someone preach, they are still so lean on the inside, and do not have any real joy or peace in their lives. You cannot get peace from noise, because noise does not minister to the spirit-man.

All a minister has to do is to proclaim the Word to you, but you have to decide what you are going to do with it. You can accept it or you can reject it. The choice is yours; no one can make you receive the Word of faith — not even Almighty God. He will have the Word put out there for you and say, "Here it is, tiger, take it or leave it — it is all up to you." You can walk away from it, but if you do, you can never be able to say you did not have an opportunity to receive God's Word.

The very fact that it says, "faith cometh..." means that faith was not there before, and that is why it "cometh," so that it can be there. Now, it is up to you to do something about it.

You will not get faith by reading the Bible. You will get information, you will get knowledge, but you will not get faith by reading. That is not the way God has designed the system to work. He has designed it so that faith comes by hearing.

Someone might ask, "What if you can't hear?" Don't you think God knows that you cannot hear? Do you think God would penalize someone because he cannot hear? God will take care of that person in some way. A minority of people cannot hear. God will take care of those people. He is not going to hold someone accountable who cannot hear, but He will hold those who can hear accountable.

Some people are always arguing about, "Well, I just don't know about this Christianity business. I don't know how God could love the world. What about all those people over there in the jungles who have never heard about Jesus?" That is not your problem. Don't you think God knows where those folk are in the jungle? He will take care of them; you are responsible for taking care of you. Your responsibility is to deal with the truth that comes to you. You can rest assured of one thing, that the Judge of all the Earth will do right, and if the man in the jungle dies before he has heard the Word, God will or has taken care of him in some way.

Notice that it does not say, "So then faith cometh by having heard." Did you get that? This is an excuse that people try to drum up by saying, "Well, I went to church last Easter, and I heard." No, it does not say faith comes by having heard (past tense). It says, "Faith comes by hearing" (present tense, continuum, ad infinitum — that implies an ongoing process, forever)!

You may have been exposed to something, but that does not mean you heard it. Did you ever tell something to someone, and they did not hear what you said? You were looking at him or her right in the eye, and later on you reminded him or her, "Now I told you so-and-so," and with a look of surprise, the person replies, "You did?" That person did not hear, because he was not really listening.

I believe that is why the Spirit of God has led me in my ministry to do so much repetition. I do not do that on purpose. But it is something the Spirit of God gives me an unction to do. And it never ceases to amaze me when, even after I have repeated something ninety-nine times, people will come up to me after a service and say, "Did you say so-and-so?" They were sitting right there, watching me, seemingly listening to me, and they never heard what I said.

Jesus said: **"Take heed what you hear"** (Mark 4:24). Why did he say this? Because what you hear is going to affect your faith.

That is why Jesus also said, **"Go ye into all the world, and preach the gospel to every creature"** (Mark 16:15).

The gospel is the good news about God's great love for mankind. It is God's good news about the fact that a person can have his sins blotted out, washed away, and he can become a child of God. It is the good news that a person can be set free from the prison house of degradation.

Since we know that faith comes by hearing, and hearing by the Word of God, if we do not go and preach the gospel to every creature, then every creature is not going to hear, and if people do not get to hear, faith is not going to come. And if faith does not come, they cannot believe. And if they cannot believe, they are going to hell!

When we go preach the gospel, faith will come, and when it does, the unsaved can exercise their wills and receive the salvation that follows on the heels of God's Word being preached.

For by grace are you saved through faith....

(Eph. 2:8)

Let's pinpoint this truth because many people have been confused on this issue. I know I was for a long time. I thought that salvation had to do with the way I felt. I thought I had to have a "salvation feeling." But notice that this verse says, **"For by *grace* are ye saved through faith"** — it is not by *feeling*, not by *emotion*, not by *experience*, but by *faith*. Feelings, emotions, and experience have nothing at all to do with your becoming a child of God.

You may experience feelings at the moment when you receive salvation, but do not make the mistake of determining the validity of that salvation by virtue of the fact that you either have or you do not have a feeling. That is where many people have gotten all confused. I know it had me confused.

I was not brought up in the church. I got saved the same year that I was married. My wife and I started going to church. In the church we went to, the members were very emotional and demonstrative. They said they were worshiping the Lord. I did not know any differently, and I had no reason to doubt their sincerity. Some of the members would holler and dance all around the church. They called it "shouting."

The church leaders led me to believe that my relationship with God was based on my having an emotional experience every week like they did. So I tried to work up my emotions, but I could not. I did not feel like running up and down the aisles or shouting like some of the deacons did. One of them would jump straight up in the air and take off running. I am not making fun of that; that was his thing to do, but it was not mine. And as a result, Satan used that against me and made me think that I was not genuinely saved because I never had those kinds of feelings.

I was trying to base my relationship with God and my encounter with Jesus on some kind of emotional experience, or some kind of feeling, when all the time, the Bible very plainly says: **"For by grace are ye saved through faith"** — it is not by feeling!

Faith means taking God at His Word. If God said it, that settles it, I believe it, and that is that! Faith does not have anything to do with feelings. If you get some feelings, count them as fringe benefits, but when I work on a job I do not work for the fringe benefits, I work for the paycheck. Now, if you have some fringe benefits coming along with the paycheck, I will have those too, but when payday comes, I am not going to settle for fringe benefits!

I understand that I have a reputation of being a pastor who does not like feelings. This is a misunderstanding. It is not that I do not like feelings, but I have been tricked by feelings too many times in the past, and

I am not going to be tricked any longer. I'll take the uncompromising Word of God every time in place of feelings. When you are standing in the center of the intersections of life, and Satan is coming in like a flood by bringing cancer, or some other sickness or disease, or poverty and fear against you, you had better know more than "shouting." You had better know how to take the Word of God and say, "In the name of Jesus, I rebuke you, devil" and have the Word of God coming out of your spirit and through your mouth.

You cannot go by feelings all the time. That is one of the reasons why some couples have problems in their marriages. That is why many of them get divorces. When the feelings of romance wear off, they think they do not love each other anymore, and then they think they are ready for a divorce. They have not understood what love is really all about; it is deeper than just some kind of palpitating heart syndrome. The palpitating heart is a part of love, but you need to realize that if that is all you are basing your marital relationship on, you might as well go on to the divorce court. Love is deeper than feelings. It is deeper than emotions. It is actually a commitment.

These couples do not realize that they have to get into the mature aspect of the marriage relationship. Part of the reason why this happens is that our society, the movies, and the media exploit hugging and kissing and the show of affection. Most of the time after marriage you do not have a great deal of time for hugging and kissing. Instead, you find yourself "out there," making a living and when you are at home, you are taking care of the family. Certainly there are times for hugging and kissing, but not at the expense of daily living.

Romanticism is real, and it has its place, but you have to grow from that into a mature loving relationship that is based on more than just a palpitating heart, hugging, kissing, and holding hands.

The things of the Lord develop in our lives in a similar fashion. There will always be the explosive power of the new-found affection — like a bomb going off, and it will be glorious. But if you use those feelings as your guide and you say, "I know that I am saved because I feel like this," then when the day comes that you do not feel like that, you will start wondering, "Am I really saved?" There are many people who go up and down this way all of their lives.

The Word says the same thing on Monday that it does on Tuesday that it does on Wednesday, Thursday, Friday, Saturday, and Sunday. It says the same thing on Easter Sunday, Christmas Day, New Year's Day, Mother's Day, and on your birthday. The Word of God stays the same; it never changes. When you base your faith on the Word of God, you will always be up and never down, because the Word is always the same.

In fact, your relationship with the Lord should develop to such a place that you do not even have to think about it. As long as you find yourself wondering, "Am I saved or not saved," you are in trouble; such thinking will keep you off-balance. But when you get to the point when you do not think about it, you will have a firmer foundation on which to develop your spiritual life.

Summarizing what we have covered thus far, Paul says, **"For by grace are ye saved through faith; and that not of yourselves: it is the gift of God"** (Eph. 2:8). Salvation is a gift, Jesus is a gift, but so is the faith by which you procure that salvation. It is a gift, and it is brought to you by the preaching of the Word. When the Word comes, faith comes; when faith comes, you can exercise your will to receive or reject Christ. We can see this principle demonstrated clearly in the tenth chapter of Romans:

> **But what saith it? The word is nigh thee [or near thee], even in thy mouth, and in thy heart: that is, the word of faith, which we preach: That if thou shalt confess with thy mouth the Lord Jesus, and shalt believe in thine heart that God hath raised him from the dead, thou shalt be saved. For with the heart man believeth unto righteousness; and with the mouth confession is made unto salvation.**
>
> **(Rom. 10:8-10)**

Salvation is simply a matter of you exercising your will in line with the clearly revealed Word of God. It is not a feeling; it has nothing to do with feelings; it only has to do with God's Word.

Notice it does not say anything about: "If thou shalt stand on your head, or hang from the chandeliers, or roll down the aisle, or have goose bumps running up and down your spine, or green lights flashing off and on in sequential order." No, Paul said, **"That if thou shalt confess with thy mouth the Lord Jesus...."** That separates the wheat from the chaff. You have to get to the point where you are willing and able to say, "Jesus Christ is my Lord. I believe in Him, I accept Him, as the Lord of my life."

You have to do it with your mouth. "Well, the Lord knows that I have a praise in my heart. And though I do not say, 'Praise the Lord,' and though I do not say, 'I love Jesus,' and though I do not say that 'Jesus is my Lord,' the Lord knows that I have a praise in my heart." And the Lord knows you are telling a lie, too!

Jesus said, **"Out of the abundance of the heart the mouth speaketh"** (Matt. 12:34). So, if it is in your heart, it will come out of your mouth. And if it is not coming out of your mouth, you must not have it in your heart, because if you are believing in your heart, and saying what you believe with your mouth, it is going to show up in what you do, in what you say, and in the way you live. And people are going to know it.

Part 2 — Ephesians 2:9-22

Not of works, lest any man should boast.

(Eph. 2:9)

You cannot do anything to merit salvation. There are some churches that teach that women cannot get saved with makeup on. They say to their female members, "You have to take that lipstick off, because God will not save you with lipstick on."

That is ridiculous! Yet, there are some churches that are very strict concerning women wearing makeup. They tell their female members, "No, you cannot be filled with the Spirit with all that paint on. You have to take all that makeup off."

It would be funny if it were not so pathetic. Paul says, **"Not of works...."** It is a matter of faith — not of works. God does not care whether you have lipstick on, or whether you do not. He is not concerned with how you dress your face up; rather, He is focused on what you are believing in your heart (spirit). That is what concerns Him.

Personally, I believe women look better with makeup on, and that, on the whole, it enhances their natural beauty.

People are confused regarding so many issues concerning salvation and pleasing God. We have made so many religious rules and regulations regarding what people can or cannot do to serve the Lord.

If you are not wearing this or that because you think it is a mark of spirituality, or if you think that because of doing this, or not doing that, that God is going to hear your prayers, or you think that doing something or not doing it is going to have something to do with you being filled with the Holy Spirit, you are missing it. God does not fill you with the Holy Ghost because you do not have makeup on, and He does not fill you because you do. He fills you because you believe, and because you receive by faith.

Those people who have all those rules and regulations concerning the wearing of makeup do not leave their church buildings and houses in the color of the raw materials they were built with; they paint the walls. I have not seen anyone put carpeting on the floor of any church that was in its natural wool coloring that came from the sheep. It is always dyed with a color. If people say, "You cannot put any paint on your body because the Lord wants to fill you with the Holy Ghost," then to be consistent, they would have to say that God could not live in their painted church buildings either.

If God will not live inside their bodies with paint on them, then He will not live inside their church buildings with paint on them! But this is human tradition, not the Word of God.

I have never seen any holy person order a car from the factory and tell the manufacturer, "I want to leave the car in its natural metal color; do not put any paint on it." No, they always get their cars with some type of color. I have not seen many people, particularly in this society, who wear clothes that have the undyed natural color of their fabrics. There is usually some kind of pattern or color on the material. Yet, some of these same people who look down on ladies who wear makeup (or "paint," as they call it) expect God to come into their painted churches but not into the bodies of women with "painted" faces. It does not make sense because it is not logical.

All these things about not doing this or not doing that are really attempts on the part of people to work their way up to God. Do you know what that is called? It is called *religion*.

The Bible very clearly states, **"Man looketh on the outward appearance, but the Lord looketh on the heart"** (1 Sam. 16:7). God looks on the inside of the individual. So whatever you do to try and earn your salvation is irrelevant and immaterial. It is a matter of what Jesus has done, and simply accepting His provisions by faith is what brings a person into the family of God.

Sometimes I hear people say, "Well, I don't have to go to church with all of those hypocrites. I am doing my good deeds in the community and I am feeding the hungry, and I am clothing the naked, and I am housing the poor. I work on this committee and I work on that committee, and we give this to those people, and we give that to these people. Surely God is going to accept me in the end."

If you are not doing things in line with the Word of God, I do not care how many so-called "good deeds" you do, it will not bring you salvation. Granted, they may be very good deeds, and they may help many people, but it is not what you do that gets you into the Kingdom of God, it is what Jesus Christ has already done, and your acceptance of what He has done that gets you in.

> **For we are his workmanship, created in Christ Jesus unto good works, which God hath before ordained that we should walk in them.**
>
> **(Eph. 2:10)**

This means that God has programmed into the system the fact that we are to do good works. This truth immediately alerts you to the fact that there must be some bad works, because if there were no bad works, then God would not have to designate and make a distinction by saying, "good works." That means that some things are good, and some things are bad, and that means that you have the opportunity, the privilege, and the responsibility to examine your works to find out if they are good or if they are bad.

The Bible says, **"...God hath before ordained that we should walk in them"** (Eph. 2:10). The *them* in this verse refers to good works.

It did not say we *would*, but it says we *should*. Unfortunately, there are some Christians, even though they are created in Christ Jesus, who do not do good works, and that is very sad. It is up to us whether we do good or bad — it is a matter of choice.

It is really easy to do good works once you make up your mind to do them. The hardest part about it is making up your mind. Satan will lie to you and tell you there are more benefits to be gained from doing bad things, but this is not so. No, if more benefits came from doing bad things, then God would have created us to do bad things rather than good.

> **Wherefore remember, that ye being in time past Gentiles in the flesh, who are called Uncircumcision by that which is called the Circumcision in the flesh made by hands.**
>
> **(Eph. 2:11)**

The church at Ephesus was what we would refer to as a Gentile church. Since the Redemption, there are only three groups of people God sees on the Earth: Jews, Gentiles, and the Church of Jesus Christ. And everyone on this planet belongs to one of these three groups. The Church of Jesus Christ is made up of both Jew and Gentile Christians.

The Letter to the Ephesians was written primarily to the Gentile church at Ephesus. All the letters or all the books which are written in the New Covenant, of course, are written to the Body of Christ, to both Jews and Gentiles in the faith. But it so happens that Paul is specifying the Gentiles in this passage.

When he says, **"Wherefore remember, that ye being in time past Gentiles..."** implies that apparently they are not considered Gentiles now. Therefore, they must have been considered something else, or Paul would not have said **"in time past."** The statement, "in time past," means a point in time that preceded the present time.

Once a person accepts Christ as his or her personal Savior and Lord, he or she ceases to be a Jew or a Gentile, and becomes a child of God. Others might refer to this person as a Jew or a Gentile, but God refers to the individual as "my son," or "my daughter," or "my child." He does not make any distinction as to whether one is a Jew or a Gentile once that person becomes a part of His family.

A long time ago, God called a man named Abraham and He made a promise to him: "If you follow me, I will make you a father of many nations. Out of you kings will come; out of you a mighty nation shall come." Abraham believed God, followed Him, and it was accounted to him for righteousness.

Out of Abraham Isaac came; out of Isaac Jacob came, and out of Jacob came the twelve sons or the twelve tribes that eventually became the nation of Israel — the Jewish people.

The Jews were to be God's channel through which His Word was to be promulgated throughout the Earth. But they, being human, did not always do everything right, just as you and I have not always done everything right.

Jesus came out of the lineage of the Jews. That is why the Jews are known as God's chosen people. Jesus was actually the end of the Law (the rules and regulations the Jews were supposed to follow). The Law was the schoolmaster to bring the world to Christ. Once the world got there, it would not need the schoolmaster anymore.

God made a very peculiar covenant with Israel. The sign of that covenant was the sign of physical circumcision. It was a sign that God made in their flesh, so they would always remember that they had this covenant with Him.

Over a period of years, instead of saying, "the children of Israel," or "the Hebrews," or "the Jews," people would refer to them as "the circumcision," because no one else had this peculiar relationship with Almighty God. The Jews considered everyone outside of the nation of Israel to be a Gentile; therefore, the Jews would refer to the Gentiles as "the uncircumcision."

This is what is meant in verse 11 where it says, **"...who are called Uncircumcision by that which is called the Circumcision...."**

> **That at that time ye were [No. 1] without Christ, [No. 2] being aliens from the commonwealth of Israel, [No. 3] and strangers from the covenants of promise, [No. 4] having no hope, [No. 5] and without God in the world.**
>
> **(Eph. 2:12)**

That is a heavy, heavy indictment. The fourth one is absolutely staggering in its import:

...having no hope...

There is no statement that is as earth-shattering as that one. When a man, woman, boy, or girl gets to the point where it could be said of them that they have no hope — friend, they are about as far out and as far down as they can ever get.

I do not say this in a condemning way, but I say it from the standpoint of God's Word: If you have never accepted Jesus Christ as your personal Savior, you are without hope, and that is an awesome thing to think about. There is no hope for the world outside of Christ.

Do you realize that a man who is without Christ is without God? This blows a hole in that statement about, "I do not accept Jesus as my Savior and Lord, but I believe in God." According to God and according to the Bible this statement still renders you hopeless, without God.

There are many people who are deceived. They are going around talking about, "I believe in God, but I do not go to church and I do not believe in Jesus. I believe He was a good man, that He was a prophet, and that He lived many years ago, but I do not believe that He was the Son of God, but I do believe in God."

These people are being deceived and they do not even know it. They may believe in God, but which god? There is another one that is called the god of this world. His name is Satan. He transforms himself into an angel of light so that he can deceive the people into thinking that he is the true, living, and real God.

The Bible teaches that if you do not have Jesus, you do not have God. And it is not what you think that counts; it is what God thinks.

No one has to be without God. That is why Jesus came. That is the beautiful part about it, God did not leave us in the dark. He made himself available to us through Jesus, and that is the reason the devil fights so tenaciously to keep people away from Christ. Because once you get into Jesus, you will get into God. And once you do that and get knowledge of spiritual things and start walking in the Word and walking by the power of the Spirit, the devil is finished with his intimidation of your life.

> **But now in Christ Jesus ye who sometimes were
> far off are made nigh [near] by the blood of Christ.**
>
> **(Eph. 2:13)**

I say this to any one who belongs to a so-called Christian religion that denies the blood of Jesus Christ: GET OUT OF THAT PLACE AS THOUGH IT WERE ON FIRE! Because it is — it is on fire of hell, and it will take you right down to hell!

We are made near by the blood of Jesus, which simply means that Jesus shed His blood to take away our sins. And when we acknowledge and accept that fact, and confess Him as the Lord of our lives, His precious blood brings us into a relationship with the Father. Any religion, or any school of thought that denies the blood of Jesus, is on dangerous ground, and should be avoided at all cost.

The Bible plainly states that it is by the blood that we have been brought nigh (near).

> **For he is our peace, who hath made both one,
> and hath broken down the middle wall of partition
> between us.**
>
> **(Eph. 2:14)**

In the beginning of God's dealings with mankind, there were two groups of people in the earth-realm — the Jews and the Gentiles. The Law of Moses stood between the two. Jesus brought the Gentiles and the Jews together into one new body, the Body of Christ. Jesus tore down the wall that separated the two, and brought us together in himself.

Having abolished in his flesh the enmity [that is, the "feud" or the "estrangement"], even the law of commandments contained in ordinances; for to make in himself of twain [that is, of two — Gentile and Jew] one new man, so making peace.

(Eph. 2:15)

And that he might reconcile both unto God in one body [one group] by the cross, having slain the enmity thereby.

(Eph. 2:16)

Notice what Paul says here, **"and that he might reconcile both...."** If Jesus had to reconcile both Jew and Gentile, it is obvious that both must have been estranged, or they would not have needed to be reconciled.

...that he might reconcile both unto God in one body...

That body is the Body of Christ — the Church of the Lord Jesus Christ. No, not the buildings that sit on corners of streets — each with a different name out front — but those of us who have accepted Jesus as Savior and Lord.

The cross is where it all started. The empty tomb is where it ends. The reconciling process began at Calvary, and it ended when Jesus came out of hell (or Hades) itself — picked up His body, and went back to heaven. That is the total action of the three days and three nights — all of that action together is what made this new body.

> **And came and preached peace to you which were afar off, and to them that were nigh** [near].
>
> **(Eph. 2:17)**

In Old Testament days, the closest people to God were the children of Israel. The Gentiles were "far off." The Bible has already said that we were without hope; we were without Christ; we were aliens from the commonwealth of Israel; we had no part in the covenants; we were far off.

So if Jesus preached the same thing to both of them, guess what? Both of them must have needed what He was preaching, whether near or far.

God is doing a new thing. He has been doing a new thing for the last 1,900 years — creating a new body, the Body of Christ, and every person who accepts Jesus as Savior and Lord becomes an integral part of this new body — both Jews and Gentiles. We are all one in Christ Jesus!

> **For through him we both have access by one Spirit unto the Father.**
>
> **(Eph. 2:18)**

This verse confirms what I said earlier about getting to God. It is very clear.

...for through him...

Him refers to Jesus.

...we both have access by one Spirit unto the Father.

Turn that verse around and it reads, "For without him, we do not have access to the Father." This confirms that you cannot get to God without Jesus. You can try every way you want, but it is as Jesus, in effect, said, "Anyone who tries to come in any other way than through the door is the same as a thief and a robber." (See John 10:1).

> Now therefore ye are no more strangers and foreigners, but fellow-citizens with the saints, and of the household of God.
>
> (Eph. 2:19)

I am a citizen, and the Bible is my passport. I have a right to be in the Kingdom. My documents (the Word of God) prove it. I am a citizen, and so are you, if you are in Jesus Christ.

If you are not in the family of God, you have no citizenship or rights in the Kingdom of God. As citizens of the Kingdom, we have a constitution and a bill of rights that guarantee us everything we will ever need and anything that we will ever dare to dream about that is consistent with a godly life.

And are built upon the foundation of the apostles and prophets, Jesus Christ himself being the chief
corner stone; In whom all the building fitly framed
together groweth unto an holy temple in the Lord.
(Eph. 2:20-21)

There are two temples: one is individual — my
body is the temple of the Holy Spirit. The other consists
of all Christians, who, together, are a temple. Jesus is
the chief cornerstone. All of us who dare to walk by the
Word, all of us who have received Him as our Savior
and confessed Him as the Lord of our lives are the
temple of God. The church building is not the temple
Paul is referring to.

God is working in and through us to bring enlight-
enment to the world. He is in the midst of us by His
Spirit in the earth-realm. And yet God is in me and in
you, and we, along with every other Christian
throughout the entire world, in whatever age or time
they live, are the temple of God collectively.

Some people still have problems with their lives as
Christians. Usually, the problem is with the flesh or the
body. They may not know what to do with their bodies,
and what not to do with them; where to take them, and
where not to take them; what to put into them and what
not to put into them. People who have these problems
usually don't have any problem whatsoever with their
conduct in a church building, however.

I have been a pastor for a number of years, and I
have watched the churches that I have pastored fill up
and run to overflowing with people. During all this

time, I have never seen anyone commit fornication or adultery in church (speaking about the church building itself). I have not seen anyone pop pills in church. I have never seen anyone pull out a pack of cigarettes and light one up in church. I have never seen anyone stand up and start cursing in a church setting. All these things are problems for the flesh, and I have never seen anyone have these problems when we come together as the Body of Christ inside a church building. The reason is because people respect the building, even if they are atheists, even if they are agnostics, or even if they are from some other kind of religious persuasion. Ninety-nine out of 100 people will show respect for a church they enter.

Yet, away from a corporate collection of Christians and the church structure, some people have all kinds of problems with their flesh: cigarettes, sex, narcotics, gambling, temper, cursing, foul mouths, foul thoughts — they have to struggle with those things in their physical bodies, but they do not have these problems in a church building. Why is that true? It is because they have been taught that the church building is to be respected as being the house of God.

Just as you respect a church structure as a holy place, you ought to be respectful with your body, because that is where God really lives. God does not live inside a building. A building is just a building. The only thing that makes it of any value is because we — the Body of Christ — are there. When we leave the church building, it is exactly what it looks like: cement, concrete, wood, carpet, etc. If Christians controlled their bodies the way they do in church, they would not have the problems so many of them experience with regard to controlling the actions of their bodies. They treat their bodies as though they were nothing, but our bodies are what Christ paid His life for. Our bodies are what Jesus bled and died for. Our bodies are what they whipped Him and beat Him for until the flesh came off His back. Our bodies, not a building, are what He came to redeem.

> **In whom ye also are builded together for an habitation of God through the Spirit.**
>
> **(Eph. 2:22)**

Do you know that God wants to live among us? There are many people who are afraid of God. You start talking about God and they start "getting nervous in the service." They do not want to get too close to God because He represents holiness.

I have news for you: your best friend is God. The reason some people are afraid of Him is because they do not really know Him. They are going by what they heard someone say.

Contrary to what some people have been taught, God is not interested in hurting anyone. He is not interested in our not having a good time. God wants us to enjoy ourselves. The thing about it is that the things some people consider to be good times are not proper behaviors. What some folks call having a good time involves illicit sex, drinking, drugs, and the whole bad scene. God wants us to enjoy life, but there is a way to do so. Sin does not have to be involved in order for someone to have a good time.

God wants to live among us, to help us, to bless us, to enhance our lives. He does not want to stifle us, to take things away from us, but to get our joy and our good times in their proper focus.

3

The Believer's Ability in Christ
(Ephesians 3:1-21)

> **For this cause I Paul, the prisoner of Jesus Christ for you Gentiles....**
>
> **(Eph. 3:1)**

For what cause? For the cause of this holy temple. For the cause of God building us together into a habitation in which He can dwell.

> **If ye have heard of the dispensation of the grace of God which is given me to you-ward: How that by revelation he made known unto me the mystery; (as I wrote afore in few words, Whereby, when ye read, ye may understand my knowledge in the mystery of Christ).**
>
> **(Eph. 3:2-4)**

The word *mystery,* in this context, almost sounds as if Paul is contradicting himself. Usually the term *mystery* connotes something that is unsolvable, something you cannot know or understand; however, this word *mystery* that Paul uses is not talking about some-

113

thing you cannot know. It is talking about something that you can only know by the Spirit of God. The things of God are a mystery to those outside of the Kingdom. Unless you are in the family, you are not going to have knowledge of what is going on in the family.

There are two kinds of knowledge. One kind of knowledge is called sense knowledge, because you learn this type of knowledge through your eyes, through your touch, through your sense of smell, through your taste, and through your hearing.

But there is another kind of information that is higher than sense-knowledge information. It is called "revelation knowledge," and it only comes from God by His Spirit. It is knowledge that you cannot find through your senses. It has to come through your spirit. And then your spirit has to educate your mind, which will, in turn, direct your body in line with God's Word. *It is revelation knowledge, which comes from the Word of God.*

There are some things you can learn in school, but there are some things about God you cannot learn in seminary, Bible school, or any other kind of school. You have to learn these things directly from the Spirit of God, through revelation knowledge.

Revelation knowledge is the highest kind of knowledge. It is the kind of knowledge that I want to operate in all the time, because revelation knowledge reveals the deeper truths of God's Word, which you cannot get in any other way.

> **Which in other ages was not made known unto the sons of men, as it is now revealed unto his holy apostles and prophets by the Spirit.**
>
> **(Eph. 3:5)**

I am going to share some revelation knowledge with you. I realize there are some people who will feel threatened by this, and I apologize in advance because it is not my purpose to antagonize or threaten anyone. Let's look at verse 5 again:

which in other ages was not...

It is obvious that when Paul says "other ages," he is not talking about the age in which he lived, because he would not use the expression "in other ages" if he were.

was not made known...

The mystery of God was not made known. Therefore, if it was not made known in other ages, then everyone who lived in the other ages did not know anything about this revelation. Consequently, if they did not know anything about this revelation, they could not live in this revelation.

Here is my point: If someone who lived in an age gone by had started writing down all of the information and insights they had accumulated in their era, their writing would not contain all we need to know to solve mysteries of the present age. Anyone, therefore, who would take the time to go back to the other age in order to get the information that had been written down in the previous epoch in an effort to try to live according to that information in the present, would miss what God is presently revealing entirely. This would be true because what is revealed now was not revealed back then.

This phenomenon is taking place in many churches today. Such churches and denominations are still trying to get people to walk by the Old Testament, trying to get them to live by the Old Covenant, trying to get them to do, say, and act the things that were under the Law. However, the Bible says, "That the mystery was not revealed unto them." When people put themselves in bondage by trying to live up to what was true for people in another era, they are missing out on the present picture, because they are not operating where the revelation is.

You have to get into the new era in order to understand and live according to what is revealed in the new era. It is fallacious, and ridiculous, and nonproductive to try to live in the present by what was given in the past, because what was given in the past does not have the present revelation.

Which in other ages was not made known unto the sons of men, as it is now revealed....

(Eph. 3:5)

How in the world are you going to live your present life based on an old revelation? Yet, there are still multitudes of Christians who are bound by the Old Testament. And there are many people who are going to churches today that are telling them, "Well, you cannot go to church on this day, and you cannot go to church on that day, and you cannot eat this, and you cannot eat that, and you cannot wear this and you cannot wear that. You cannot do this and you cannot do that." These people are utterly in bondage to these restrictions and rules. Paul is plainly telling us, in verse 5, that it "was not made known unto them."

Apparently, if it was not made known unto them back then, and it is now made known to us, it is obvious that the present revelation supersedes the old one, because if the old one was good enough to live by, we would not need a new one.

The very word *new,* as opposed to *old,* tells us that the new must be better than the old, because if the old were good enough you would not need a new. Since the Bible is divided into the Old Testament and the New Testament, it is obvious that the new must supersede the old.

Someone might ask, "Well, what is the Old Testament for?" It is for us to look at and find out what not to do. It is for us to examine and find out how they missed it back there in some cases, and how they achieved certain things in others, so that we can gain insight into finding out how we can make it in life and be successful. If they could not get away with certain things, then we are not going to get away with them either. If they made it by obeying God's Word, based on the amount of revelation they had, then it is obvious that we can make it based on operating in the revelation that God gives us. The Old Testament is there for us to learn lessons from, not to lead us into bondage.

That the Gentiles should be fellowheirs, and of the same body, and partakers of his promise in Christ by the gospel.

(Eph. 3:6)

In the Old Covenant, Christ was not revealed. Some passages mentioned that He was to come, but He was not revealed then as He is revealed now under the New Covenant. We have to follow the New Covenant in order to find out about Jesus.

Note three important things Paul says here: **"That the Gentiles should be fellowheirs...."** A Gentile is every person who is outside the nation of Israel, regardless of his geographical location, the color of his skin, or the texture of his hair and slant of his eyes. An heir is someone who inherits something. We are inheritors of the promises of God.

....and of the same body...

What is that body? We read about it in the first part of the second chapter of Ephesians, where God took those who were far away and those who were near, and brought them together into one body. That body is the Body of Christ — the Church of the Lord Jesus Christ. This does not refer to the buildings with crosses on top of them, situated on street corners in towns and cities all over the world. I am talking about the people in those buildings who have accepted Christ and confessed Him as the Lord of their lives.

...and partakers of his promise in Christ by the gospel.

You cannot partake or inherit the promise in Christ if you do not know Him. How are you going to be a partaker without even knowing Him? You cannot; it is impossible. You are going to have to at least know Jesus, and the way you do that is by getting into His Body. That is what the ministry of the Word is all about.

> **Whereof I was made a minister, according to the gift of the grace of God given unto me by the effectual working of his power.**
>
> **(Eph. 3:7)**

Let me stick a pin here. I firmly believe that there are many men and women who are in the wrong place, doing the wrong thing. What I mean is that there are people who call themselves preachers who should not be preaching. God is not a failure. If He has called you, He is going to confirm His call on your life, and your calling is going to produce fruit.

There is a story in the Old Testament that tells of a king who was waiting for a word from the battlefront. A messenger was sent. The messenger was instructed to take the message directly to the king.

Another man who was not sent decided that he was going to run also. Although he did not have the message or the authority to go forth, he outran the legitimate messenger. When the false messenger ran up to the king, the king asked, "Do you bring good tidings? What of the battle?" The false messenger was standing there, huffing and puffing, while off in the distance, the real messenger who had the true message and the royal authority could be seen approaching. When the king asked concerning the battle, the false messenger opened his mouth to speak and fell over dead.

He dropped dead! He was not called to bring the message. He was operating in a realm where he had no business, and it did not work, and it will not work. Someone might ask, "But how do you know whether you are called or not?" Let me clarify something for you. When I say *called*, I mean that God calls some to function in the Body of Christ as ministry gifts to the body, such as the five-fold ministry gifts recorded in Ephesians 4:8-11; and 1 Corinthians 12:28. According to Acts 8:4, it appears that every Christian is a "preacher," but obviously every preacher is not a ministry gift to the Body of Christ. Such a person is not called; therefore, they do not have to worry about it. If you are called, you will know it!

If God calls you, He is going to hold you accountable for fulfilling that which He has called you to do. Since He is going to hold you accountable for what He has called you to do, He is obligated to make what He has called you to do very plain, so that you will never be able to say, "Lord, I did not know you called me." Yes, God is obligated to make your calling plain, and if it is not plain, then He did not call you. It is just that simple.

There are many men and women who are calling themselves, "Reverend So-and-So." And they are standing in the way of people coming into the Kingdom of God, because there is no anointing on what they are saying or doing.

Notice that Paul says, **"Whereof I was made a minister."** He did not say that he had made himself one.

Being a minister is a gift or calling of God. You are called or you are not. It is not something you can buy.

I knew a man some years ago who wanted to be a preacher so badly that he bought himself a doctor of divinity degree for fifty dollars. He bought this degree seemingly thinking that if he hung it on the wall it would somehow make him a minister of the gospel. Only the Spirit of God can make you a minister of God. Only the anointing of the Holy Spirit can produce fruit, only the call of Jesus on your life can make you a minister of the gospel, and if God did not make you a minister, do not try to be one.

...according to the gift of the grace of God...

It is the grace of God. None of us who stand in the office of a minister is worthy to be there on our own merits. God's calling on our lives makes us able to do what He has called us to do. God spoke to me one day in an audible voice and said, *"You are to preach my gospel."*

I replied, *"Yes, Lord."* And when I said yes to His calling, it made me able to do what He called me to do. I would rather be a minister of the gospel than anything else in the world. There is no greater calling; there is no greater vocation; there is no greater work; there is no greater anything in all this world than to stand and be able to preach the Word of Life. But it is God's calling that makes you able and worthy.

...by the effectual working of his power.

It is God's power that makes it work. If His power is there, there will be some confirmation of that power.

There will be some results of that power. There will be some benefits of that power.

A minister should not just drag along year after year, hardly breaking ground, hardly doing anything but just being there. If the power of God is there, it is going to produce life. I would be very upset if I started out as a pastor with twelve people in my congregation and ended up with eleven people some twenty-five years later. Such an experience would lead one to conclude that either something is wrong with God or with pastor. If God's power is working in me, it has to produce life because there is life in God. When His power is working in and through you, it has to produce life in those to whom you are ministering. If that power is not being generated, you are missing something. In such a case, you may not have been filled with the Spirit of God, you are not called, or you are not operating in the Word. Something is lacking, and it is certainly not on God's part.

Unto me, who am less than the least of all saints, is this grace given, that I should preach among the Gentiles the unsearchable riches of Christ.

(Eph. 3:8)

I know what Paul is talking about in this verse. It is amazing how God chooses things to work through that the world would never choose. I think about all the times when I walked the streets of Los Angeles, trying to find a job to take care of my family. I could not qualify for this, I could not qualify for that, or I could not pass certain tests for particular types of jobs.

Many times we think God wants the child who comes out of his mother's womb to be a genius with an IQ of 200! You would think God would choose a man who has scholastic ability, a man who is eloquent, a man who can stand and command the masses to listen to him by the resonant tone of his voice. You would think God would choose a man like that to be a minister of the gospel. No, God takes the thing that no one else wants. God takes the thing that men reject and He makes something out of it.

You might say, "Why? That does not make sense." It is not sense. God does not operate by sense; God operates by faith. Because if God took the man with all the qualities I have described, the man with all the brains, the man with the eloquent voice, and the looks to go with the voice, the man who could command the masses, if it were that man whom God used, then everyone would say, "Why, he is supposed to succeed; look at him. He is so smart, he is so handsome, he has such an eloquent voice. What do you expect? He has a Ph.D., he has an IQ of 200; he is supposed to be a wonderful success."

No, God takes someone whom no one wants. And when someone looks at that individual and says, "I do not understand it. I do not see how that person can be where he is. He does not have the brains, he does not have the looks, and he does not have the strength to do what he is doing." That is when the power of God can be seen.

When God takes an ordinary man and fills him with His Spirit and lays His hands upon him, that ordinary man becomes extraordinary. You cannot give credit to his education, you cannot give credit to his eloquence; you have to give all the credit to the power of God, to the Spirit of God, and to the Word of God.

The Scriptures say, **"Not by might, nor by power, but by my spirit, saith the Lord"** (Zech. 4:6), and it is the Spirit of God that gives a man the ability to operate in the power of God!

A minister, a real minister, an anointed minister of the Lord Jesus Christ, is a gift to the Body of Christ.

> But unto every one of us is given grace according to the measure of the gift of Christ. Wherefore He saith, When he ascended up on high, he led captivity captive, and gave gifts unto men. (Now that he ascended, what is it but that he also descended first into the lower parts of the earth? He that descended is the same also that ascended up far above all heavens, that he might fill all things.) And he gave some, apostles; and some prophets; and some evangelists; and some, pastors and teachers.
>
> (Eph. 4:7-11)

We should really read verse 8 and then go right into verse 11, because verses 9 and 10 are actually parenthetical statements, and not necessary to the context. Read it as follows:

> Wherefore he saith, When he ascended up on high, he led captivity captive, and gave gifts unto men. And he gave some, apostles; and some, prophets; and some, evangelists; and some, pastors

and teachers; For the perfecting [or maturing] **of the saints, for the work of the ministry, for the edifying** [or building up] **of the body of Christ.**

(Eph. 4:8,11-12)

I stand in the office of pastor and teacher. According to these verses of Scripture, I am a gift to the Church of the Lord Jesus Christ. My purpose is three-fold: **to perfect or mature the saints, to do the work of the ministry, and to edify or spiritually build up the Body of Christ.** Not only am I a ministry gift to the Church, but so are all the other people who are a part of my ministry, both those who are paid and those who are not paid, because these folks help me do the job God called me to do. They are called to assist me in ministering to the saints.

God never made anything with two heads on it. Anything that has two heads is a monster. There may be many fingers to help the head do what it is supposed to do, but there will only be one head. That is God's order. All ministers of the gospel who are anointed by the Spirit of God are gifts to the Church, and they should be received as gifts.

...that I should preach among the Gentiles the unsearchable riches of Christ.

(Eph. 3:8)

Notice that Paul did not say, "unsearchable poverty." He said, "the unsearchable riches of Christ."

125

There is no poverty in Jesus. There is no lack or want in Him. In Jesus Christ, there is an abundant supply for every area of our lives, more than enough to put us on top.

When something is unsearchable, you cannot dig deeply enough to find its bottom. You can search and search, but you never come to its end. And yet, think of all the Christians who are poor and do not have enough to make it in this world.

Not long ago, I read a pamphlet that was written by a minister. Its topic was prosperity. He said that we (speaking about preachers) should not talk so much about prosperity and having material possessions.

He went on to ask how one could go about preaching prosperity in a country that is undeveloped, "near pagan," and in a part of the world that is called the Third World. My answer to him is that I would preach prosperity there in the same way I am preaching it in America. This minister does not understand that prosperity is not predicated upon the economy of the land, prosperity is predicated upon God's "unsearchable riches."

God is not poor because a nation is poor. God is not rich just because a nation is rich. God is rich because He is God. I would preach the same message of prosperity I am preaching now wherever I would go. I would preach it even if the listeners did not have a pot to cook in. If the people who are in destitute situations will learn how to operate in the Word of God, they will start rising from their poverty and lack. There are many people who think the same way this minister thought. They feel we should not preach prosperity and make such a big thing out of it, but they have to understand that it is not the fault of those who preach prosperity that people do not have prosperity. When we arrived on the scene, there were the "haves" and the "have nots." In fact, I was among the "have nots" for a long, long time. I was living in a nation that had plenty, and I had nothing but a hard way to go and a hard way to get there.

But I found out that God is not a respecter of persons. I found out that my success is not predicated on the society I live in; it is not predicated on the system of government I am under; it is not predicated on the geographical area of the Earth that I occupy, my prosperity and my success are tied into Almighty God.

I have news for you. It does not matter what part of the world you live in. God is still God, and His Word teaches the "unsearchable riches of Christ." Paul did not tell us just to preach the riches of Christ in America; he did not say we were to preach it only in the Western World; he did not tell us to preach it only in Asia or Europe — He simply said to preach "the unsearchable riches of Christ"! And if people will keep listening to the Word and seeking the "unsearchable riches of Christ," it will not be long before they will have those riches.

There is no reason for the Church of the Lord Jesus Christ to be in lack, to be in want, to go without, to not have enough, to have to struggle, to have to beg, to have to resort to rummage sales and bake sales, bingo games and all the other activities that are designed to raise funds.

One of the reasons the Church has not been able to do what it is supposed to do is because it has been operating in the poverty syndrome for too long. You cannot buy something with nothing. You cannot go on television or buy television equipment with rummage sales. Yet, think of how many people we can minister to in an hour — millions of people — through television. There are approximately 7,000,000 people in New York City alone. Think of it. In one hour, we have the potential of ministering to 7,000,000 people! Think of all the people in Los Angeles, Washington, D.C., Chicago, and the other major cities of America that we can minister to through the medium of television. You cannot do that based on income from bake sales, car washes, and barbecues. Thank God for the "unsearchable riches of Christ"!

The riches are available to us, not to squander on our own lusts, but rather so that they may become a means to an end — reaching people for Christ.

God surely does not want you to be poor. How could He want you to be poor, and for you to go through life with your needs unmet, to always be struggling to pay your bills and to keep food on the table, when He talks about the "unsearchable riches of Christ"?

It is inconsistent to think that God would will poverty for any of His children, but this is the portrayal that many churches, down through the years, have presented to the world. Their philosophy is that God does not want us to lead the good life, because we may become covetous and sinful. If He did not want us to enjoy the good life, why did He tell us about "the unsearchable riches"? That is like holding out a carrot in front of a horse — a carrot he cannot eat.

The Bible says that God does not tempt people. (See James 1:13.) In light of this truth, why would He hold out to us the impossible dream of something we could not achieve or rise to? God would not do this. When He tells us about riches, He is telling us about them so that we can set our sights higher, so that we can come up out of the bottomless pit of lack and into the rarefied atmosphere of God's best.

Jesus said, **"If ye continue in my word, then are ye my disciples indeed; And ye shall know the truth, and the truth shall make you free"** (John 8:31-32).

I am not free if I cannot pay my bills. I am not free if I cannot feed my family. I am not free if I cannot take care of my automobile. I am not free if I do not have something to give toward the work of the gospel. I am not free if I am in fear. I am not free if I am chained to a bottle of pills, or to a dialysis machine or to any other kind of machine.

I am not free if I have hate and prejudice in my heart. Jesus said the truth will make you free. He did not say the truth would lead you to freedom. He said, **"...And the truth shall make you free."**

> **And to make all men see what is the fellowship of the mystery, which from the beginning of the world hath been hid in God, who created all things by Jesus Christ.**
>
> **(Eph. 3:9)**

In verse 10, Paul is getting ready to tell us why the mystery has been hidden in other ages, and why it is coming to pass now.

> To the intent that now unto the principalities and powers in heavenly places might be known by the church the manifold wisdom of God.
>
> (Eph. 3:10)

To the intent...

Everything contained in the verses from 1 to 9 in Ephesians 3 represents the intent Paul is referring to.

Through the Body of Christ, God is going to display His "manifold wisdom." Do you realize how important that makes us? Do you realize now why the devil tries to drive us into the ground? It is because he does not want anyone to know about this wisdom of God.

That is why he puts pressure on us. That is why he tries to bomb us out. That is why he tries to discourage us with fear, sickness, disease, poverty, and all the rest of the ills that plague mankind. Satan knows that if the Church ever gets loose, the "manifold wisdom of God" is going to be displayed for all time and eternity through the Church.

...that now unto the principalities and powers in heavenly places...

When I first read this Scripture, I thought Paul was saying that God was going to display His "manifold wisdom" through the angels. Then I realized that we hold a higher position with God than the angels. The angels are the servants of Jehovah God. They are His angelic messengers and workers. We are the children of God.

As mighty and as powerful as the angels are said to be, we stand head and shoulders above them, because Jesus raised us to that higher position.

Hear what the Apostle John says by inspiration of the Holy Spirit: **"Beloved, now are we the sons of God, and it doth not yet appear what we shall be: but we know that, when he shall appear, we shall be like him; for we shall see him as he is"** (1 John 3:2).

God is going to use the Church, and He is going to show the angels — all those He has called to be servants or **"ministering spirits, sent forth to minister for them who shall be heirs of salvation"** (Heb. 1:14) — that it is through the Church that He is going to display His "manifold wisdom."

God lives in what is referred to as the third heaven, or the heaven of heavens. This is in contrast to the heaven that is actually the atmosphere around the Earth, and the middle realm that is called "the heavenlies," where Satan and his demons operate.

I like to compare these three heavens to a salami sandwich. Think of the top slice of bread as being the heaven of heavens where God dwells, and the bottom slice of bread as being the heaven, or the firmament around the Earth, and the piece of salami as being the heavenlies.

The angels of God live in the third heaven with God (on the top slice of bread). Satan's headquarters (the heavenlies) are in the salami area, and just as the salami touches the top slice of bread and the bottom slice, so Satan has access both to the heaven of heavens and to the earth-realm. That is why we have to contend with his influence in human affairs.

The Bible confirms this configuration in Ephesians 6:12: **"For we wrestle not against flesh and blood, but against principalities, against powers, against the rulers of the darkness of this world, against spiritual wickedness in high** [or heavenly] **places."**

Satan's primary area of operation is in the earth-realm. The Book of the Revelation says that he is called, **"The accuser of our brethren"** (Rev. 12:10). This Scripture lets us know that the devil does have access to the throne of God, where he accuses the Christian.

Satan's headquarters, however, is in the heavenlies where his emissaries go forth into the earth-realm to do his bidding.

...the principalities and powers...

Principalities are spirit-creatures. The word *powers* means *authorities*. They are those evil spirits who have rulership in certain areas over certain situations. Satan has the world divided into certain geographical areas, and he has assigned certain demons to these areas.

In the Book of Daniel, we read that Daniel had a vision, which he did not fully comprehend. He prayed and asked for understanding. Twenty-one days after he had prayed, the angel Gabriel came to him with the interpretation of the vision.

In explaining why it took him twenty-one days to come with the answer, Gabriel said to Daniel: **"...Fear**

not, Daniel: for from the first day that thou didst set thine heart to understand, and to chasten thyself before thy God, thy words were heard, and I am come for thy words. But the prince of the kingdom of Persia withstood me one and twenty days: but, lo, Michael, one of the chief princes, came to help me; and I remained there with the kings of Persia" (Dan. 10:12-13).

That prince of Persia was not the actual prince who sat on the physical throne of Persia, but it was the demon spirit that operated through that monarch to cause havoc upon the Earth.

In every area of the world, these spirits exist, and Satan has them doing his work. That is why certain adverse and tragic things are always happening in certain parts of the Earth. When you look at the geography of the Earth, it is interesting to note how certain negative things seem to be so prevalent in certain areas of the globe. That is because particular types of spirit-creatures inhabit those locations and work through men to bring about adverse situations.

There is a story in the Bible about a man called the Gadarene demoniac. He was demon-possessed and ran naked around the tombs, cutting himself. When Jesus came into the area, the spirit that was in this man recognized Him. When Jesus told the evil spirit to come out, the demon spirit in the man said: **"...My name is Legion: for we are many"** (Mark 5:9). When Jesus again told the spirit to come out of the man, the Bible says the spirit, **"...besought him [Jesus] much that he would not send them away out of the country"** (Mark 5:10).

The Bible tells us that these demons left the man and went into a herd of swine, which threw itself over a cliff and drowned in the sea below. Even pigs have enough sense not to be demon-possessed! Those spirits did not want to leave that area of the world because that was where they were assigned to operate.

In certain parts of the world there is rampant starvation. That is because there are poverty spirits that operate in those areas, and these spirits keep the people and the land poor.

There are gambling spirits that gather in certain parts of the world, and most things in those areas have to do with some form of gambling. Similarly, there are areas where prostitution and other vices prevail because there are evil spirits assigned to these locations and these spirits promote these immoral activities.

The Father God intends to bring all of these negative activities to an end. The group he is using to do this is a group that no one would ever dream could get the job done, and that group is the Church of the Lord Jesus Christ.

This is astounding, because most denominations have not taught this. They have acted as though we are to remain in some type of holding pattern, and we, the Church of the living God, are supposed to stand and say, "Here we are, and we are not going to be moved."

One day Jesus asked His apostles, **"...Whom do men say that I the Son of man am? And they said, Some say that thou art John the Baptist: some, Elias; and others, Jeremias, or one of the prophets. He saith unto them, But whom say ye that I am? And Simon Peter answered and said, Thou art the Christ, the Son** of the living God. **And Jesus answered and said unto him, Blessed art thou, Simon Bar-jona: for flesh and blood hath not revealed it unto thee, but my Father which is in heaven. And I say also unto thee, That thou art Peter, and upon this rock** [the rock of the confession of Peter's lips that Jesus was the Christ — the Anointed One] **I will build my church; and the gates of hell shall not prevail against it"** (Matt. 16:13-18).

The Church has never seen this statement the way God meant for us to see it. I saw this Scripture for years and did not understand it correctly. I thought we, as Christians, were supposed to anchor our feet into the ground and let Satan and his demon hosts come against us, and we would not be moved.

That is the concept the Church has had, but that was not what Jesus meant at all. When He said that the gates of hell will not prevail against the Church, we have to realize where gates are located. Gates are anchored to walls, and walls are around cities, and the city that He is talking about is hell itself.

This means that if we take the Word of God, which is the sword of the Spirit and the power of God, and we launch an offensive attack against Satan and all of his demon cohorts, against sickness and disease, and poverty and fear, that those gates will not be able to stand, because we can knock them down with the Word of God.

That is what Jesus is talking about. We are not supposed to be standing still somewhere in some kind of a holding pattern. There is a song about "holding the fort." Jesus did not say anything about "holding the fort." He said for us to take the land.

However, we cannot do it when we are whipped and defeated; we cannot do it when we are poor and sick; we cannot do it when we are fearful and afraid. We have to get into the **"unsearchable riches of Christ."** We have to stand on the Word of God. We have to stand by the power of God. We have to put on the whole armor of God and take the helmet of salvation, and the sword of the Spirit, and the shield of faith, and go after the enemy and knock his gates down. And those gates will not be able to stand against the Christian who is prepared for battle!

I believe Jesus is not coming back until we have completed our job. I hear the Father God saying to Jesus, **"Sit thou on my right hand, Till I make thine enemies thy footstool"** (Luke 20:42-43 and Heb. 1:13).

How is God going to do that? The Father is seated on the central throne, Jesus is seated at His right hand, and the only One of the Godhead that is in the earth-realm today is the Holy Spirit. And the Holy Spirit does not do anything by himself. He works through human vessels that are yielded to Him. Those human vessels are better known as the Church of the Lord Jesus Christ. God is doing it through the Church, and by the Church, and His "manifold wisdom" is going to be seen.

When the end of the ages comes and the consummation of all things has been achieved, everyone for all time and eternity will realize that God was just, that God was mighty, that God was perfect and that God knew exactly what He was doing when He created this new group — the family of God — the Church of the Lord Jesus Christ. I am talking about a Church composed of blood-washed, Spirit-filled, Word-toting,

Word-believing faith people. I am talking about a Church comprised of people who know their God. The Bible says that **"the people that do know their God shall be strong, and do exploits"** (Dan. 11:32).

Jesus did exploits. He was the "Man for all seasons." He was on top of every situation, never showing any anxiety or fear. One day some people came to Him and said, "You had better be careful; Herod is going to get you."

Jesus told them, "Go tell that fox, I cast out devils, and I do cures today and tomorrow and I am going to Jerusalem and that is that!" (Luke 13:31-32). Jesus let everyone know who He was — and we are to be like Him.

> **According to the eternal purpose which he purposed in Christ Jesus our Lord: In whom we have boldness and access with confidence by the faith of Him.**
> **(Eph. 3:11-12)**

In the fourth chapter of Hebrews, we see a corresponding passage of Scripture that shows this very clearly.

> **Let us therefore come boldly unto the throne of grace, that we may obtain mercy, and find grace to help in time of need.**
> **(Heb. 4:16)**

You cannot come boldly to the throne of grace unless you have access to the throne. The "throne of grace" is the throne of Almighty God, and we, as His children, have a right to come into the presence of God and make our petitions known to Him and expect to be heard. We can confidently talk to our heavenly Father. We can have a counseling session with Him, and we can fellowship with Him. In other words, we can talk with God whenever we want to, because we have access to the throne of grace through Jesus Christ.

Christians have been led to believe that we are supposed to be docile, little kittens, and anyone who wants to can kick us around. The traditional church has misunderstood what humility is all about. Humility does not mean to be taken advantage of, walked on, cheated, robbed, killed, or defeated.

This kind of humility is not the same kind of humility Jesus displayed when He went to the cross to redeem mankind. He willingly became sin for us and gave himself over to the Jews and to Pilate in order to become our sacrifice. That is an entirely different thing. When Jesus walked the Earth and ministered to the people, He walked boldly and no one spit on or took advantage of Him.

We, too, are to be bold like Jesus, and that boldness should be based on our relationship to and with Almighty God. As I said before, there are some people who are afraid of God. Someone might say, "Yes, Brother Price, but the Bible says that **'the fear of the Lord is the beginning of wisdom'** (Prov. 9:10)." They need to understand what the word *fear* means in the Bible when it is used in reference to God. It does not mean to be scared or afraid of God. The kind of fear spoken of in the Bible is a reverential kind of fear — it is the same kind of fear one should have for anything that can harm you if you are not careful to observe the rules and regulations governing the power that operates it, as in the case of electricity, fire, etc.

For example, I have a hot water heater in my house which has a gas pilot. When the water temperature goes down, the pilot automatically causes the burners to go on, and the fire starts and the water gets heated. When there is enough hot water, the burners go off. I am not afraid of the fire that heats the water, but then I do not play with it either. Fire burns, and it can harm me, but I am not afraid of it, because I know its dangers and I treat it accordingly. If I were afraid of fire, I would not have the heater in my house. No, I am not afraid of fire, I just have a reverential fear or an awe or respect for it.

In other words, we recognize that God is almighty and that He is not to be trifled with. But we should not be afraid of Him in the sense of trying to run and hide from Him. Yet, that is what some people do. Some people are so afraid of God that they will not even pray to Him. They will come and ask me to pray for them. They believe I can get to God before they can. They feel inadequate and unworthy. If God believed we were unworthy, He never would have said **"Come boldly unto the throne of grace..."** (Heb. 4:16). The reason we can come boldly is because we have a right to be there because of Jesus.

> **Wherefore I desire that ye faint not at my tribulations for you, which is your glory.**
>
> **(Eph. 3:13)**

When Paul uses the word *tribulations* here, it is because he had to go through quite a few negative experiences. Satan will always shoot at those who are in the forefront of the ministry. If he can stop God's ministers, he can stop their influence on other people.

If God has called you to any kind of ministry and you cannot stand pressure, you had better get out of the ministry, because Satan is going to put pressure on you in order to try and discourage you. He will have people talking about you and calling you everything but a child of God. All of it is designed to frustrate you, and to get you so upset that you will throw in the towel and say, "Oh, I am not going to preach anymore. They are talking about me and calling me a false prophet. My feelings are hurt, and I am not going to preach anymore." That is just what the devil wants you to do.

If you let such criticisms bother you, you will never be effective for God — you will never be able to be a worker together with Him. Satan will see to it that you will experience pressure, because he knows if he can stop the leaders, he will stop the followers.

You have to understand that you, as a Christian, are on enemy-held ground; consequently, you can expect the devil to shoot at you. Thank God, the Word says, **"...this is the victory that overcometh the world, even our faith"** (1 John 5:4). Thank God, the Word says, **"...greater is he that is in you, than he that is in the world"** (1 John 4:4).

The tribulations may come, but I use tribulations as steppingstones to step up higher and keep on rising in the things of God. I just use them as launching pads. Trials and tribulations did not stop Paul, and they will not stop you, unless you let them.

> **For this cause I bow my knees unto the Father of our Lord Jesus Christ, Of whom the whole family in heaven and earth is named.**
>
> **(Eph. 3:14-15)**

The family in heaven consists of all our brothers and sisters in Christ who have physically died and have gone on to glory. They are still part of the family.

When a Christian physically dies, his spirit and soul leave his body to go to be with the Lord in a place called paradise, which is located in the third heaven, to await the great day of Jesus' return. When Jesus comes back to the Earth, He is going to bring with Him all the family that is now in heaven. Then those of us who are still alive at that time will be caught up together in the air with the ones who return with the Lord. The bodies of those spirits and souls who are in heaven will be raised from the dead (that is what resurrection is), and reunited with their spirits and souls. Then we will all be with the Lord forever — in our glorified spirits, souls and bodies.

> **That he would grant you, according to the riches of his glory, to be strengthened with might by his Spirit in the inner man.**
>
> **(Eph. 3:16)**

If there is an inner man, there must be an outer man. The outer man is your flesh. The inner man is your spirit — this is the real you. God strengthens us with **"might by His Spirit,"** and that is the reason Jesus wants us to be filled with the Holy Spirit. Jesus does His work in us through His Spirit. That is why Satan fights against the baptism with the Holy Spirit so vigorously. He knows that if he can keep a believer from receiving the gift of the Holy Spirit, he can virtually control that person's life.

The way the devil operates is, first, to keep you from coming to Christ. If he can do that, he has you going to hell with him. If that does not work, and somehow you get saved, then the second part of his game plan is to keep you ignorant of who you are in Christ, ignorant of your rights in Christ, ignorant of what you can do in Christ, and ignorant of the Holy Spirit.

Satan knows that if he can keep you spiritually ignorant, keep you in your own ability, and keep you from being filled with the Spirit, then he can cause what God said would happen in Hosea 4:6: **"My people are destroyed for lack of knowledge."** Satan believes he can destroy your life because he believes you will not have the ability to supernaturally withstand the onslaught he can bring against you by his demon hordes. That is what he has been doing to the Church for years.

In most churches today, there is no victory in the people's lives. They are scared, sick, poor, struggling, hateful, mean, strifeful, prejudiced, and all the rest.

God works through His Spirit. But the Holy Spirit is a gift, just as salvation is a gift. We must receive this gift that God has made available to us.

The early churches that are spoken of in the Bible were Spirit-filled churches — the people in them operated in the gifts of the Spirit. You cannot operate in the gifts of the Spirit without being filled with the Spirit. What happens much of the time is that when people read the Bible, they read it through their denominational glasses, so to speak. And since their particular denomination does not believe in speaking with tongues, when they read those passages about being filled with the Spirit, their minds draw a blank, and they reject that part of the Word of God.

This is what I did for seventeen years. Whenever I read about speaking with tongues or being filled with the Spirit, my mind drew a blank. I do not remember ever reading those passages of the Scriptures about the Holy Spirit. When I received the Holy Spirit, I thought God had slipped something into my Bible. I wondered where in the world these passages had been, because I had been reading the Bible for seventeen years and I never saw that I needed to be filled with the Holy Spirit. It happened that way because the churches I belonged to said we did not need to speak with other tongues. God never said that. The Bible never said that; people said that! When I stopped listening to people and started listening to the Word, I climbed out of the bag I was in and got turned on to the real truth of God's Word.

...to be strengthened with might by his Spirit in the inner man.

This means to be strengthened in the inner man, the spirit-man, the man who is in contact with God. Some people think they are in contact with God through their bodies, but they are not. You cannot contact God with your physical body. That is why so many people have a problem with finding God, because they are trying to relate to Him physically. God is a Spirit, and in order to contact Him, you must do it through your spirit. Some people have the idea that God is a mind. God is not a mind. God is a Spirit.

In the fourth chapter of John, Jesus is seen going through a particular part of the country called Samaria. He stopped by Jacob's well, near a city called Sychar. He sent His disciples into the village to buy some food and other things for their travels. While He was there, a woman came to draw water. Jesus engaged her in conversation. In the course of the conversation, they began to talk about spiritual thirst. In the process, Jesus made a statement to the woman concerning the nature of the heavenly Father.

> Jesus saith unto her, Woman, believe me, the hour cometh, when ye shall neither in this mountain, nor yet at Jerusalem, worship the Father. Ye worship ye know not what: we know what we worship: for salvation is of the Jews. But the hour cometh, and now is, when the true worshippers shall worship the Father in spirit and in truth: for the Father seeketh such to worship him. God is a Spirit: and they that worship him must worship him in spirit and in truth.
> (John 4:21-24)

Notice the word *must* — this is not an option. You have no other choice if you are going to worship God. We have to worship in spirit and in truth — not in the flesh, but in the spirit.

It is true that we live our Christian lives in the physical world through our flesh. But when it comes to contacting Almighty God, we do so through our spirits, not through our minds.

Some ministers teach that God is mind because in Philippians 2:5 Paul said, **"Let this mind be in you, which was also in Christ Jesus."** They say God was in Christ, so *mind* was in Christ, so God is *mind*. But that is not what Paul said. He was using a figure of speech, which we use all the time. For instance, we say, "Why don't you make up your *mind*?" What we are actually saying is, "Why don't you make a decision?" When Paul said, "Let this *mind* be in you," he meant, "Let the same commitment, the same love, the same dedication, the same purpose that Christ had be in you as well."

> **That Christ may dwell in your hearts by faith; that ye, being rooted and grounded in love....**
> **(Eph. 3:17)**

The word *dwell* means to *live in, settle down in, and take up residence in.* God calls those things which be not as though they were. (See Rom. 4:17.) God says, "I live in you and dwell in you and walk in you." How does He do this? By His Spirit. Now there really is no way for us to comprehend this, and really there is no reason to try, because there is no way we could ever fathom this phenomenon of Almighty God. So, just accept it.

The Holy Spirit has the ability to be everywhere at the same time. How? I do not know. But He does. And God is in us by His Spirit. We do not know what constitutes the Holy Spirit. He is referred to as a Person. References to Him are in the forms of the masculine personal pronoun, *He, Him,* or *His.* He is the third Person of the Godhead, and He has the ability to be in us — the Christian — around us, beside us, everywhere at all times.

You might say, "I don't understand." I know it, because it is in a realm that we cannot comprehend with our human intellect. Just think about it, some seventy-five years ago when people started talking about going to the moon, many people said these folks were crazy. They said this was just science fiction. They asked questions, such as: "How could you possibly get there? How would you get away from the pull of the Earth's gravity?" They had all kinds of questions, because at that time, scientists did not have the capability or technology to accomplish such a feat. Now it is not such a big thing. In fact, when scientists talk about launching a rocket, most of the time people do not even pay any attention. It is not news anymore. Why? Because we have the technology to do it. We know that it is possible. It has become commonplace.

The same ideology can be applied to the operation of the Holy Spirit. We cannot comprehend the Spirit with our human minds, but we will be able to do so someday when we receive our eternal minds. In the meantime, all we have to do is to accept what the Word of God tells us about the power of the Holy Spirit.

...That Christ may dwell in your hearts by faith...

Some Christians are like yo-yos, up one day and down the next. They are not really sure whether they are saved or not, they are going by their feelings. As long as they feel it, they are fine, but when that feeling begins to wax and wane, they start getting into doubt, wondering, "Am I really saved?"

God is not a feeling. The Bible says that Christ is to dwell in our hearts "by faith" — not by feelings, not by emotions, not by signs and wonders, but by faith. That means that because the Word says Jesus is in us, we confess that He is there, we believe that He is there, and we act in accord with what the Bible says is true. Physically, Jesus is not there. He is seated at the right hand of the heavenly Father. But the Holy Spirit, who causes us to become new creatures in Christ Jesus when we become born again, is Christ's representative as the Spirit of Christ in us. Jesus is there by faith. The Bible says it, I believe it, and that settles it.

This means that I have to act as though Jesus is dwelling in my spirit. If He is in there, I cannot tell a lie. Can I? Because if I tell a lie, He that is in me has heard the lie. I have lied in the presence of the Almighty. I cannot fornicate. Can I? Because Jesus is right there in the room with me; He is in me.

Someone who reads this may be a fornicator or an adulterer. If so, I want you to remember you are taking Jesus to bed with you in an illicit affair. In all of your sexual fantasies and your sexual excursions within the realm of your mind, Jesus is there.

In all of the malice you hold against certain people, against certain races or ethnic groups, Jesus is right there. He is aware of your wrong attitude. He is in you by faith.

If Jesus Christ came to you right now in the flesh — just suddenly appeared in the flesh — and said, "I am going to travel with you for the next week. I want to spend a week with you." You would be watching your P's and Q's, to be sure. You would be crossing your T's and dotting your I's. You know you would. You would be on your best behavior. You would not let one of your little vulgar words escape your lips — not with *the Man* standing right next to you. But even though He is not standing there where you can see Him, He is in your spirit. Cursing your brothers and sisters in Christ, using profanity, thinking no one hears you — He hears you, and you grieve Him. You grieve Him just as you would if He were standing beside you physically. You have to get that picture of Jesus established inside of your mind and in your spirit — Jesus is in you by faith! Once you get that settled, you will never have a problem about whether you are saved or not, because it will not matter how you feel.

I have heard some people say, "Well, I tell you what, if you cannot feel it, you do not have it. I have to feel my religion!"

I usually reply to such a person, "Do you have brains?"

When they answer in the affirmative, my response is, "Have you ever felt them? Have you ever felt the physical blood pump that pumps the blood through your body? What does a heart feel like? Do you have intelligence? What does intelligence feel like?" The point I am making by these questions is that feelings have nothing at all to do with the reality of God. That does not mean that there may not be some feelings associated with your relationship with God, but you have to learn how to base your relationship with the Lord on faith, and not on feelings.

...that ye, being rooted and grounded in love.

The only way you can be rooted and grounded in love is by being rooted and grounded in the Word. The Father and Jesus are not here, and the Holy Ghost you cannot see. But the Word of God is here. And God's Word is God's will and plan revealed to us. God wants us to be anchored and permanently settled in the knowledge of Him. The only way we are going to get to that point is by being taught the Word, by studying the Word, by confessing the Word, and by living the Word.

...rooted and grounded in love...

Love is the underlying foundation of our Christian life. **"For God so loved the world, that he gave..."** (John 3:16). Likewise, we should so love that we give, giving our lives to the Lord, and giving our lives to one another. God does not want us to waste our lives. The days of sacrifices are over, in the sense that God would want us to sacrifice our lives to the death. Our dying is not going to do God any good. He needs us to be alive.

He needs us to be healthy. He needs us to be wealthy. He needs us to be filled with His Holy Spirit. God cannot get anything accomplished through a corpse.

The Jews sacrificed animals under the Old Covenant, but Jesus became our Sacrifice, and He ended sacrifices once and for all.

Are you rooted and grounded in love? If you are not, thank God, you can be. Some people do not know what love is. They think love is going to a church where you hug and kiss all the time. True love is based on how we treat one another. Love is being honest and truthful with one another. Love is being concerned about one another and looking out for one another's welfare. Love is doing things that will edify and build one another up to make us better people, better Christians. Love is giving of ourselves for Jesus' sake and for the Word of God; it is not just kissing and hugging. Sometimes there are situations where that will be okay, but you cannot make hugging and kissing a rule for showing love, because you can very easily get into the flesh that way.

> **May be able to comprehend with all saints what**
> **is the breadth, and length, and depth, and height.**
>
> **(Eph. 3:18)**

Paul did not say that you would comprehend, but rather he indicated that if you are strengthened by God's Spirit in the inner man, if Christ dwells in your heart by faith, and if you are rooted and grounded in love, that you would be in a position to comprehend —

which means to understand, to come to know — what is the breadth, length, depth, and height of the love of God.

Let me paraphrase what Paul meant with modern terminology. He is saying that the love of God, the grace of God, the mercy of God, the caring of God are so tall that you cannot go over them. God's love goes down so far that you cannot tunnel under it; it is so wide that you could go forever and never be able to get around it. The length, the height, and the breadth of God's great love for us cannot be comprehended by the natural mind. It can only be understood through the Spirit of God. It is mind-boggling when you think that God knows every person who has ever lived on this planet as well as those who live on it now, and that He loves us all. Just think, God knows you; He knows me. And He is personally concerned about us. God loves us so much that He sent His Son, Jesus, to die for us, that we might be raised from spiritual death into spiritual life and become His children. In the natural, we cannot comprehend His great love, but in the Spirit, by "being strengthened with might by His Spirit in the inner man," we can understand it.

> **And to know the love of Christ, which passeth knowledge, that ye might be filled with all the fullness of God.**
>
> **(Eph. 3:19)**

To someone who does not understand that statement, it would appear to be a contradiction. Usually, when we think of knowledge, we think of information being imparted to us. Here, however, Paul is talking about the love of Christ which passes knowledge. He is saying you can only understand this love by the Spirit of God in your spirit-man, not with your head or mind. He explains:

...that ye might be filled with all the fullness of God.

What does the word *full* mean? It means there is no more room. One of my areas of ministry is divine healing. You may wonder how I can get divine healing out of that verse, but that verse is full of divine healing.

...that ye might be filled...

Not that you might have a little of it, but that you would be filled,

...with all the fullness of God.

How much sickness is there in God? Of course, the answer is none. If you are filled with the fullness of God, there is no room for sickness in you. If you are filled with all the fullness of God, there is no room for any poverty. If you are filled with all the fullness of God, there is no room for fear or hate or racial prejudice or any other kind of prejudice.

Notice the word *all*, which means nothing is left out. In God there is everything we will ever need, everything we will ever desire that is consistent with a godly life.

The Bible says, **"Every good gift and perfect gift is from above, and cometh down from the Father of lights, in whom is no variableness, neither shadow of turning"** (James 1:17). That good comes from God, and He wants us to be full of that good.

If you are full of good, how are you going to do bad to your brother? There is no envy or jealousy in God. There is no strife in God. In God, there can be no husbands and wives sitting in church not talking to each other or choir members not speaking to one another. Such people cannot be filled with all the fullness of God, because if they were, they could not sit by people and not speak. The Spirit of God is One. He is a Spirit of unity, not division, not strife, not schism.

Oh, that we might be filled with all the fullness of God: full of joy, full of peace, full of good health, full of wealth, full of all that we need, so much so that we have it to give away to others. Give love away, give joy away, give peace away.

Notice that Paul says, "that you might be." He did not say that you would be. The will of God is for you to be filled with His fullness, but the decision is really up to you whether you will be or not, because you are going to have to receive that fullness by faith and then allow God to manifest that fullness in you. If you do not receive it and do not act on it, then you will nullify and short-circuit that fullness, and it will not work on your behalf.

> **Now unto Him** [that is, God] **that is able to do exceeding abundantly above all that we ask or think, according to the power that worketh in us.**
>
> **(Eph. 3:20)**

There is that word *able* again. There are qualifiers in the Word of God that we need to be cognizant of, because they are so very important.

God does not do just what we ask or think, but He does **"exceeding abundantly"** above all that we ask or think. Notice again, that it says that "He is able" to do it. It does not say that He *will* do it. The very fact that it says He is able alerts us to the fact that there is a responsibility factor involved.

We know God has the ability, but He cannot do anything unless we let Him do it. You hear people saying all the time, "Well, you know the Lord is able." That the Lord is able is a foregone conclusion. What we need to know is, will He? For me to get the benefits of His ability, I have to know, that I know, that I know that He will expend His ability on my behalf.

...according to the power...

God's ability to do "exceeding abundantly" above all that we ask or think is predicated, governed, controlled, and limited by the operation of the power in us.

With that in mind, it is easy to understand why so many Christians are not receiving the blessings of God. Number one, they go to a church that does not even believe in being filled with the Spirit, and it is from the

Spirit that the power and God's ability to accomplish things come to us. So we see that if you have no power working in you, that God is not able to do exceeding abundantly above all you ask or think. This means your needs will not be met, because God cannot meet them except by the power that works in you. And if you are one of those Christians who is going to a church where they are teaching that the Holy Spirit's power went out with the early church, and that God is not filling us with His Spirit anymore, there is no power that is going to work in you. And if that power is not working in you, God does not have a channel in you to do exceeding abundantly above all you ask or think.

Yes, we know that God is able, but how does His ability become ours? I know God is able to heal, but will He heal me? I know God is able to make a way out of no way, but will He make a way out of no way for me? I know God is able to take away fear and doubt and condemnation, but will He do it for me? That is what I need to know. Just to glibly say, "Well, the Lord is able." That is not going to do me any good; I have to *know* that He will.

God's ability is programmed in us by the Holy Spirit — "the power that worketh in us." That is why the devil fights the baptism with the Holy Spirit so tenaciously. If you are not filled with the Holy Spirit, His power is not working in you, and God's ability is not going to be operating on your behalf. That is what has kept the Church powerless for so long, and that is what has kept the Church an embarrassment to Jesus, traditionally speaking.

God is sitting on the throne in a city that has streets of gold. His people are down here on planet Earth which is full of gold also. Everything in the heavenly realm is duplicated in the earthly realm. There are gates of pearl in heaven, and we have pearls here on the Earth.

There are beautiful precious gems that garnish the twelve foundations of the city in heaven, and every one of those gems, plus more, can be found in the earth-realm. The Earth is a miniature of heaven and all that is in it.

I can imagine how embarrassed Jesus must be when He sees His blood-bought, blood-washed, redeemed people resorting to rummage sales, barbecue dinners, and bake sales in order to raise money to finance the work of the Kingdom, while the cattle on a thousand hills belongs to Him, the hills on which the cattle graze belong to Him, and the grass that the cattle eat on those hills belongs to Him. Jesus is there in a city with streets made of gold; and, yet, His people are down here begging. What an embarrassment that must be to Him!

Humans are designed to breathe air. That is how we stay alive. Try breathing water, and you die. Try breathing sand, and you die. Breathe air, all other things being equal, and you will live. That is how God has designed the body to work. We cannot change it. We came from the factory that way. And until the designer makes a change in the design plan, we have to follow the instructions, or we are going to be up a creek in a boat with no oars.

God has designed the system to operate by "the power that worketh in you." That is the reason Jesus told His disciples to go back to Jerusalem and not to preach any sermons or teach anyone anything until they had received power from on high. (See Luke 24:49.)

If the disciples, who walked with Jesus three and a half years, and who were commissioned by Him to go out as His ambassadors to work miracles and prepare the way for Him, needed the power before they could be ready and equipped to do the work of God, how can Christians today do the work of God without that same power? Yet, this is what the Church is trying to do.

Bible schools, ministerial schools, and seminaries all over the world are turning out men and women who are not even born again, let alone filled with the Holy Spirit. Many a church is staffed with ministers who do not even believe in the Virgin Birth, who do not believe in the miracles recorded in the Bible, or believe in divine healing.

The spiritual level of any congregation is measured by the spiritual ministry it receives. If you have a minister in the pulpit who does not believe in divine healing, you are going to have a congregation that does not believe in divine healing.

If you have a man in the pulpit who is telling the people, "Well, the Lord is able," but little else, you will have a congregation who will end up saying, "the Lord is able," but never go beyond that. And the people in those congregations will end up going down the tubes.

The Bible tells us that God is **"able to do exceeding abundantly."** The very fact that it says He is able implies that He is willing to do. Because if God were not willing, why would He tell us that He is able? What is He able to do? **"Exceeding abundantly above all that we ask or think!"** How does He do it? — **"According to the power that worketh in us,"** — but the power is not in you if you are not filled with the Spirit.

It is one thing to be born of the Spirit, but it is something entirely different to be filled with the Spirit. There are many Christians that believe being born of the Spirit is the same thing as being filled with the Spirit. But it is not — not according to the Bible.

I thank God that I found out about the power. And I am glad that that power is working in me. I have been accused of overemphasizing the material aspects of life. The reason that I do so is because for too long Christians have heard negative things about prosperity, healing, and faith. For too long, Christians have been told to stay humble by being poor and going with their needs unmet. But the Bible says that God is able to do exceeding abundantly above all that we can ask or think. That has to do with more than just houses and lands and cars and clothes, and all of the other material things of life. It also has to do with living a holy life.

Do you realize what a job it is, what a fight it is, and what a challenge it is to try to live a holy life in this day and time? You are trying to do right, and it seems as though every time you turn around, there is a temptation that would try to keep you from doing it. But if you will put it in your mind to live right and do right, by the power of the Holy Spirit within you, God will be able to help you live a clean, holy life.

The Bible tells us to love one another. But how do we love? We love according to the power that worketh within us. We have to, because there are many people, including some Christians, who are not very lovable, and it is hard to love them in the natural. They are ornery, undependable, critical, jealous, strifeful, and seem to have all the other negative attitudes that make it difficult to love them. However, we can love them by that power that worketh in us, because that power will overcome all of the negativity inside of them. We can then be able to see Christ in them, and the Christ in them is easy to love by the power that worketh in us. But if you do not have that power working in you, you will find yourself looking down your nose at other people.

Some Christians have problems with giving or tithing to the ministry. They would rather keep their money and give it away to the tax people. They ought to be giving into the Kingdom of God. It irks them to have to tithe 10 percent, but they do not mind paying 19 percent prime interest. They will give the bank 19 percent, but they will not give God 10 percent to save their lives. If they ever get the power of God and the Spirit of God and the revelation of the Word of God, they will find out that you cannot beat God in giving. They will find out that it is to their advantage to give God that 10 percent. If they learn how to give God the 10 percent, it will be very easy to pay the 19 percent.

I asked the heavenly Father how to prosper financially so that I could be a blessing to other people. I wanted to be a giver. I wanted to give to other ministries; I wanted to give into the ministry that God gave me. At that time, I did not have enough money to pay my own bills, so how could I give anyone anything? I found out that it works by the power that worketh in me. I found out that if I would yield to the power that is in me, that God is able to do exceeding abundantly above all that I could ever ask or think.

I began to say, "Lord, I am going to take you at your Word. You told me to bring all the tithes into the storehouse and you would open the windows of heaven and pour me out a blessing where I would not have enough room to receive it. If I do not have enough room to receive the blessing, then it is obvious that all my needs are going to be met, coming and going. If I do not have enough room to receive it, that means there is going to be some left over. So with what is left over, I can give that away, and as I give that away, I am planting more seed, and that means I am going to have more harvest coming in." (See Mal. 3:8-10.)

I began to tithe. I began to do it God's way. I did it according to the power that worketh in me. I said, "Now, Lord, I would rather have 10 percent of a million dollars every year as my income than to have 90 percent of nothing." It would not bother me a bit to make a million dollars a year and just live on the 10 percent and give God the 90 percent. You can live a prosperous life on 10 percent of a million dollars.

At first, it was hard for me to separate myself from my money, because that money came hard. But I began to see that the way to receive from God is by giving. I first tithed 10 percent, then 12½ percent, then I went to 15 percent, 20 percent, and now I am tithing 25 percent of my income. If every believer had that same kind of desire and that same kind of goal, and did it, we could build churches all over the world with few problems. All it takes is money. And the money is going to have to come from those who are in the Kingdom of God.

How can we give it if we do not have it? I guarantee you, you are not going to get it from the world system. The world will see to it that you, as a Christian, do not get it. If you will learn how to operate by the power that works within you, you can begin to flow in God's financial plan of prosperity. No, it is not for you to squander and waste on your own lusts, but to be a blessing to the Church and a channel of blessing to other people.

Some Christians are having problems with their bodies. They can hardly live a whole week without committing fornication or adultery, or some other ugly thing that they know is wrong. They did not really want to do the wrong thing, but they could not help themselves. They will never be able to help themselves until they let the power work in them. The flesh, and the lusts of the flesh, are mighty strong. Your body will keep pulling at you and nagging you all the time, if you are weak. Satan will never let up. He will drive you into the ground. He will get you while you are asleep, in your dreams and in your thought life. But, thank God, according to the power that worketh in you, you can put that junk under your feet and live a holy life for God.

Unto him be glory in the church by Christ Jesus throughout all ages, world without end. Amen.

(Eph. 3:21)

It is important to understand what Paul is talking about here when he says **"world without end."** He is not talking about this present evil world, because this present world is coming to an end. There is a day appointed by God when He will judge this Earth in righteousness. This world system, as we know it today, is by and large ungodly, and it is going to end. In fact, it is gearing up now for the final countdown.

What Paul is talking about here is the world of the Kingdom of God. This Earth, as we know it, is not going to be destroyed. This Earth will always be here. But it is going to be changed; it is going to be renovated by fire. All of the evil will be burned up, and the Earth will be purified. It will be restored back to what it was in the very beginning when God created it.

We have to understand that we were made for this earth-realm. Yes, we are spirits that have souls, but we live in flesh-and-blood bodies made out of the Earth. When Christians die, our spirits and souls will go to heaven to be with Jesus. Our bodies will go back to the Earth, from which they came. However, this is only a temporary thing. When Christ returns to set up His Kingdom, we as Christians are going to return with Him to enjoy the Earth in all its fullness.

People are concerned about a population explosion. They are saying that there is not enough room or food or other things for all the people on the Earth. The only reason it appears there is not enough is because of the greed of men. It has been scientifically determined that if you would take everyone who has lived on the Earth from its beginning up to the present time and place them on a square foot of ground, you could put everyone who ever lived in the state of Texas, with the rest of the world left over.

God knew when He created the world how long it was going to last. He knew His children were going to be here and He knows how much we all need before Jesus comes back. He is not going to let us run short of anything. There are still deposits in the Earth of everything you can name that have not even been discovered, which God is holding in abeyance for the people of His Kingdom.

Rest assured that we are not going to run out of anything. God has it all mapped out; He knows exactly how much is here and how much we need to make it through. When this present world comes to an end, God is going to revamp it and fix it up. He is going to get rid of Satan and all of his demon forces. Once we get rid of them, we will not have any more decay or destruction or wars.

In Revelation 21:5, God stated, **"...Behold, I make all things new."** He did not say, "Behold, I make all new things." He is going to renovate the world, just as He is going to renovate us and give us brand-new, glorified bodies. He is going to give us bodies that are not subject to decay or death or any of the other things that have tripped us up in life. There will be no old age or sickness or disease or decay — just life everlasting, lived in the glory of the Lord.

4
The Believer's Walk in Christ
(Ephesians 4 & 5)

Part 1 — Ephesians 4:1-32

> **I therefore, the prisoner of the Lord, beseech you that ye walk worthy of the vocation wherewith ye are called.**
>
> **(Eph. 4:1)**

Paul is speaking figuratively when he says:

I therefore, the prisoner of the Lord...

There are two ways in which you can be a prisoner. You can be a prisoner by being arrested and incarcerated against your will. And you can voluntarily imprison yourself by living a certain restrictive life-style.

Many years ago, I placed myself into voluntary servitude when I asked my wife to marry me. I made myself a prisoner to her, and she made herself a prisoner to me. She told me that she loved me, and I told her that I loved her, and so we agreed to share our lives together in holy matrimony, and we became prisoners to each other.

That is what Paul meant when he said, "I am a prisoner of the Lord." Jesus did not tie a rope around Paul and demand that he do thus and so, or he would be put into prison. Jesus simply said, "Come, follow me," and Paul made himself a prisoner of the Lord by doing just that.

...that ye walk worthy of the vocation...

The word *vocation* implies a "career, occupation, job, or a profession." A vocation is whatever you commit yourself to do.

...wherewith ye are called.

Paul is talking about all of us who are in the family of God, all of us who are in the Body of Christ. And he is also talking about all those who are not Christians, those who have not accepted Jesus Christ as their Lord and Savior.

People may think that their vocations are to be doctors, lawyers, ministers, or whatever. That may be so in this earth-realm, but God has called everyone of us to another vocation, a vocation that will last throughout eternity, and that vocation is to be a son of God. We are called to be members of the family of God.

Because of intellectual teachings in some quarters there are those who adhere to a vain doctrine known as the "Fatherhood of God and the brotherhood of man" — an idea which says, "God is the Father of all mankind." That is not biblically true.

You have two choices: Either you can go by tradition and the academic or intellectual surmisings of people, or you can go by what the Bible says. Let's see what the Bible has to say:

> **But as many as received him, to them gave he power** [the right or the privilege or the authority] **to become the sons of God, even to them that believe on his name: Which were born, not of blood, nor of the will of the flesh, nor of the will of man, but of God.**
>
> **(John 1:12-13)**

It is obvious from these Scriptures that God has to give you the authority and the right and the privilege to become His son. You must not have been a son of God before that authority, right or privilege was given to you. If you already were a son, why would He have to give you the authority to become what you already were?

No one is a child of God until he is adopted into the family, and he is not adopted into the family until he has accepted Jesus Christ as Savior and Lord. That is the way God has designed the system to work.

God is calling every person on planet Earth to a vocation, and that vocation is sonship with Him. He is giving us the privilege to become His children. I thank

God, through Jesus Christ, I am one of the children of God. He has given me that privilege and that is the vocation He has called me to.

...that ye walk worthy...

There are many Christians who are not walking worthy of that vocation. They are a disgrace to the family name. They bring embarrassment to our Father because they are not living like they are supposed to live. They give lip service to God, they talk about how much they love the Lord, they quote the Scriptures and speak with tongues, but they live like dogs: fornicating, lying, stealing, cheating, committing adultery, causing strife, being envious and jealous, and practicing all the rest of the sins of mankind.

It is a privilege to be a child of the King. It is a privilege to be a son of God. I know some families that I would not want to be a part of. I count it to be **"joy unspeakable and full of glory"** (1 Pet. 1:8) to be able to name the heavenly Father as my personal Father, to name Jesus as my Elder Brother, and my Savior and Lord. That is a privilege, and I dare not walk any other way than the way that is worthy of Him.

God is calling us to sonship, and Paul tells us to walk worthy of the vocation of that sonship wherewith we are called. We are called to live a life of holiness, a life of commitment, a life of dedication, a life of truthfulness, and a life of honesty and integrity — not a life of double standards, one way on Sunday and another way the rest of the week, one way at church and another way on the job, or one way at church and living like someone else at home. That is not walking worthy of sonship, that is not walking worthy of the vocation we are called to, and that is not walking worthy of the Lord Jesus Christ.

I can understand a person committing a sin, even after he or she has become a Christian, even after he or she has been filled with the Holy Spirit, even after he or she has become knowledgeable in the Word. I can understand it. I do not agree with it, but I can understand how some people can commit sin. It is because they are human and are still in the flesh. They are still subject to the trials and temptations Satan brings against them, and I understand that it is possible to yield to that pressure.

But one of the things I find hard to understand is that if they have made a commitment to Christ and a commitment to walk as Christians, why such people do not have a desire to participate in and like the kinds of things that are consistent with a godly life. I cannot understand how people can be born again and filled with the Spirit and still be so attached to the things of the devil or the world. That I cannot understand — particularly if they are knowledgeable in the Word.

Paul tells us that we are to walk worthy. The very fact that he uses the words *walk worthy* means there is a way in which we can walk that is worthy, and a way that is unworthy.

There is a companion Scripture that corroborates what we have just covered:

That ye might walk worthy of the Lord unto all pleasing, being fruitful in every good work, and increasing in the knowledge of God.

(Col. 1:10)

169

Friend, if you are increasing in the knowledge of God, somewhere along the line you should start thinking like God. You should start having the mind of Christ, and you should not have any desire to hold onto the devil's way or the world's way of doing things.

In other words, we are to walk in a way that is pleasing to the Lord — that is our responsibility. Too many Christians are praising the Lord and receiving the blessings of God, then giving credit to the devil by their life-styles.

Christians are to walk worthy of the vocation wherewith we are called. Every human is called to the same vocation, that is sonship with God. But it is up to us believers to show the world how to live that sonship life-style.

> **With all lowliness and meekness, with longsuffering, forbearing one another in love.**
>
> **(Eph. 4:2)**

The word *longsuffering* does not mean to suffer a long time. It means "enduring," "endurance," or "the ability to endure." Paul says, "forbearing one another," which means to "put up with one another."

The only way we can put up with one another is by having the divine love of God working in us. Because of God's love, we can do it, particularly when we remember how God puts up with us so graciously.

> **Endeavouring to keep the unity of the Spirit in the bond of peace.**
>
> **(Eph. 4:3).**

There is supposed to be peace, not only in our individual hearts, but there ought to be peace in the entire family of God. There is no reason for division, turmoil, or strife in the family. When these things exist, an individual needs to look at his or her commitment to the Lord, and see where the fault lies.

Even though Satan is the author and originator of strife and confusion, he cannot cause any turmoil or confusion unless we let him. I made up my mind long ago that I would never allow the devil to cause me to bring strife and confusion into the Body of Christ. I made up my mind that I would not let people's ugly talking and ugly acting make me react in an unkind way toward them.

The natural reaction of the human mind is to retaliate when someone says something bad about you. I have had people say very unkind things about me. I just said, "Father, I pray for them. You said in your Word that no weapon formed against me can prosper. [See Isa. 54:17.] Father, I ask you to forgive those who have spoken out against me, because I know they did it out of ignorance, jealousy, and envy and not out of knowledge, because if they really knew me, they would not have said what they said. So, Father, I am asking you to forgive them just as I have forgiven them." That keeps the doors open for the blessings of God to continue to flow.

If I see strife operating in my ministry or even hear about it, I get on it like white on rice. I expose it for what it is and bring it out into the open, because I made up my mind years ago that I would not be a party to any strife in my personal life or in my ministry. When you put the Word of God on strife, everything is brought into the open and you can get rid of it quickly. That is what believers are supposed to do. We are supposed to endeavor **"to keep the unity of the Spirit in the bond of peace"** (Eph. 4:3).

In this third verse, Paul has implied a very beautiful truth.

We have to understand that if it is not possible to keep the unity of the Spirit, and if it is not possible to operate in the bond of peace, why would God tell us to do something we could not do? This Scripture tells us that Christians can keep the unity of the Spirit, and we can do it in the bond of peace. In fact, I do not think that Jesus Christ is coming back until this happens in the Church. When you look at the way things are now, with different doctrines being taught on just about every church corner, it seems that this unity among churches will never happen. But it will.

All that has to take place is for all those who are unwilling to be unified to die out, and when they are out of the way, the only ones left will be those who are willing to walk in the bond of peace and the unity of the Spirit.

> **There is one body** [this is talking about the Body of Christ] **and one Spirit** [talking about the Holy Spirit], **even as ye are called in one hope of your calling.**
> **(Eph. 4:4)**

The one hope is the same as that vocation, that sonship with God — the hope of the deliverance from the powers of darkness, into the family of God.

One Lord, one faith, one baptism.

(Eph. 4:5)

There is a great deal of misunderstanding about the word *baptism*.

When Paul says, **"One Lord,"** he is telling us that there is only one way to get saved, and that way is Jesus Christ. The Bible tells us in Acts 4:12, **"Neither is there salvation in any other: for there is none other name under heaven given among men, whereby we must be saved."**

I have heard some people say, "Christians should not be so narrow-minded." Christians are not narrow-minded; God is!

Jesus himself said in John 14:6, **"...I am the way, the truth, and the life: no man cometh unto the Father, but by me."** Now if that is being narrow-minded, Jesus is the originator of narrow-mindedness. He never said, "I am one of the many ways up the mountain." No, He clearly and definitely stated that He was the *only way*! You can take it or leave it — but that is the way it is.

...one faith...

What is this faith Paul is talking about here? It is faith in Christ as Savior and Lord. Then Paul says,

...one baptism...

The Bible actually teaches more than one baptism. And yet it says here, **"one baptism."**

Hebrews 6:1 verifies this fact:

> **Therefore leaving the principles of the doctrine of Christ....**

Notice that it says the doctrine of Christ, and not the doctrine of Price, or the doctrine of Crenshaw Christian Center, or the doctrine of the Methodist Church, or the Baptist Church, or whatever church. It says the doctrine of Jesus Christ.

> **...let us go on unto perfection** [the word *perfection* means maturity or full growth]; **not laying again the foundation of repentance from dead works, and of faith toward God, Of the doctrine of baptisms, and of laying on of hands, and of resurrection of the dead, and of eternal judgment.**
>
> **(Heb. 6:1-2)**

Notice that the word *baptisms* has an "s" on the end — showing plurality — more than one.

A superficial reader of the Bible will pick up the Bible and read something in it and say, "You cannot depend on the Bible because it contradicts itself. It says one thing in one place and then it turns around and says just the opposite in another place." A person who does not know how to rightly divide the Word of God spiritually, reads it academically, and academically it does appear as if the Bible contradicts itself in places.

For example, it appears as though there is a contradiction between Ephesians 4:5 and Hebrews 6:2, but there is no contradiction here. Paul is talking about two entirely different things in these Scriptures.

In Hebrews, he is talking about the doctrine of Christ, and there are several principles in this doctrine. One of these principles is the doctrine of "baptisms."

In Ephesians, Paul is talking about "the vocation wherewith we are called" — that's sonship with God. And in that principle, or in that transaction, there is only one baptism that saves you. If you are not baptized in that particular way, you are not saved.

There are some people who believe that if you are not baptized in the name of the Father and of the Son and of the Holy Ghost, you are not saved. Ephesians 4:5 is not talking about water baptism. It refers to another kind of baptism. We just saw that in Hebrews 6:2 in the word *baptisms.*

The New Testament teaches that there are three types of baptisms. One, you absolutely, unequivocally have to experience in order to get into the family of God and experience the other two. The other two baptisms, you ought to have because Jesus said you should.

Let me first explain the baptisms that do not involve salvation, but that you should participate in, and then I will conclude by explaining the one that does save you.

I will cover water baptism first. Water baptism is an outward manifestation to the world that something has happened to you on the inside. It is an identification with Christ.

Water baptism will not save you, because if it could, all ministers would have to do is to dip people in water, and they would be saved.

> **What shall we say then? Shall we continue in sin, that grace may abound? God forbid. How shall we, that are dead to sin, live any longer therein? Know ye not, that so many of us as were baptized into Jesus Christ were baptized into his death? Therefore we are buried with him by baptism into death: that like as Christ was raised up from the dead by the glory of the Father, even so we also should walk in newness of life. For if we have been planted together in the likeness of his death, we shall be also in the likeness of his resurrection.**
>
> **(Rom. 6:1-5)**

Jesus died, was buried, and He rose from the dead. Water baptism is a symbol of that identification with Christ in His death, burial, and resurrection. We die to the old man, and we become a new creature in Christ Jesus.

Since the old spirit (or old man) in us is dead, we bury him. When you bury something, you cover it up. Consequently, when you baptize someone, you put him or her under the water and that represents the burial process. When he or she comes up out of the water, that represents the resurrection, and that is how we are symbolically identified with Christ in our new-birth experience. That is what water baptism is all about — it is an announcement to the world that the person being baptized is being identified with Jesus Christ in His death, burial, and resurrection.

As I said before, not being baptized in water will not keep you from going to heaven, but every Christian should be baptized because Jesus said so. But it will not save you, just as reading the Bible will not save you, but you should read the Bible because 2 Timothy 2:15 says, **"Study to shew thyself approved unto God, a workman that needeth not to be ashamed, rightly dividing the word of truth."**

If you want to be approved unto God, you have to study the Bible. In Hebrews 10:25, Christians are told not to forsake the assembling of themselves together, **"as the manner of some is."** This means we should go to church, but going to church in and of itself will not save anyone. We ought to do it simply because the Word of God tells us to.

Similarly, we are told to **"pray without ceasing"** (1 Thess. 5:17), but praying will not save you. We ought to pray simply because God has instructed us to do so in His Word. There are many things the Bible tells us to do, but those things in and of themselves will not save anyone. Nevertheless, we ought to do them because God wants us to, usually because it will benefit us in some way.

Let us see what the Bible has to say about the next baptism. In the third chapter of Matthew's Gospel, we find a the narration concerning John the Baptist at the Jordan River. Many people were coming to be baptized by him, and there were inquiries regarding who he was. John informed them that he was not the One, but a messenger sent before Him to prepare His pathway.

> **I indeed baptize you with water unto repentance:**
> **but he that cometh after me [Jesus] is mightier than I,**
> **whose shoes I am not worthy to bear: he shall baptize**
> **you with the Holy Ghost, and with fire.**
>
> **(Matt. 3:11)**

"With fire" refers to the Day of Pentecost when **"...cloven tongues like as of fire..."** (Acts 2:3) appeared above the heads of all those who were present. The fire was a signal to the apostles that this was what John had been talking about when he said they would be baptized with the Holy Ghost.

Notice that John said: **"He shall baptize you with the Holy Ghost"** (Matt. 3:11). The other terms the Bible uses in reference to the baptism with the Holy Ghost are **"filled with the Spirit"** or **"receiving the gift of the Holy Spirit."** These are the three different terminologies that have reference to being filled with the Spirit, or baptized with the Spirit — and Jesus is the Baptizer.

Every born-again believer ought to be baptized with the Holy Ghost, just as he ought to be baptized in water. Being baptized in water is not going to save you and being baptized with the Holy Ghost is not going to save you. To be baptized with the Holy Spirit is for divine supernatural power, to be imparted to you in the person of the Holy Spirit.

The reason that the three different references are used — *gift, filled, and baptized with* — is because when a person is filled with the Holy Spirit, there are three different entities involved. And each of the three has something separate to do.

On man's side of the ledger, it is us receiving the gift of the Holy Spirit. On Jesus' side, it is Him baptizing us with the Spirit. And on the Holy Spirit's side, it is Him filling us. That is the reason for the three different designations.

Let us now look closely at the number-one baptism, the one that saves you.

One Lord, one faith, one baptism.

(Eph. 4:5)

Verse 5 relates to verse 1. It has to do with the vocation that we are called to. Without this baptism, you are spiritually dead, separated from God. You are heading for the lake of fire by way of hell. Hell is only a temporary place. Your final destination is the lake of fire; even hell is going to be put into the lake of fire. I do not know where the lake of fire is and I do not really care to know because I do not plan to go there.

One Lord, one faith, one baptism.

It is unfortunate that in the church world, especially in what we might call the Charismatic or Pentecostal movements, you hear terms that are not scripturally accurate. For example, you hear the term, "the baptism *of* the Holy Spirit or Holy Ghost." Usually when people use that terminology, what they really mean is "the baptism *with* the Holy Ghost," which means being filled with the Spirit.

There is a baptism *of* the Holy Ghost, but it is not the same thing as being filled *with* the Holy Ghost. It is possible not to know the terms but still have the experience. To me, it is always nice to know the terminology and to have the experience. In that way, I can help someone else without giving them false information and having them say things that are not scripturally correct.

> **For as the body** [the human body] **is one, and hath many members** [Paul is using the physical body as an illustration], **and all the members of that one body, being many, are one body: so also is Christ. For by one Spirit are we all baptized into one body, whether we be Jews or Gentiles, whether we be bond or free; and have been all made to drink into one Spirit.**
>
> **(1 Cor. 12:12-13)**

That means it is the Spirit who is doing the baptizing. It is the Holy Spirit who takes us out of the family of Satan and puts us into the family of God. It is the Holy Spirit who takes us out of sin and puts us into righteousness. It is the Holy Spirit who causes the new birth to take place. It is the Holy Spirit who re-creates us and makes us new creatures in Christ Jesus.

We can see this more clearly in the Gospel of John.

This was the occasion when Jesus was speaking to the man Nicodemus. As they were talking, Nicodemus asked Jesus about certain spiritual things, and Jesus began to tell him about becoming a part of the family of God by experiencing the new birth.

> That which is born of the flesh is flesh; and that
> which is born of the Spirit is spirit.
>
> **(John 3:6)**

Notice that the first time the word *Spirit* is used it is capitalized, referring to the Holy Spirit. The second usage of the word *spirit* is in the lower case, referring to man's spirit.

What Jesus said, in essence, is that the new birth is the rebirth of the human spirit. How does this take place? It takes place by the activity and the action of the Holy Spirit.

It is the Holy Spirit who takes a person and immerses him or her into the Body of Christ. That is what the word *baptism* means. The word *baptize* or *baptism*, as it is used in the New Testament, comes from the Greek Word *baptiso*,[6] which means "to dip into or immerse or submerge."

This transaction is known as "the baptism *of* the Holy Spirit." You can now see the difference between "the baptism *of* the Holy Spirit, and "being filled *with* the Holy Spirit." One is for salvation and the other is for power. And the baptism in water is for identification with Christ. One is essential for salvation, the other two are accompanying factors necessary for the total Christian life-style.

> One God and Father of all, who is above all, and
> through all, and in you all.
>
> **(Eph. 4:6)**

Here, Paul is talking about the Body of Christ, because this letter is written to Christians. This is not a letter written to the world. The Bible is God's love letter, blueprint, schematic diagram, a book for God's people to learn how to live the God-kind of life.

The Book is a coded book, and if you do not understand the code, you cannot understand the Bible. You have to be born *of* the Holy Spirit to have the capacity to understand the Word. That is why unsaved people cannot really comprehend the Bible. Yes, they can read the words, but they cannot understand the meaning behind the words. They try to interpret the Scriptures intellectually, and they cannot; confusion is the result.

...and in you all.

That is, He is in all of us — those who have accepted His Son, Jesus Christ, as our personal Savior. God is in us by His Spirit. Christ is in us by His Spirit. The Holy Spirit is in the earth-realm today in order to be the ambassador and the representative for both the Father and the Son.

God is not in everyone who is on the Earth. It is important to understand this fact. **God is only the Father of those who have been adopted into His family.**

It is very important to recognize that when Paul says **"...and in you all,"** he is referring to those to whom the letter is addressed — namely, those in the Body of Christ.

> **But unto every one of us is given grace according to the measure of the gift of Christ.**
>
> **(Eph. 4:7)**

In this verse, Paul is talking about two things: salvation and faith. In the second chapter of the Book of Ephesians, we are told that **by grace we are saved.** The grace of God is what saves us, because it gives us the privilege and the opportunity to become the sons of God. We do not deserve this privilege, and we cannot demand it. But out of His great love, God gives us His grace. However, it is up to us to receive it. **"For by grace are ye saved through faith; and that not of yourselves: it is the gift of God"** (Eph. 2:8).

Salvation is a gift, and the faith by which we obtain the salvation is a gift also. We can see this very clearly in the twelfth chapter of Romans. You have to keep in mind that these letters or epistles are addressed to the Body of Christ, to the Church, to Christians, and not to the world.

> **For I say, through the grace** [there's that word *grace* again] **given unto me, to every man that is among you** [that is, among you who are in the family of God], **not to think of himself more highly than he ought to think; but to think soberly, according as God hath dealt to every man** [that is, every man who is a Christian] **the measure of faith.**
>
> **(Rom. 12:3)**

Faith and salvation are both given to us by God out of His love and His grace. Faith is given, and salvation is given, and with the faith, we obtain the salvation.

That grace — God's unmerited favor — is available to every person. All one has to do is to receive it. God does not cram it down our throats. He does not force it on anyone. If you do not want it, you do not have to take it, but the good news is that it is available. **"Whosoever will, let him take the water of life freely"** (Rev. 22:17) is the spiritual injunction. Turn it around, and it says, "Whosoever will not, will not take the water of life...." Those who do not take freely will be left out in the cold. But, thank God, they do not have to be; they can enter in and be welcome — if they want to.

> **Wherefore he saith, When he ascended up on high, he led captivity captive, and gave gifts unto men.**
> **(Eph. 4:8)**

This is referring to Jesus in His death, burial, and resurrection. This is talking about the time when Jesus came up from the underworld (hell). He went into the tomb and picked up His body, which was instantly changed and glorified. Then He went up to heaven. When Jesus went to heaven, He led "captivity captive." A more accurate translation is that He led "captive captivity." What does this mean?

Before Jesus came into the earth-realm, there were no people who were called Christians. There could not have been because Jesus had not yet come and paid the price for man's redemption.

When men died under the Old Covenant, their spirits and their souls left their bodies (just as happens now when people die), and went into a place located in the bowels of the Earth.

When a man who followed God in the Old Testament died, his spirit and his soul went down into the underworld (hell), into the section known as paradise (or Abraham's Bosom). Those who did not follow God, or do what was right, according to the Law, went into the section called Hades. Between these two locations, there was a great gulf fixed so that no one could cross over from one side to the other.

The people who died under the Old Covenant had a promissory note from God. They had the promise of a better day. They had a promise of a Redeemer. They had the promise of a Messiah. If they lived faithful to that promise, God accounted their faithfulness for righteousness. They were held in paradise — the air-conditioned part of the underworld — awaiting the fulfillment of the promise.

Jesus came to redeem all men — those under the Old Covenant, those who were alive at the time He physically walked the Earth, as well as those who would come afterward. When Jesus died to take away the sin of the world, He became sin for all mankind. He became our substitute in hell. Calvary was His entrance into hell.

We have so conditioned ourselves concerning the cross and Calvary that most Christians think it was the cross that saved them. Salvation only began at Calvary; it was the first stage. Salvation actually began when Jesus hung on the cross, but salvation was not completed until He ascended into heaven after being three days and three nights in the bowels of the Earth.

If Jesus had died at Calvary and remained in the grave, mankind would still be up the creek in a boat with no oars, still headed for hell. There would be no salvation and no redemption. He had to come out of that grave and rise from the dead. His resurrection is what secured redemption for us. The cross only happened to be the method of capital punishment for that time — that is why Jesus went to Calvary.

When He died, His spirit and soul left His body. His physical body was placed in the tomb; His spirit and soul went down into the underworld, into Hades. As Jesus spent three days and three nights in that place, God saw us spending that time there. At the end of that period, just before His physical body began to decompose, God raised Him from the dead. (The body begins to decompose around the fourth day of death. That is why Jesus had to rise after three days and nights.)

God made a promise through David many years ago concerning Jesus' sojourn in hell. David wrote in Psalm 16:10, **"For thou wilt not leave my soul in hell [Hades]; neither wilt thou suffer thine Holy One to see corruption."** This is further substantiated in Acts 2:27 and 2:31.

When divine justice was satisfied by Jesus spending our time in hell [Hades], mankind was acquitted. Jesus then left the Hades section of the underworld and crossed over into the paradise section to announce to all of the Old Testament saints that salvation had been accomplished, the Law had been fulfilled, and they were free to leave. He gathered them all together and took them as captives, as it were, up to heaven.

In Ephesians 4:8, where it says, **"...he led captivity captive...,"** Paul does not mean that Jesus drove them as someone would drive a herd of cows. It says, **"he led"** them; this means that Jesus went first. These people had been held captive in paradise, but now that salvation had been accomplished, their redemption had been bought and paid for. The promissory note was taken back because they now had the actual promise. When Jesus led these Old Testament saints out of the underworld, the paradise section was transferred up to the third heaven, and it is now a "suburb" of the third heaven.

When Paul had a vision of heaven, he said that he was **"caught up into paradise"** (2 Cor. 12:4) — not down, but *up*!

When land developers build cities, usually the cities continue to grow and grow. Eventually, these cities start running out of room, and the city planners begin annexing areas of land adjacent to these growing communities so that people will have places to live. These cities usually keep spreading farther and farther out from the main city.

It is much the same with the Hades section of the underworld. There has been such a great increase in the population of hell that it has moved over into the paradise section, which was left empty, and now that section is being filled up with the inhabitants of hell. The Bible says in Isaiah 5:14, **"Therefore hell hath enlarged herself...."** Hell has enlarged itself so that it can take in more customers.

When Jesus led captive captivity, the angels of heaven stood on the walls on that great day to observe His entry. These angels began to shout and say, **"Lift up your heads, O ye gates; and be ye lift up, ye everlasting**

doors, and the King of glory shall come in. Who is this King of glory? The Lord strong and mighty, the Lord mighty in battle" (Ps. 24:7-8). This is talking about Jesus Christ, our champion — the King of kings and the Lord of lords! This is what the fourth chapter of Ephesians is talking about also:

> **Wherefore he saith, When he ascended up on high, he led captivity captive, and gave gifts unto men.**
> **(Eph. 4:8)**

Verse 9 begins with parentheses and verse 10 ends with parentheses. Therefore, we would call these verses parenthetical statements. In other words, we could lift out this section of Scripture and not destroy the meaning of verses 8 and 11.

Notice that the word *gifts* is plural, meaning more than one gift. Jesus gave us some gifts, so that immediately alerts us to the fact that if He gave us some gifts, He must have wanted us to have them. And until such time as we are able to determine that He has taken these gifts back, then we can assume that these gifts are still here, and we ought to have them in operation.

> **(Now that he ascended, what is it but that he also descended first into the lower parts of the earth?**
> **(Eph. 4:9)**

You do not call a graveyard the lower parts of the Earth. Notice also that the word *parts* is plural — meaning more than one part. This confirms the existence of Hades and paradise.

> He that descended is the same also that ascended
> up far above all heavens, that he might fill all things.)
> (Eph. 4:10)

Let's bypass verses 9 and 10, and read verses 8 and 11:

> **Wherefore he saith, When he ascended up on high, he led captivity captive, and gave gifts unto men....And he gave some, apostles; and some, prophets; and some, evangelists; and some, pastors and teachers.**
>
> **(Eph. 4:8,11)**

The gifts were apostles, prophets, evangelists, pastors, and teachers. These are the gifts Jesus gave to mankind.

The technical definition of the word *apostle* means a "sent one." The office of an apostle is really the office of a missionary that we have in churches today. In order to stand in the office of an apostle of the Lord Jesus Christ, a person would have to be a Spirit-filled, tongue-talking, faith-believing, divine-healing, gifts-of-the-Spirit-operating person. An apostle is one who goes into virgin territories to establish churches. In fact, the apostle just about performs all of the ministry gifts. He may operate as a prophet on occasion. He may do the work of an evangelist. He may do the work of a pastor and teacher. But primarily, an apostle is a sent one.

The ministry gifts work in conjunction with the nine spiritual gifts, which are recorded in 1 Corinthians 12:8-10. These nine gifts are the spiritual tools that equip the fivefold ministry gifts. They are: (1) Word of Wisdom; (2) Word of Knowledge; (3) Discerning of Spirits; (4) (Special) Faith; (5) Working of Miracles; (6) Gifts of Healings; (7) Divers Kinds of Tongues; (8) Interpretation of Tongues; and (9) Prophecy.

If one is not a Spirit-filled believer from the standpoint of Acts 2:4, then he or she cannot really stand in the ministry offices to the extent that Jesus wants him or her to. If one could, then why are the spiritual gifts listed in the Bible?

The word *missionary* is not a biblical term; however, most churches have missionaries who go out into the world. Often they are struggling all the time and do not really operate in the supernatural realm. This is not to put them down, but we are trying to bring into reality what the Bible is talking about concerning these gifts that Jesus left to His Church. When Jesus left these gifts here, He did not leave us powerless. He did not go off to heaven and leave His Church down here to be whipped, defeated, walked on, and beat into the ground by the devil and his crowd. He left us well-equipped to do the work. He said, **"Go ye into all the world, and preach the gospel to every creature"** (Mark 16:15). He left us fully equipped to do just that.

The apostle is a *sent one* by Jesus Christ, and his job is to go out and get churches started, place a pastor over the particular church, and then move on to another virgin territory. As I said before, he may function in all of the other ministry offices at one time or another while he is getting a church established, but once it is up and running, he leaves that area, and goes on to the next.

A prophet is a person who has visions and revelations. We have a good example of a New Testament prophet in the person of Kenneth Hagin. Reverend Hagin, founder of the Rhema Bible Training Center and Kenneth Hagin Ministries, in Tulsa, Oklahoma, is a prophet and a teacher. Sometimes one can function in a combination of the ministry offices, but primarily Kenneth Hagin is a prophet. Jesus has appeared to him several times, validating this office that receives visions and revelations.

There is some controversy surrounding the office of an evangelist because many people do not understand what an evangelist is. Today, we have very few New Testament-style evangelists. Most of the people who call themselves evangelists go from church to church holding revival services, basically preaching salvation sermons. To qualify as a New Testament evangelist, one has to have the gifts of healings and/or the working of miracles operating in his or her ministry.

Most evangelists today are really exhorters, and what they do is exhort people to get saved. That is great, but they really are not evangelists in the truest sense of the word. In the eighth chapter of Acts, we see an example of an evangelist. In fact, Phillip is the only example we have in the Bible of a New Testament evangelist, and the gifts of healings and miracles worked in his ministry.

What is prominent in all these offices is the presence of the supernatural. If the supernatural is not operating, one is not standing in that office. One may be called to an office, but he or she has not yet moved into the fullness of that office until the spiritual gifts are functioning. That is the Bible way, that is God's way.

A pastor is one who has the oversight under Jesus of a local congregation. Jesus said to Peter on the banks of the Sea of Galilee, **"Feed my lambs...Feed my sheep"** (John 21:15-16). The office of a pastor is to feed, not entertain, not emotionalize. A true New Testament pastor will feed the people God's Word, whether they like it or not, because he gets his orders from the Holy Spirit, not the people.

The last office is that of teacher. And as the title implies, the teacher teaches. People can operate in combinations of these offices, as I said about Kenneth Hagin. My ministry office is that of pastor and teacher.

I thank God that I finally found out what I am supposed to do. I was a minister for seventeen years, and I really did not know what I was supposed to do, because the churches I belonged to did not believe in being filled with the Spirit. Therefore, we did not have the Divine Revelator to show us what ministry was all about. I am grateful to the Lord that I finally found my place as pastor and teacher in God's scheme of things.

And he gave some...

Notice the word *some*. This means everyone is not going to be one of these ministry gifts. There are many people who have this idea (especially in this latter move of the Spirit in these last days) that everyone has a ministry. Everybody is not called to a ministry gift. The Bible says *some*.

To stand in the ministry office of apostle, prophet, evangelist, pastor or teacher, you have to be *called* and *anointed* by the Spirit of God. You cannot claim one of these ministry gifts and make yourself one. You cannot buy some degree and hang it on a wall and call yourself one. Yet, there are many ministers passing out business cards with the title "Apostle So-and-So" on them, trying to drum up speaking engagements. You do not have to tell anyone that you are an apostle or a prophet or an evangelist. If you are one of these, it will be demonstrated in your ministry.

Some of these so-called ministers need to find themselves jobs. Some women are running all over town, leaving their children, leaving their husbands, calling themselves "Prophetess So-and-So." Their calling is to take care of their children and stop putting them off on someone else. They had them, and they should take care of them. I do not believe that God called any woman into some kind of ministry to leave her husband and leave her children while she travels all over the country preaching. That is not conducive to a good, harmonious family relationship. They have to remember that God created the family before He instituted the ministry, and good family relationships are important to Him.

What are these gifts for? Paul tells us in Ephesians 4:12 that they are:

> **For the perfecting of the saints, for the work of the ministry, for the edifying of the body of Christ.**
> **(Eph. 4:12)**

The word *perfecting* there does not mean "flawless." Literally, it means the maturing of the saints — bringing them into full spiritual understanding, growth, and development.

...for the edifying...

Edifying means the building up of the Body of Christ, making it strong in the Lord and in the power of His might.

The ministry gifts are given to the Church for three things: (1) for perfecting or maturing the saints; (2) for the work of the ministry; and (3) for the edifying or building up of the Body of Christ.

If the saints are to be perfected, and the work of the ministry is to be carried out, and the Body of Christ is to be edified by the apostles, prophets, evangelists, pastors, and teachers, then that means we still have to have these gifts working today. If not, the saints will not be perfected, the work of the ministry will not be carried out, and the Body will not be edified.

You might say, "Well, my goodness, Brother Price, I can read the Bible. Why did you go through all of that?" I will tell you why. Because there are some denominations today and some churches which tell us that we do not have apostles or prophets or teachers today. The only ministry gifts most churches presently recognize are pastors and evangelists, and that is why the Church is sadly lacking in power. That is why the Church has not been able to do the job that Jesus gave us to do because we are only operating on two cylinders when we ought to be operating on all five.

Paul said, "Jesus gave." And I am here to tell you that no bearded professor standing in some room in some seminary, or any other kind of Bible school, or any denomination or any church council or any other place that calls itself religious has a right to say that we do not have these ministry gifts operating today.

The Bible clearly shows us that Jesus gave these gifts and there is no indication anywhere in the entire Bible that these gifts have ceased or will cease to operate as long as the Church is here on planet Earth. I have heard people ask, "Well, if this is true, why don't we have these gifts operating today?" The reason we do not have them functioning fully today is because there are many ministers who do not have enough sense and enough time to sit down and find out what God has called them to do. Instead, they are running around, copying what someone else may be doing, or getting a church like so-and-so, or getting a television ministry like so-and-so, or getting a tape ministry like so-and-so instead of waiting to find out what God has called them to do. We do not have them because there are very few churches that are teaching about these gifts. There are very few ministries that are telling you that these gifts are still available. So, every young person who thinks he has a call to the ministry, all he knows to do is to try and be an evangelist or a pastor. All he does is run around all over the countryside having revival meetings.

Most of them are not even filled with the Holy
Spirit. They do not have the gifts of the Spirit in operation, so the supernatural cannot work for them.
Consequently, what they are doing is not going to inspire
anyone. They work all week and have services for five
nights and get three people saved. When, if they would
do it God's way, they would have a landslide. They
would not have enough room for the people, because
there is no shortage of customers.

> **Till we all come in the unity of the faith, and of
> the knowledge of the Son of God, unto a perfect man,
> unto the measure of the stature of the fulness of Christ.**
> **(Eph. 4:13)**

Till literally is the word *until*. And *until* means *until*.
Jesus gave these gifts, and He told us what the gifts were,
and He told us the purpose of the gifts, and then He
qualified how long they are to be in operation. All we
have to do is find out how longs *until* is, then we will
know whether the gifts ought to still be working today.

I have actually heard some minsters of the gospel
say, "Brother Price, we do not have these things operating
anymore. They went out with the early church. When
the last apostle died, miracles, healing, signs, and
wonders ceased operating. They were only temporary,
just until such time as the Church became established.
The Church has been established for well over 1,900
years, and so we do not have these things anymore." The
sad thing about this is that the Church has accepted this
statement as truth. I used to think that these so-called
ministers knew what they were talking about because,

after all, they were the ones called by God and they had the degrees, so they must know what they are talking about. I did not know a thing about what I am teaching today, because no one in the churches I belonged to ever told me anything about these gifts.

Jesus said these gifts would be in operation until "we all come in the unity of the faith." *All* does not mean all white folk, or all black folk, or all red, brown or yellow folk. It said, *all* — meaning every one of us who becomes born again by accepting Jesus Christ as our Lord and Savior.

Can you see how far we are from that? And people are running around with their suitcases packed, talking about the Lord is coming soon. How is He going to come when there is no unity?

I believe that before we can come into this unity, that denominations, as we know them today, are going to have to die out, because the division caused by denominationalism has hindered the Gospel of Christ. I am not talking about individual men, and I am not castigating any person, but denominational theologies have hung us up and strung us out.

I want to apologize beforehand for what I am about to say, because it is never my intent to ridicule or purposely hurt or criticize anyone or any church. Rather, I want to challenge and provoke us to seriously think about what is going on in the world today.

It is a fact that someone who is a staunch Catholic, who was raised as a Catholic, and has been a Catholic all of his or her life, would never darken the doors of a Baptist church. And vice versa. That is a hindrance to unity, because if God is in that Baptist church, that

Catholic person ought to be able to go there and worship God. It should not matter what name is over the door. A Christian seeking to worship God should be able to go to any Christian church. But the doctrines of men and the so-called tenets of the different denominations have hindered people from joining together in the worship of God instead of bringing them together.

Denominations have the Body of Christ divided up into different camps of either Protestant or Catholic. There is no such animal in the Bible. Jesus did not die to have His Body segmented. There is one Body, one Head, and one Lord!

Jesus Christ is not coming back until His Word is accomplished. That is why He went back to heaven and left the gifts here to prepare the way so that He could come back.

The Church is still sectarian, the Church is still schismatic, and the Church is still divided. Jesus said these gifts will continue to operate until the Church comes into the unity of the faith.

Paul said, **"Till we all come in the unity..."** — not division — of the faith. How is this going to be accomplished? Through the ministry gifts. By the apostles, the prophets, the evangelists, the pastors and the teachers, who are filled with the Holy Spirit and operating in the supernatural gifts of the Spirit.

The Body of Christ is not united; it is divided. There are white Christians who would not come to a black church to save their lives, and there are some blacks who would not go to a white church to save their lives. There are some Hispanics who would not go to an Oriental church and vice versa.

Jesus did not shed His blood for the junk that has been going on under the guise of Christianity — prejudice, division, chicken dinners, bake sales, rummage sales, bingo games, and all the rest.

But, praise God, there is a new breed rising up in the Earth. It has been rising for a few years now, a new breed of men and women, boys and girls who believe the Word, who are filled with the Spirit of God, who know how to walk by faith and not by sight, and who know how to be world-overcomers. This is their battle cry: **"This is the victory that overcometh the world, even our faith"** (1 John 5:4).

> **That we henceforth be no more children, tossed to and fro, and carried about with every wind of doctrine, by the sleight of men, and cunning craftiness, whereby they lie in wait to deceive.**
>
> **(Eph. 4:14)**

There are still too many Christians who are babies in the faith. There are some people who have been Christians for forty-five years, and they are just as infantile now as they were the day they got saved. This is all because they have never been properly taught the Word.

...carried about with every wind of doctrine...

There are all kinds of doctrines going around. Someone is always coming up with some new thing to grab the people's attention. And there are many baby Christians who have never really grown up that are always listening to these new things. Their motto seems to be: "A revelation a day keeps the blues away." That is the way some of them appear to think, judging by their actions. They run to every church, to every meeting, day and night, leaving their husbands or their wives, leaving their children, leaving their responsibilities. They want to hear something *new*. They have not mastered the old yet, but they want to hear something new. Such people never really grow and develop in the things of God.

> But speaking the truth in love, may grow up into him in all things, which is the head, even Christ. From whom the whole body fitly joined together and compacted by that which every joint supplieth, according to the effectual working in the measure of every part, maketh increase of the body unto the edifying of itself in love.
>
> **(Eph. 4:15-16)**

The Body can "edify itself" because the ministry gifts are a part of the Body of Christ. For example, I am a pastor and a teacher. I am born again and filled with the Spirit. Therefore, I am as much a part of the Body of Christ as any other Christian. Consequently, when I minister to other Christians, it is the Body edifying itself. I edify when I minister to other Christians, and these same Christians edify one another when they share the Word with others in the family of God.

...by that which every joint supplieth...

Every born-again person is a part of the Body of Christ. Every joint or member in the Body is essential to the whole. That is why we should never downgrade ourselves or any other Christian. I am a joint, you are a joint, we are all members in the Body of Christ. Each Christian counts for something in the Body.

I used to have a problem with that, because I wanted to be like so-and-so; I either wanted to be able to preach like so-and-so, or I would say, "I wish I could sing like so-and-so."

God never called me or you to be like "so-and-so"; He called you to be you and me to be me. There is no one else in the entire universe like you. You are unique; I am unique. And each one of us is important to God. We do not have to try to be like someone else; all God wants us to do is to be ourselves. God can work through you just as you are. Every joint supplies something. That means every one of us is important to the Body.

The Bible uses the analogy of the human body as an illustration of the Body of Christ. It talks about each of us being a member in this Body. Stop and think about it. If you drop something heavy on your little toe, your whole body hurts, even though it is only your little toe that is injured. When one part is not working properly, your whole body is affected.

Do you realize that when you do not yield yourself to the Spirit of God and let God work through you, you have hindered the whole Body of Christ? You are one of those joints. You are supplying something. Find out from God what He wants you to do. Find out from Him where you ought to be. Say, "Lord, here am I, send me. What do you want me to do?" It may involve the signing of some documents, it may involve carrying boxes somewhere — but whatever it is, it is important to God. Everyone wants to look for big things to do, but such "big things" may not be what God has for you to do.

You may be thinking, "Yes, you can talk, you big-shot preacher. You have a big church." Wait a minute! I did not start out with a big church. I started out to do nothing more than please my heavenly Father. I wanted only to fulfill the calling He had placed in my heart. I never asked the Lord for a big ministry. I never asked the Lord to be on television. I never asked the Lord for any of that. All I was trying to do was to be pleasing to God and to do what I believed He was leading me to do by His Holy Spirit. Every time I would do the best that I knew how to fulfill what I believed He told me to do, I would hear in my spirit, *"Now, I want you to do this, and I want you to do that,"* and everything He told me to do prospered.

You are a part, you are a joint, you are a member. Are you carrying out and fulfilling your function?

...edifying of itself in love.

Love is the motive for our acting and being. Christians should always be motivated by love one for another when it comes to ministering to the Body in whatever way God leads us. **"For God so loved the world, that He gave..."** (John 3:16). We should so love that we give of our time, of our talents, of our energies, and of our expertise in any way we can to benefit the Body of the Lord Jesus Christ. If you say you love the

Lord, then you need to be about your Father's business. You need to find out what you can do, and whatever it is, you need to start doing it.

> This I say therefore, and testify in the Lord, that ye henceforth walk not as other Gentiles walk, in the vanity of their mind, Having the understanding darkened, being alienated from the life of God through the ignorance that is in them, because of the blindness of their heart.
>
> **(Eph. 4:17-18)**

Every man outside of Christ is spiritually dead. He is blind to the things of God. Just as a blind man cannot tell whether the sun is shining or whether a heat lamp is putting out warm rays, so it is with spiritually dead men. They do not know what is going on when it comes to the things of God because they do not have the capacity to know.

...being alienated...

Alienation means *separation*. If you are alienated from someone, you are not in fellowship with him or her. It means you are not having communion with others. It means you are out there all by yourself. Without Christ, people are alienated from God. But, thank God, through Jesus and the power of the Holy Spirit, those who are alienated can be reunited with God. That is, if they want to be.

> **Who being past feeling have given themselves over unto lasciviousness, to work all uncleanness with greediness. But ye have not so learned Christ; If so be that ye have heard him, and have been taught by him, as the truth is in Jesus.**
>
> **(Eph. 4:19-21)**

The truth is in Jesus. Jesus said: "If ye continue in my word, then are ye my disciples indeed; And ye shall know the truth, and the truth shall make you free" (John 8:31-32). Because He is the truth, if you have Him, you are free.

> **That ye put off concerning the former conversation the old man, which is corrupt according to the deceitful lusts.**
>
> **(Eph. 4:22)**

The word *conversation*[7] is a very interesting word. In the context of the original Greek, it does not refer to verbiage or talking. It means behavior, or your manner of living or your total life-style, which also includes the words you speak.

Paul tells us here that it is our responsibility to put off the old manner of life.

> **And be renewed in the spirit of your mind.**
>
> **(Eph. 4:23)**

Paul tells us that even though we are born again, we still live within the framework of a nature that is like it was before we came in contact with Jesus. In other words, that which is in the flesh will still function and do what it did before it became born again, if we do not do something about it.

The inner man, the spirit-man, has been renewed. We have become new creatures in Christ Jesus, but what the spirit-man has to do is to exert its influence on the outward man, and not let the old way of life control our actions.

Notice that Paul does not say "that ye pray off" the former conversation or life-style. He did not say that you cast it out like you would cast out an evil spirit. No, he told us to "put it off." That clearly means we can stop living ungodly life-styles because we are in control of our lives.

In Romans 12:2, Paul is basically saying the same thing:

> **And be not conformed to this world: but be ye transformed by the renewing of your mind, that ye may prove what is that good, and acceptable, and perfect, will of God.**

It is our responsibility to be renewed in our minds. The mind contains our intellect. It is really the soul part of the human nature. The soul also contains our wills, our desires, our emotions, as well as our intellects. When Paul tells us to be renewed in the spirit of our minds, he is telling us that this action has to take place in the center and core of the soul realm. The renewal of the mind is what has to take place in order for anyone to be able to put off the old conversation, or the old way of life.

That is why the Word of God is so important. Many people do not understand why studying the Word is so essential to living a Christian life. Some Christians even consider going to church as just a part of their social life.

Many times people go to specialized schools to learn special crafts and trades, so they can be better at doing the things they have a talent for doing. We have enough sense to know that the more we know, and the more we can do, the better we can perform. This means that we will have a better opportunity to make more money or achieve a higher position, and, therefore, a better economic life for ourselves and for our families.

It is the same way in the spiritual dimension. We do not go to church just to be going to church. We are not talking about things in the Bible just to be talking about things in the Bible. Whether we realize it or not, we are always in school. All of life is an education. If you stop learning, you stop living. In church, we are simply dealing with spiritual truths, and spiritual truths give us the ability to function in the realm of God's kingdom so that we can function at the highest level in this physical and material world.

Many Christians today are "missing it" because they are carrying on just as they did in their math class, or English class, or history class. They are dragging their feet; they are not doing their homework and are making F's in the important issues of life. We are in a constant state of learning. Every time I teach, I hear the message, too; so I am teaching me as well as those in the congregation. The message produces change in me. It puts me over, it makes me a winner, and I continue to learn new things all the time. This is because you can never exhaust God's supply of wisdom and knowledge. But you have to renew your mind with God's Word by programming your mind with God's Word in order to get His wisdom! That is what the Bible is all about. It is our blueprint for successful living.

You have to train yourself, through the renewing of the mind with God's Word, so that when your spirit receives orders from the Holy Spirit, your spirit will direct your soul. And your soul, in turn, will direct your body and bring it in line with God's will, plan, and purpose. That way, you can be a winner in life, coming in and going out!

> **And that ye put on the new man, which after God is created in righteousness and true holiness.**
> **(Eph. 4:24)**

Notice again that Paul is telling us that it is our responsibility to put on the new man. I cannot do it for you, and you cannot do it for me. We each have to do it for ourselves in order to achieve the victorious, overcoming life.

> **Wherefore putting away lying, speak every man truth with his neighbour: for we are members one of another.**
> **(Eph. 4:25)**

Paul is saying that if you lie to me, you are lying to yourself, because we are one in Christ. Unfortunately, society has so conditioned us, that most people live a lie.

Words do not have a great deal of meaning to most people. But they ought to, especially to the children of God! Your word ought to be your bond. If you say it, you ought to do it, and if you do not intend to do it, do not say it!

Again, notice where the responsibility lies. It is our responsibility to do it, and, again, that means that we can. "Well, I don't want to hurt their feelings. I knew it was not true, but I did not want them to get upset." You hear people make statements like this all the time. A lie is a lie is a lie! "...and all liars, shall have their part in the lake which burneth with fire and brimstone..." (Rev. 21:8).

A lie will catch up with you, because when you tell one lie, you often have to tell a second lie to cover up the first, and this may require a third to cover up the second, and so on and so forth. It just keeps snowballing, and eventually you end up trying to live that lie. When you do that, you cut off the power of God from operating effectively in your life.

...speak every man truth with his neighbor...

The most tragic person you can ever meet is a self-deceived person. It is bad enough when someone else tricks you, but when you trick yourself, you are in bad shape. There are many people who lie to themselves all the time. When you lie to yourself, you are eventually going to try and lie to God. When you do that, the devil will be on your case like white on rice.

You have to tell the truth, even if it hurts; you have to always tell the truth. I maintain that posture in my life. I will tell the truth no matter what. It is not because I am super-spiritual; it is because I have made up my mind that that is the way I intend to live. Jesus said, "The truth shall make you free" (John 8:32), and I believe in being free.

> **Be ye angry, and sin not: let not the sun go down upon your wrath.**
>
> **(Eph. 4:26)**

The words *be ye angry* really mean *be ye wrathful and sin not*. There are many things that can agitate you, that will cause you to rise up in indignation. Just be sure that the indignation is righteous indignation. That is what Jesus had when He went into the Temple and found the Temple authorities selling animals for sacrifices and cheating the people. Jesus told these men that they had turned His Father's house, a house of prayer, into **"a den of thieves"** (Luke 19:46).

The Bible tells us that Jesus took a rope, tied some knots in it, made a whip, and went into the Temple and drove the money changers out. (See Matt. 21:12-13.) Do you think He went through the Temple whipping and striking these men with a smile on His face? No, He would not have been smiling and grinning from ear to ear as He did so. He was righteously indignant because of how His Father's house was being mistreated.

There ought to be some things that we do get angry about. We ought to get righteously indignant about injustice. We ought to be righteously indignant about sin, as well, but our indignation should lead us to do something constructive, not destructive, about the situation.

We read throughout the Bible about the wrath of God. If it is all right for the Father to get angry, then it is all right for the child. But it depends on the kind of anger that you are talking about. Paul says, "Be ye angry, and sin not." That means I can be angry and not sin, but, by the same token, there is a kind of anger that consumes a person to such an extent that he or she would act in a destructive manner, and to respond to anger in this way is a sin.

It makes me righteously angry when I see Satan lording it over the lives of my brothers and sisters in Christ. It upsets me when I see Christian men and women, boys and girls who are sick and their bodies are diseased and their organs and limbs are not functioning properly because of the diseases Satan has put on them. That makes me righteously indignant, and I want to lay hands on them and see them made whole.

I get righteously indignant when I see one person mistreating another person, especially when those people are Christians. This is justifiable wrath; it is the same kind of anger that Jesus exercised.

There is a fine line between righteous indignation and human indignation. If you do not know how to govern yourself accordingly, you can go from something that is righteous and appropriate into something that is human and carnal.

Whatever it is that has caused you to become angry, get it out of your system before the day is over. Paul tells us to get rid of that anger as quickly as possible — do not let it go on and on and on, because it can become a thing of the flesh if you are not careful.

Neither give place to the devil.

(Eph. 4:27)

I want to emphasize this, because there are many people who do not like to talk about the devil. I have heard them say such things as: "Let us not speak about the devil, Brother Price. We do not want to glorify him."

Actually, not saying anything about the devil is often what glorifies him. We need to call a dog a dog, and a hog a hog, and the devil the devil!

There is a belief in some circles that there is no such thing as a personal devil (in reference to Satan). These folk are deceived. We need to say what the Bible says. If the Bible speaks on the issue, then we ought to speak on it. If the Bible is silent on an issue, then we ought to be silent about it.

I have even heard some people say, "The concept of a devil is something that was dreamed up by the clergy to frighten people. But those of us who are intelligent know that there is no such thing as a personal devil. Rather it is simply a maladjustment of one's intellect. But once you get your mind straightened out, you will see that there could not be any such thing as a devil."

What these people are actually saying is that they are more intelligent than God. God believes in the devil, and you had better have enough sense to know there is a devil so that you can know who your enemy really is.

I want to cover several Scriptures concerning this entity known as Satan, the one who is commonly called the devil. I believe it is vitally important to cover this information because there are many things that are going on in the world today that are so unrighteous, unholy, and unjust. That there has to be a reason why these things are happening in our world.

If you study elementary science, you will find out that there is a principle of cause and effect in operation. If there is an effect, there had to be a cause. All over the world, we see disease, sickness, rape, murder, prejudice, and all kinds of maladies that are designed to cause misery to mankind.

With all of our superior intellectualism, social studies, and all of the information we have available to us concerning human behavior and environment, things do not really change. People are still just as hateful, warlike, and unholy as they have ever been. It is a known fact that the crime rate is escalating year by year. Mankind is more educated than ever in the history of the world, and yet we have not been able to stop or even control the negative things that are going on around us. We see "effects" everywhere. Hospitals are filled with "effects." What are the causes? Where does all that misery and devastation come from?

Traditionally, most people have blamed God for the calamities that impact mankind. "Well, the Lord is working something out, Brother Price. We know the Lord has a purpose in this. God works in a mysterious way, His wonders to perform." And so we have been blaming God for everything. The thinking, of course, is that, "Well, if God did it, you cannot fight city hall — so what are you going to do? You just have to accept it." But deep down on the inside, no one really believes that garbage.

For example, if people really believed that sickness and disease were God's perfect will, that God had a purpose in bringing those things upon them, they would never seek medical aid. The moment they applied any kind of medication to their illness or disease, they would be interrupting the will, the plan, and the purpose of Almighty God.

There are causes for all effects. And Christians, as the children of God, need to know what those causes are so that we can know how to deal with them.

In Matthew's Gospel, chapter 4, beginning at the first verse, we are given valuable information concerning this personage known as Satan and his mode of operation.

> **Then was Jesus led up of the Spirit into the wilderness to be tempted of the devil. And when he had fasted forty days and forty nights, he was afterward an hungred. And when the tempter came to him, he said, If thou be the Son of God, command that these stones be made bread.**
>
> **(Matt. 4:1-3)**

Notice that the devil is called "the tempter." The word *tempter* comes from the same root word as *tempted, tried,* or *tested.* Satan is the tester. His purpose for testing you is to push you to the breaking point, to destroy you, to annihilate you, to wipe you out. And he came to Jesus for that same purpose.

> But he answered and said, It is written, Man shall not live by bread alone, but by every word that proceedeth out of the mouth of God. Then the devil taketh him up into the holy city, and setteth him on a pinnacle of the temple. And saith unto him, If thou be the Son of God, cast thyself down: for it is written, He shall give his angels charge concerning thee: and in their hands they shall bear thee up, lest at any time thou dash thy foot against a stone. Jesus said unto him, It is written again, Thou shalt not tempt the Lord thy God. Again, the devil taketh him up into an exceeding high mountain, and sheweth him all the kingdoms of the world, and the glory of them; And saith unto him, All these things will I give thee, if thou wilt fall down and worship me. Then saith Jesus unto him, Get thee hence, Satan....
>
> **(Matt. 4:4-10)**

This latter statement is what I want you to pay particular attention to. Would you accuse Jesus of being a psychological aberration? Would you consider Jesus as having delusions of grandeur? Would you say that Jesus was having hallucinations because of not having eaten for forty days and nights? No, Jesus was talking to the tempter! Apparently the tempter must have had some ears with which to hear, or it would not have done Jesus any good to have talked to him. **"Get thee hence, Satan!"** How could Jesus say that if there is no person called Satan?

> Submit yourselves therefore to God. Resist the devil, and he will flee from you.
>
> **(James 4:7)**

214

How can you resist something that is not there? How can you resist someone who does not exist? Notice the use of the personal pronoun *he*. Notice that it does not say *it* will flee, but *"he* will flee...." The devil will flee from you, provided you have submitted yourself to God.

The way you submit yourself to God is by submitting yourself to God's Word. For God and His Word are one.

It is an impossibility to be submitted to God and simultaneously to be out of line with His Word — because they are one.

In John's Gospel, chapter 10, beginning at verse 10, we see Satan being called by one of his aliases. An alias is an assumed name, and we see Satan being referred to by his alias of "thief."

> **The thief cometh not, but for to steal, and to kill, and to destroy: I [Jesus] am come that they might have life, and that they might have it more abundantly.**
>
> **(John 10:10)**

I believe this is a spiritual picture of the contrast between Jesus and Satan, because they are the two entities who are standing, as it were, on the rim of eternity vying for the lives of men.

Jesus very clearly tells us what the thief's purpose is — **"to steal, and to kill, and to destroy"** — that is the work of the devil. It is Satan who steals our lives, our good health, our finances, our homes, our relatives, our children, our husbands, our wives, etc. And he is the one who steals the peace from the Earth. He is a thief, and he does exist.

But, thank God, we do not have to be passive about his existence. We can render him ineffective in our lives, despite his power. Thank God, we are in touch with Someone who is all-powerful. Satan may be mighty, but our God is all-mighty!

Neither give place to the devil.

The word *place*, as it is used here, is a pregnant word in that it gives birth to many facets of revelation. The word in the Greek for *place* is the the word *topos*[8]. It is the same root word from which we derive the English word *topography*, which has to do with land masses, surfaces, contours, islands, seas, rivers, inlets, hills, mountains, lakes, etc.

In essence, **"Neither give place..."** is literally saying, "Do not give the devil a rock, a rim, a ridge, a lake, a pond, a river, a mountain." In other words, "Do not give him any place whatsoever!" This implies that Satan cannot have a place unless I give it to him. That is thrilling to know, because so often we have thought that we were just victims of life, victims of the circumstances, victims of "whatever will be, will be." But, thank God, we who have knowledge of the Word, who know how to walk by faith, who are filled with the Holy Spirit, and who are born again know what is happening and who is behind the happenings of life.

Do you know how you give Satan place in your life? By getting away from the Word of God. The moment that you get away from the Word, you get onto the devil's territory. And the moment you get on his territory, he is going to try to destroy you. He will cut you down and blow you away. That is, if you let him.

It is good news to know that I have something to say about my life. It is good news to know that I am not a victim of the circumstances; I am the master! It is good news to know that Satan cannot rush in like a flood and overwhelm me. Thank God, I can walk in the light of the Word of God. I can do what the Word says, **"Neither give place to the devil."** The way you give place to him is by playing his game. And the way you play his game is to not play God's game. There are only two games to play — either the devil's or God's. If you are not playing God's game, you are automatically playing Satan's. And if you are playing God's game, the devil has no jurisdiction over you.

> **Let him that stole steal no more: but rather let him labour, working with his hands the thing which is good, that he may have to give to him that needeth. Let no corrupt communication proceed out of your mouth, but** [only let out of your mouth] **that which is good to the use of edifying, that it may minister grace unto the hearers.**
>
> **(Eph. 4:28-29)**

Paul is saying that the only things that ought to come out of our mouths are those things that are going to build people up, not things that will tear them down. He told us earlier, in the 22nd verse, to "put off the old man," and then in verse 24, he told us to **"put on the new man."** These are not just suggestions — they are commandments! These are not arbitrary things that we decide whether we want to do or not. The Holy Spirit is telling us, through the Apostle Paul, that this is how we are supposed to live. If we would do what we are told to do, the gossiper would be out of business, the slanderer would be out of business, and people's reputations would no longer be maligned and destroyed by wagging tongues.

Gossip is not edifying; it is always destructive — it tears down, it destroys, it casts a shadow on people's good names. Gossip can stop with you! You can become a committee of one, and thereby stop gossip. If you do not listen to gossip, the gossiper is out of business. A gossiper is dependent upon someone's ear to stay in business. If you do not give him your ear, he is out of business.

We ought to be slow to speak. We ought to take time to be sure that what we are saying is the truth, the whole truth, and nothing but the truth. Some things are left better unsaid. There is no good that comes out of saying a lot of things, even though they are true, if they do not build up. We need to learn how to control our mouths, and that is a responsibility that we all have.

It is great to exercise faith and believe God for our needs to be met. It is wonderful to believe for cars, houses, and all of the other things that make for a good life. But it is also wonderful to keep our mouths shut unless we can say something that is good. If you cannot say something good, then do not say anything. Say, "Praise the Lord," or "Glory to God," or "Bless God!" If you keep on praising God, you will not be able to gossip.

And grieve not the holy Spirit of God, whereby ye are sealed unto the day of redemption.

(Eph. 4:30)

It is very important for us to be aware of grieving the Holy Spirit. There are three things that we can do relative to the Spirit: (1) We can quench the Spirit; (2) We can resist the Spirit; and (3) We can grieve the Spirit.

"To grieve" means to cause Him pain, in the sense of doing things that are ungodly, that are not according to the Word of God. And when we grieve the Spirit, we will cause Him to withdraw His manifestation.

In the eleventh chapter of First Corinthians, verse 30, it talks about how many believers are weak, and sickly, and how many actually sleep (or die) prematurely. Paul tells us that the cause of these conditions is not discerning, not seeking, not appreciating, not treasuring the Lord's Body. His Body means more than the elements — the bread and wine — that symbolically represent the body and blood of the Lord Jesus, but it means Christians appreciating and respecting one another.

Sometimes we grieve the Spirit of God because of our mistreatment of our other brothers and sisters in Christ. You can pray all day long, and make all of the right confessions concerning the gifts of the Spirit being in operation, but they will be withdrawn, or they will not operate if we do not operate in love toward one another.

So when Paul says, "Grieve not the Holy Spirit," he is saying we *can* grieve Him. We need to be careful that we do not do anything that would stop the Holy Spirit from operating in our midst.

Sometimes we do things ignorantly. For instance, you can be in a service, and the Spirit of God may want to move through tongues and interpretation or prophecy, and you get an urge in your spirit to speak out, but you are not really sure and you do not want to do something presumptuously, so you end up not speaking out, and someone else does.

Inside, you are left with a feeling of emptiness because you feel you should have spoken up. I believe this is an area where we can grieve the Holy Spirit, but I also believe that this is a kind of grieving that does not cause Him to withdraw His presence because He knows our hearts, and knows that we do not want to do anything that would bring discredit to the Kingdom of God.

I believe the Lord appreciates it more when we are slower to speak than when we are too fast to blurt something out.

However, I also believe that what Paul is talking about here when he says, **"Grieve not the holy Spirit,"** is that when we commit a deliberate, knowledgeable act that is absolutely opposed to the revealed Word of God, we do grieve the Holy Spirit. This will cause the Spirit grief, and it will cause a withdrawal of His manifestations.

Some people think that the Holy Spirit can do whatever He wants to. Yes, He can from the standpoint of ability, but His ability to work in our midst is governed by our receptivity, our love, our faith, and by an atmosphere in which He is made to feel welcome.

> Let all bitterness, and wrath, and anger, and clamour, and evil speaking, be put away from you, with all malice.
>
> (Eph. 4:31)

The wrath and anger Paul is talking about here is soulish human anger. People have all kinds of bad habits, such as smoking. I personally consider smoking to be very bad, indeed. Evidently, so did a former Surgeon General of the United States, since he placed a warning of the dangers of cigarette smoking on every pack of cigarettes.

There are all kinds of things that people do that are bad for them. Some people would not consider putting a cigarette in their mouths. They would not think of using narcotics, and they would not ever touch a drop of alcohol, but they do not mind worrying. Do you know that worrying will kill you faster than alcohol will? Alcohol will put you out, but worrying will kill you — dead! Worry is a sin. Anything contrary to the Word of God is a sin. Worry is a lack of trust in God. If you were trusting God, why would you worry? Worry comes simply from you taking matters into your own hands.

Do you know that anger is a sin? I am not speaking of the "righteous" kind of anger that I mentioned previously. I am talking about the human kind of anger that makes you lose control. The kind of anger that makes you tear things up, act ugly, and say bad things to others.

I am talking about the kind of anger that can be a habit just as bad as smoking cigarettes or taking narcotics. You can be addicted to anger in the same way you can be addicted to anything. Paul tells us to put away this kind of anger.

We like to talk about faith and healing, but we do not want to talk about anger and wrath, clamor, evil speaking, and putting away malice. But that is what Paul tells us to do. We are to continually exercise the spirit of sweetness and love, particularly toward our brothers and sisters in Christ.

> **And be ye kind one to another, tenderhearted, forgiving one another, even as God for Christ's sake hath forgiven you.**
>
> **(Eph. 4:32)**

Are you kind? Are you tenderhearted, or are you cold? Do you show tenderness and mercy? Sometimes Christians can be so mean to other Christians. It is bad enough being mean to people in the world — but it is terrible to be mean toward our brothers and sisters in the Lord.

You should never hold anything against anyone. Just stop and think, what if God, the Father, ever held anything against us, all the garbage we have done — where would we be?

Husbands hold things against their wives; wives hold things against their husbands; children hold things against their parents, and on and on it goes. Think about the love of God.

Think about how many times the Lord has forgiven you. And then think about how He keeps on blessing you. For you or me not to forgive someone and then go to the Lord and ask Him for forgiveness is like the man in the eighteenth chapter of Matthew. This man owed his king 10,000 talents. He went to the king and told him that he could not pay him because he did not have it to pay. The king, in essence, told him, "Well, everything you have is going to have to be sold until your debt is paid."

The man fell on the floor and said, "Please have mercy on me. I know I owe you this debt, but I cannot pay you, so I am asking you to please have mercy on me."

And the king said, "All right, forget the debt."

The man went outside, wiping the sweat off his brow, and when he happened to see one of his friends going by, he said, "Hey, don't you owe me twenty-eight pence?"

The friend fell on the ground and said, "Have patience with me, have mercy, and I will pay you everything."

But the first man did not listen to the pleas of his friend and had him thrown in jail.

The analogy here is that when we go to the Father God and ask for forgiveness, and He forgives us (the Bible tells us that He does so in 1 John 1:9), and then we hold something against someone else, that is being an ungrateful wretch, just like the man in the parable. But take heed, because the parable tells us that when the good master heard about what the man had done to his friend, he sent for the man and said, "I forgave you all your debt just because you asked me to, and yet you would not forgive your brother." And he had the man thrown into jail and withdrew his forgiveness. (See Matt. 18:23-35.)

Are you a forgiving person? Exercising forgiveness is a part of the Christian life-style. It goes right along with claiming houses and cars and healing and saying, "Praise the Lord." Make sure you are quick to forgive, just as the Lord is quick to forgive you.

Part 2 — Ephesians 5:1-33

> **Be ye therefore followers of God, as dear children; And walk in love, as Christ also hath loved us, and hath given himself for us an offering and a sacrifice to God for a sweetsmelling savour.**
>
> **(Eph. 5:1-2)**

These verses are talking about the pattern of the Christian life. So many times you hear people say, "Well, I do not know how I am supposed to act as a Christian." If they would read the Bible, they would know, if they understand what they are reading.

The Lord has made very plain to us how we are supposed to exemplify the Christian life to the world. And these are some of the things we should not be doing:

> **But fornication, and all uncleanness, or covetousness, let it not be once named among you, as becometh saints.**
>
> **(Eph. 5:3)**

It would have been well enough if Paul had said, after the second or third time, let it not be named among you. That would have given us an out. But the Bible does not allow for any time. Paul said, "Not once, let it be named among you!" He could not have made it any plainer or simpler.

Fornication simply means sexual intercourse outside of marriage. It is a sin, it is un-Christian, ungodly, and unspiritual, and there really is no excuse for it because people can get married and avoid this sin. The Bible says, **"Let every man have his own wife, and let every woman have her own husband"** (1 Cor. 7:2).

Paul tells us that fornication is uncleanness.

Covetousness is the desire to have something that does not belong to you. It is all right to desire, let us say, a new car that is sitting in an automobile showroom, which does not belong to anyone specifically. However, you should not desire to have a car that is actually in the possession of another person.

Satan can tempt you into being covetous. And as a result, covetousness can cause you to end up telling a lie, stealing, or doing something else that can get you into real trouble spiritually, as well as in the physical world.

It is possible and permissible for you to want something that is like what another person has. That is a different thing, but it is a sin to actually desire the possessions of others.

You do not have to be covetous. God will give you something that is unique, if you will believe Him for it. I hear people talk about, "I want to have a ministry like so-and-so." Not me, I want to have a ministry like the Holy

Spirit wants me to have. Now if it ends up being similar to so-and-so's, that is the Holy Spirit's problem, not mine.

Jesus told the parable about the talents. (See Matt. 25:14-30.) He said there was a servant whose master gave him five talents, and to another servant, the master gave two, and to another, he gave one. Then the master went away on a journey. When he came back, he took an accounting of the men's stewardship.

The man who had the five talents said, "Master, I took your five and I put them on the open market, and I gained five more." The master said to this man, "Well done, thou good and faithful servant." The man who had two talents came and said to the master, "Lord, you gave me two and I put them on the open market and I gained two more." The master also complimented him for his diligence. He said the same thing to the first man who had been given the five talents. He did not say anything more, nor did he say anything less. The master did not count five or two; the Lord counted the faithfulness!

The man who had the one talent thought he was being smart. He had taken his talent and buried it. He said to the master, "Lord, I knew that you were an austere man, I knew that you reap where you did not sow; I was afraid, so I took what you gave me and buried it. Here it is, I got it back for you; it is yours."

The master told him, "Thou unprofitable servant. You should have taken that talent and given it to the exchangers so that I might have received some usury (or interest) when I came back." He then said to his other servants, "Take the talent away from him and give it to the man who has ten. Bind the unprofitable servant, hand and feet, and cast him into outer darkness."

The point of the parable was not the importance of the one, two, or the five talents, but the faithfulness of the servants. You do not have to covet anything, including ministries, that someone else has. Just do what God has assigned you to do, and the Lord will reward you for it.

It is un-Christian and ungodly to covet. Covetousness is a selfish-greedy spirit that comes from Satan, and it will mess up your life if you allow such a spirit to come in.

> **Neither filthiness, nor foolish talking, nor jesting, which are not convenient: but rather giving of thanks.**
>
> **(Eph. 5:4)**

I happen to be quoting from the King James Bible, and the word *convenient*[9] is somewhat misleading in the English language. The meaning of the word in the Greek is "fitting or becoming." So the verse should actually read this way: "Neither filthiness, nor foolish talking, nor jesting, which are not fitting and becoming." Right away, you know that *foolish* means *stupid*, so you want to avoid that attitude. But then Paul says, **nor jesting.**

God built us with a capacity for a sense of humor. You can rest assured that humor does not come from the devil, because he does not laugh about anything, except the misery of mankind. But God has a sense of humor. And like I always say, anytime you doubt it, just look in the mirror! Of course, I am just jesting. God does not mind a sense of humor. But when it is just abject foolishness or something that is destructive, then we should avoid it. Such foolishness is not fitting; it is not becoming. There is a time to laugh, and a time to take things lightly, but it ought to be convenient to do so, it should be fitting for the occasion.

Many Christians, bless their hearts, think we are supposed to always have a solemn, sour demeanor. They seem to think we are supposed to go around as if we are sucking on a lemon all the time. This does not attract people; rather, such an attitude will actually keep people away from the gospel. The Bible tells us in Hebrews 1:9 that Jesus was "anointed with the oil of gladness." This lets us know that Jesus had joy, and the outflow of joy is cheerfulness and a sense of humor.

> **For this ye know, that no whoremonger, nor unclean person, nor covetous man, who is an idolater, hath any inheritance in the kingdom of Christ and of God.**
>
> **(Eph. 5:5)**

Paul is not saying that a Christian who may, in a moment of weakness, commit one of these acts has no inheritance in the Kingdom of God, but he is using this as an early warning system for us.

The Holy Spirit, through the Apostle Paul, tells us that no person who is a whoremonger (in reference to one who is not born again); the unclean person (notice, he did not say a person who does some things that are unclean. He says an *unclean person*. This is talking about a person who has never been saved, never been born again); a covetous man (not a man who commits a covetous act) has an inheritance in God's kingdom. (This is talking about one who is a sinner!)

A sinner is unclean. A sinner is covetous. A sinner is a whoremonger. Paul says no person who is an idolater (not one who commits some act of idolatry) has an inheritance in the Kingdom of God. The reason Paul is using these terms is because he is trying to alert us to some things that we, as Christians, are not supposed to do. Our life-style is supposed to be patterned after Christ, not after the world.

> **Let no man deceive you with vain words: for because of these things cometh the wrath of God upon the children of disobedience.**
>
> **(Eph. 5:6)**

The word *vain*, in this verse, connotes the idea of "empty words, void of quality."

This tells me that I cannot be deceived, unless I let myself be deceived. No one can deceive you, unless you let him. If that were not the case, this verse in Ephesians would be an empty statement. Why tell us not to be deceived by vain words if we did not have any control over the deception?

There are many people who are being deceived. They cannot tell the difference between night and day, between rain and sunshine. You see them streaming into churches where they are not learning a thing; they are not hearing the Word of God that would set them free; they are staying locked up, bound with the chains of tradition and religion, and they are being deceived by empty words, words that are void of quality. Tragically, they are listening to those empty words week after week, learning nothing, coming no closer to the truth, and growing not at all, because they are being deceived.

Paul says that because of these empty words,

...cometh the wrath of God upon the children of disobedience.

The word *disobedience* literally means unbelief — the children of unbelief.

A long time ago, before I was filled with the Spirit and knew how to rightly divide the Word, I read where the Lord appeared to Ezekiel and said, "Son of man, I have made you a watchman over the house of Israel." The Lord went on, "Son of man, I place you on the wall to warn the people. Son of man, if you see the sword coming into the land and you do not warn the wicked to flee from his wicked way, and the sword comes and devours that wicked man, I will require his blood at your hand." The Lord explained, "Son of man, if you see the sword coming into the land and you warn the wicked to flee from his wicked way and he does not flee from his wicked way, he shall perish in his wickedness, but thou has preserved thine own soul" (Ezek. 3:17-19).

The reason why I sometimes may seem to come across as being a bit stern and even a bit heavy, is that I realize I have to give the Word to the people, so that it becomes their responsibility to do something after they hear it. Once I say it, it is over and done with, and I am finished with my part in the process. It is now in their laps, and they can do whatever they want with it. I can then rest in the fact that I have delivered my soul.

There are many people today who are being deceived by vain, empty words, and they are accepting this vanity and emptiness as God's truth.

Someone said to me one time that he was going to a particular church because the church was very quiet and sedate. The music was very soft and soothing. The sad thing about this is that the people are learning nothing; in fact, they are being deceived. This church was telling the people that there is no such thing as a devil, that there is no such place as hell, and they did not need to believe in the redeeming blood of Jesus. All they had to do was to be nice, be sweet, and come to that church. Those are vain words, words that are empty and void of God!

As long as the Word is being taught, it should not matter whether there is noise or not, or whether it is quiet or not. The issue to face is: Are you being ministered life or death through what you are being taught?

> **Be not ye therefore partakers with them. For ye were sometimes darkness, but now are ye light in the Lord: walk as children of light.**
>
> **(Eph. 5:7-8)**

The world is waiting to see us walk as children of God, the children of light. They are tired of our just saying it. They want to see it. They are tired of having us hand them a Christian tract. They want to see our light. They are tired of bumper stickers that say, "Honk

If You Love Jesus"; they want to see a consistent life-style that is lived in Christ. Christians need to understand that what we do speaks so much louder than what we say.

What we, as Christians, have to do is to let our light shine. We do not produce the light, we simply have to let it shine. We are not asked to create the light, because only God can do that. We are to let the light within us shine forth to a dark world! Jesus said, **"Let your light so shine before men, that they may see your good works, and glorify your Father which is in heaven"** (Matt. 5:16).

No, you are not saved by works, but if you are saved, you will have some works. Many times, I tell baby Christians not to be so quick to go babbling all over town about who they are in Christ. All they have to do is just live it for a while. They will not have to say anything; people will see it.

(For the fruit of the Spirit is in all goodness and righteousness and truth;).

(Eph. 5:9)

I believe this verse is really talking about the human spirit, not the Holy Spirit. Our bodies are propelled by our human spirits, just as an engine propels a ship. You cannot see the engine from the outside as the ship travels across the waters, and so it is with our human spirits.

People cannot tell what is on the inside, except by what they see manifested on the outside. Jesus made it very plain when He said, **"Wherefore by their fruits ye**

shall know them" (Matt. 7:20). And, just as a tree is known by the fruit it bears, so are the children of God known by the fruit they bear.

Proving what is acceptable unto the Lord.

(Eph. 5:10)

We need to prove what is acceptable unto the Lord. There are only three passages in the Bible that talk about proving something: Romans 12:2; Malachi 3:10; and Ephesians 5:10.

Romans 12:2 tells us to **"...be not conformed to this world: but be ye transformed by the renewing of your mind, that ye may** *prove* **what is that good, and acceptable, and perfect, will of God"** (Italics mine). Note that it says that *you* may prove, and no*t God* may prove. Here again, we are told to prove what is acceptable unto the Lord.

"Proving what is acceptable unto the Lord" implies that we can know the will of God so that we can please Him. Some people have the idea that God is mysterious. You hear them say, "The Lord works in a mysterious way, His wonders to perform." Unfortunately, that concept has crept into the church world. It is as if we really cannot know God or understand His purposes and His will. The Bible very clearly tells us that **"The secret things belong unto the Lord our God: but those things which are revealed belong unto us and to our children"** (Deut. 29:29). This means there must be some things that are revealed, or they would not belong to us and to our children.

Since we are told to prove that which is acceptable to the Lord, whatever it is that is acceptable to God, we must be able to find so that we can prove it. Therefore, God cannot be a mystery. He has revealed himself to us very plainly, but we are going to have to know His Word in order to discover His revelation of himself.

"Why, you just never know what the Lord is going to do, Brother Price." Yes, you do — He told you in His Word! God does not sneak up on us. It is the devil who does that; that is the way he operates. He is a thief, a murderer, and a liar.

Whenever Jesus referred to God Almighty in the four gospels, ninety-nine percent of the time, He referred to Him as "Father."

A real father, not a pretender, not an actor, not a make-believe person, but a real father cares and protects his children and is always looking out for their best interests. A real father would not do things to cause his children to be sick, poor, or defeated in life. God is a real Father to us. That is why Jesus used the term *Father* to convey the love and care the heavenly Father has for us, His earthly children.

So, whatever it is that is acceptable to God has to be available to me. It has to be revealed in His Word so that I can know what is acceptable to Him, so that I will not go counter to His wishes. God is not a mystery — not to His family, not to His children. The Bible is not a mystery novel. The Bible is God's love letters to His children, revealing His tender, loving heart toward them.

And have no fellowship with the unfruitful works of darkness, but rather reprove them.
(Eph. 5:11)

There is a style of life that accompanies the profession of faith in Jesus Christ as Savior and Lord. There should never be a dichotomy between what you say with your mouth and your faith in God. In other words, the way you live, the things you do, the things that you are involved in, the things that you participate in, *must* correspond to what you say with your mouth, or you are then what the Bible calls a hypocrite.

The Christian boy or girl or man or woman has no business being associated with, or involved in any kind of a close relationship with a person who is a non-Christian. Some people will try to come up with this garbage about, "Well, I am trying to get him (or her) saved." You do not have to go to hell yourself to get someone saved. You do not get yourself involved with the devil to get a person saved. You can get someone saved without going steady with him (or her).

In 2 Corinthians, we see something that will help us to understand more clearly what is being said in Ephesians 5:11.

> **Be ye not unequally yoked together with unbelievers...**
>
> **(2 Cor. 6:14)**

Many times this verse has been used by ministers, and even by certain Christians, to indicate that a Christian should not be associated with a non-believer. And that is true as far as it goes; but I do not think that it goes far enough. It means more than that. Paul says:

> **Be ye not unequally yoked together with unbe-
> lievers....**

The word *yoke* is used by seamstresses in sewing. It describes the collar-type part of a dress, blouse, shirt, etc. However, biblically speaking, this term has more to do with an agrarian society where there are animals or livestock that are used as beasts of burden, animals that pull plows and carts.

In biblical times, the yoke was a wooden board that would fit over the neck of two animals, usually oxen, fastening them together so they could pull a load in tandem. When put side by side with this board around their necks, the animals could not do anything but walk together. If one went to the right, they both had to go to the right. If one went left, they both had to go left. Whatever one would do, the yoke would make the other do also.

The Spirit of God is using this word *yoke* as an analogy. He is letting us know that whenever a Christian is involved with an unbeliever, it is like being yoked with someone who is not going in the same direction he or she is going. And because of the nature of the yoke, it could end up forcing the Christian to go in the direction of the non-Christian.

Therefore, the Spirit, through the Apostle Paul, warns the Christian: **"be ye not unequally yoked together with an unbeliever."** It is, however, all right to get yoked up with someone who is going in the same direction that you are going. In other words, if both parties are going south, they have it made. But if one is going south, and the other wants to go north, they will have problems.

Most often this Scripture has been used to illustrate the fact that a Christian and a non-Christian should not associate together in any kind of an alliance that would tie them together legally, morally, or in any other way that implies a close, involved relationship, such as going into business together, or going steady, or getting married. You cannot always tell when you are going to fall in love with someone; therefore, it is best not to get tied up with anyone who is not going in the same direction. When a Christian gets involved with a non-Christian, the Christian sometimes ends up by compromising the things of the Lord.

I believe this verse is not only talking about a Christian and a non-Christian becoming involved, but it also has reference to a believer becoming involved with an "unbelieving" believer.

The church world is full of "unbelieving" believers. For instance, if I believe in divine healing, and you do not, you are an unbeliever, because the Bible teaches divine healing. God believes in divine healing, the Holy Spirit believes in divine healing, Jesus believes in divine healing, and if you do not, you are an unbeliever!

I have seen some of the worst marriages and some of the worst problems between two people who are born again, but the problem comes because one believes in divine healing and the other does not. Whenever the devil attacks one of their children, there is always a big argument. The believer wants to use faith in the Word of

God, and the unbeliever wants immediately to go to the hospital. There is nothing wrong with going to the hospital, but when you have a situation like this, you are presented with a problem of faith, because one parent wants to believe God, while the other wants to believe the doctor.

> **Be ye not unequally yoked together with unbelievers:** [Why, Paul?] **for** [or because] **what fellowship hath righteousness with unrighteousness? and what communion hath light with darkness?**
>
> **(2 Cor. 6:14-16)**

The word *righteousness* here is talking about the Christian, and *unrighteousness* is talking about the children of Satan. Christians are the righteousness of God in Christ Jesus, so we do not have any business getting tied up or involved with the children of unrighteousness. God views Christians as light and those outside of Christ as darkness, because God is light, and Satan is characterized in the Scriptures as darkness.

> **And what concord hath Christ with Belial? or what part hath he that believeth with an infidel?**
>
> **(2 Cor. 6:15)**

"Belial" is another name for Satan and his demon hosts. Paul asks, **"What concord hath Christ with Belial?"** Of course, we understand that Jesus is not going to have anything to do with the devil, and besides that,

Jesus is not even here, so why would Paul say anything about Jesus? He is talking about Jesus, because we are in Christ, and we are the Body of Christ!

If you have accepted Jesus as your personal Savior, the Bible views you as Christ. You are a part of the Body of Christ, so that means you are considered Christ. Jesus is the Head, and we are the body. Whatever the head is, so is the body. So if the Head is Christ, the body is Christ.

An infidel is one who does not believe.

> **And what agreement hath the temple of God with idols? for ye are the temple of the living God; as God hath said, I will dwell in them, and walk in them, and I will be their God, and they shall be my people.**
> **(2 Cor. 6:16)**

Now, what are you doing associating with those who are outside the family of God? Of course, we know that we have to work with non-believers; we have to ride the bus with non-believers; we have to sit on airplanes with non-believers, and we have to go to school with them. We cannot get away from non-Christians. You would have to get completely out of the world to do that.

But in these Scriptures, Paul is talking about Christians getting involved in relationships that legally lock you into a close situation, such as going into business together or getting married, or going steady. Unfortunately, I see the latter two involvements more among females than I do males. These attachments cause them to have to go through all kinds of heartache and heartbreak because they did not follow the admonition of the Holy Spirit.

We can readily see that 2 Corinthians 6:14 is tied into Ephesians 5:11, and that we, as Christians, are going to have to make some decisions in life as to with whom we will become involved, if we want to walk in the fullness of God's blessings.

> **For it is a shame even to speak of those things which are done of them in secret.**
>
> **(Eph. 5:12)**

"Of them" is referring to the unfruitful works of darkness. Paul, of course, is talking here about spiritual matters. But it is also interesting to note how evil manifests itself under the cover of darkness. Thieves usually do their work in the dark or in the nighttime. In fact, that is when most crimes take place. This is not to say that no crimes are ever committed in daylight, but the bulk of crime is committed under the cover of darkness. Light exposes evil; light exposes the unfruitful works of darkness and shows them up for what they really are.

> **But all things that are reproved** [or exposed, or discovered] **are made manifest by the light: for whatsoever doth make manifest is light.**
>
> **(Eph. 5:13)**

It is light that shows things up. When things are obscure and you cannot see, you want light. Light makes everything more easily seen and comprehended.

Although Paul is talking about spiritual things, the analogy leads us to understand that the same thing is true in the physical world.

> **Wherefore he saith, Awake thou that sleepest, and arise from the dead, and Christ shall give thee light. See then that ye walk circumspectly, not as fools, but as wise.**
>
> **(Eph. 5:14-15)**

To walk circumspectly simply means to walk in the light of God's Word. This means that you are going to have to get into the Word so you can find out how you ought to walk. It is really easy to walk circumspectly. The hard part is making the decision to want to do so.

In fact, it is a lot easier to do right than it is to do wrong. Most people wrestle with the decision to do right, but it is easy to do what is right; that is, if you really want to. The choice is yours. What do you really want to do? You can do anything you want to do, whether it is good or bad, but you are the one who has to make the choice.

> **Redeeming the time, because the days are evil.**
>
> **(Eph. 5:16)**

Redeem means to buy back. What is Paul talking about when he says, **"redeeming the time?"** Once time is gone, you cannot buy it back. Literally, what the statement means is "to make the most of the time you have."

241

Too many Christians are squandering the most valuable thing they have — their time. Time is the one thing you cannot get more of. When time has passed, that is it.

Are you making the best use of your time? You had better do it while you can. Many young people are wasting time because they believe they have a long time to live. They think, "I am only twenty years old, so I have a lot of time to do what I want to do."

Some people die at twenty! Some folk have died even younger than that. Being ten, twenty, or thirty does not guarantee anyone a long life. As Christians, we need to make the best use of our time, because this old world is winding down. We are definitely closer to the end than we are to the beginning. No one on Earth knows exactly when the end is coming, but I tell you what, we are nearer to the end than we have ever been before. Therefore, we need to take advantage of the time God gives to us.

There are many youngsters who are just going to school, messing around, and thinking they are having a good time. They do not realize the importance of studying and applying themselves in order to get the best education they can, while they can. It is harder to go back and play catch-up than it is to get it while you are there. Some people do it, but look at all that time that could have been given to something else.

There are many Christians who are the same way. They are hearing the Word of God, and are just taking it for granted without making any real commitment to applying it to their lives.

Redeeming the time. Make use of your time, friend. Some people are wasting their money on a lot of nonsensical junk when they should be using their funds to free themselves from debt so that they can then take the money they save and invest it in the Kingdom of God. Then God would have a definite avenue to provide them a return, according to His promises outlined in His Word.

It is a lot later than we think. If I did not know the Word of God, if I did not know how to walk by faith, if I did not know that God was my source, I might go out and jump out of a forty-story building and just forget it. Things are bad, and Christians had better learn how to walk in the Word.

Wherefore be ye not unwise, but understanding what the will of the Lord is.

(Eph. 5:17)

You are not going to understand what the will of the Lord is unless you know His Word.

And be not drunk with wine, wherein is excess; but be filled with the Spirit.

(Eph. 5:18)

This verse has given some people some problems. The Bible is written to Spirit-filled Christians. When I use the adjective, *Spirit-filled*, I refer to tongue-talking people who are filled with the Spirit, according to Acts 2:4, Acts 10:44-46, and Acts 19:6.

Unfortunately, Ephesians 5:18, in the King James Version, is not clearly translated. It sounds as if Paul is saying to go out and get filled with the Spirit. But he is already talking to Spirit-filled people, and once you get filled, you are full.

I heard a man one time stand up in front of the congregation, and in all sincerity, he said, "Brothers and sisters, we need to get refilled with the Spirit, because after all we all have holes in us and sometimes the Holy Ghost just leaks out and we have to get filled again."

Once you are filled with the Spirit, you are filled. You cannot get unfilled. Jesus very plainly said, **"I will pray the Father, and he shall give you another Comforter,.... Even the Spirit of truth.... for he dwelleth with you, and shall be in you** (John 14:16-17). Referring to the Holy Spirit, Jesus also said, **"He will abide with you forever"** (John 14:16). The Holy Ghost does not come and go for the New Testament believer.

Under the Old Covenant, the Holy Spirit was not a constant presence. He would come upon the prophet, the priest, or the king to anoint them for service, and if they messed up some way, the Spirit would leave. But under the New Covenant, He is residing in those of us who have received Him.

What this eighteenth verse is literally saying is this: "And be not drunk with wine, wherein is excess, but be *being* filled with the Spirit." That is an entirely different thing. "Being filled" indicates a constant ongoing manifestation. It is not talking about going out again and getting refilled; but what it is talking about is letting the filling that you have bubble out of your life. Let that filling that is in you flow out of you into the lives of other people and let it have an effect upon the environment around you.

There are churches where people have gotten filled with the Holy Spirit twenty-five years ago, and they have never done anything since then. The Holy Spirit has just been lying dormant, inactive like an inactive volcano. Once in a while, every hundred years or so, it erupts and explodes, and they have some kind of a feeling. But what Paul is saying is "be being filled." In other words, rely upon the power that is in you to be a constant source of spiritual energy.

The Holy Spirit is in the Spirit-filled believer, like a reservoir. Jesus said, **"Out of his** [your] **belly** [which represents your innermost being] **shall flow rivers of living water"** (John 7:38). What Jesus means is that we are to let the Spirit live in, through, and out of us. There is a way to do that, and we do not have to run down the aisles, hollering and jumping, or wearing some funny-looking white dress hanging down to the sidewalk in order to do it.

Christians ought to be operating in the Spirit all the time. The Holy Spirit should not be something we use as we would a spare tire. When do you spend time thinking about the spare tire in the trunk of your car? Probably not until you get a flat. That is the way most Christians are about the Holy Spirit. They only think of the Holy Spirit when something occurs in their lives to bring Him to the forefront of their minds. But when Paul says, "be being filled," he is talking about a constant flow of the power of God being activated in and through you, influencing your life and the lives of others.

> Speaking to yourselves in psalms and hymns
> and spiritual songs, singing and making melody in
> your heart to the Lord.
>
> (Eph. 5:19)

That is beautiful. I do not care what a psychiatrist or a psychologist tells you, it is all right to talk to yourself. If you are not worth you talking to you, who else is going to bother to talk to you? What is important is what you are saying to you.

The psalms that Paul refers to are the ones that are recorded in the Book of Psalms in the Bible, plus any original psalms the Holy Spirit gives to you. Psalm 150 is not the last psalm the Holy Spirit has inspired. There are other psalms He wants to give us if we will allow Him to use us to bring them forth.

How do you speak to yourself? By speaking in the Spirit, talking in tongues — "praying in the Spirit" is really the correct terminology.

Hymns must be different from psalms, and spiritual songs must be different from hymns and psalms. A good illustration of this form of praise is found in the Book of Acts, where it tells about Paul and Silas singing to the Lord while they were in jail at Philippi.

> And at midnight Paul and Silas prayed, and sang
> praises unto God: and the prisoners heard them.
>
> (Acts 16:25)

That is some singing! It caused the Earth to quake and the cell doors to clang. I can hear them now, down there in the middle of that jail at midnight. Both their hands are in stocks, their feet are in stocks, and their backs are bleeding from being whipped for the name of Jesus. I can hear them now singing the praises of God. I will wager they did not sing some old church song filled with doubt and unbelief. So many of the hymns sung in churches today do not have a spiritual base. Many of the old hymns are filled with unbelief and doubt.

Most Christian singers, even today, still minister to the souls of people, not to the spirit of man. I am interested in that which ministers to the spirit-man, rather than that which caters to our soulish nature. If we are going to sing spiritual songs, we should sing only those songs that are based on the Word of God, and not just those that arouse our emotions and cater to our feelings.

...making melody in your heart to the Lord...

(Eph. 5:19)

There are many believers who will not apply to sing in the choir of their churches because their voices do not meet the criteria established for choral singing. But I tell you what, since the Lord gave you a voice, He does not mind hearing it. So, go ahead and sing to Him; He will hear you. Maybe the choir director will not approve your audition, but you sound good enough to God.

There is a difference between singing by yourself or singing in a choir. In a choir, the sound has to be melodious; otherwise, the resulting discord would turn people off. Nothing can turn your heavenly Father off when you are making melody to Him, because He understands the motive behind your singing. And when it is coming from your heart (your spirit-man), He will receive it.

Take some time to sing to the Lord. Perhaps, no one else wants to hear you sing, but the Lord does. He inhabits our praises and worship, and He welcomes the melodies we make in our hearts to His name.

> **Giving thanks always for all things unto God and the Father in the name of our Lord Jesus Christ.**
> **(Eph. 5:20)**

We are required here by the Spirit of God to do certain things. The Father God is not unreasonable. Sometimes, because of the error of our human intellect, we think that God requires things of us that seem to be impossible. But I can assure you, on the authority of the uncompromising Word, God is not unreasonable with His children.

There was a point in my personal life when this twentieth verse of Ephesians 5 was a stumbling block for me. My dilemma was that I did not think that I could obey God and do what this verse says. Many things that happen in life seem to be inappropriate reasons for offering up thanks. Then I read one author who was an advocate of giving thanks for everything at all times. He even cited some situations of how to do it. Yet, down in my spirit, his explanations did not satisfy me.

I consider myself a stickler for the Word. That does not mean that I know everything about the Word, but I have committed myself to walking by the Word of God to the extent of my ability. Years ago, I made a vow to myself and to the Lord, that if the Word says it, and I understand it well enough to put it into action, I will do it — no matter what.

Giving thanks always for all things...

This verse caused me to wonder about many things. To think in line with this statement, would seem to mean that when something bad happens, such as a wino stumbling across a street and being hit by a car and killed, propelling him into a Christless eternity, I should thank God. Aren't we told to give thanks for all things?

Likewise, it would seem to mean we should give thanks when a beautiful, young bride who had been married only eight months and was six months pregnant, and was on her way home from the market when she was grabbed by three men in a car, raped and left for dead. Should we give thanks for such things when they happen in our society? Paul said, **"Giving thanks always for all things...."**

It was difficult for me to thank God that the wino got hit by a car before he ever had an opportunity to get saved. It was difficult for me to thank God that a woman got raped and was left for dead. It was difficult for me to thank God that a dear loved one was diagnosed with terminal cancer and died six months later. I could not do it, and yet the Bible told me to give thanks.

I began to seek the Lord regarding this somewhat confusing Scripture. I said, "Now, Lord, there has to be an explanation. I know enough about your Word to know that sometimes words do not always say everything that is intended, and sometimes a person must dig deeply into your Word to find out what is really being said and what principle is involved." The Spirit of God called my attention to one word, and this one word set me free. I want to share it with you because I believe it will help set you free from confusion, too, as far as this Ephesians 5:20 is concerned.

Giving thanks always for all things unto God and the Father...

That is a strange statement. I thought God was the Father. So, why would Paul say, "God and the Father?" Why not say, "The Father, in the name of our Lord Jesus Christ," or "Unto God, in the name of the Lord Jesus Christ?" It is almost as if Paul is talking about two different entities here: God, and the Father. But we know from other biblical teachings that there is only one Father, and He is God, and there is only one God, and He is Father. And yet, the Spirit of God says, **"Unto God and the Father in the name of our Lord Jesus Christ."**

The Spirit of God showed me something that helped me understand this principle of giving thanks. Let us examine this principle very carefully, because it is so very important.

The things that happen in life are not always sweet or nice. All too often, people get sold a bill of goods to anesthetize their pain, but they really did not get an explanation that ministered to them. Then someone told them, "Well, we cannot understand the ways of God, so we just have to accept what God does." I do not believe

that is true. I do not believe that our heavenly Father
leads us around in the dark. I do not believe that He
wants us to walk around like imbeciles and just do whatever He decrees without some explanation.

No, there is an explanation of this principle of
giving thanks. We just have to explore the Word in order
to get the revelation of it.

> Then went the Pharisees, and took counsel how
> they might entangle him in his talk [Of course, this is
> referring to Jesus]. And they sent out unto him their
> disciples with the Herodians, saying, Master, we
> know that thou art true, and teachest the way of God
> in truth, neither carest thou for any man: for thou
> regardest not the person of men. Tell us therefore,
> What thinkest thou? Is it lawful to give tribute unto
> Caesar, or not? But Jesus perceived their wickedness,
> and said, Why tempt ye me, ye hypocrites? Shew me
> the tribute money. And they brought unto him a
> penny. And he saith unto them, Whose is this image
> and superscription? They say unto him, Caesar's.
> Then saith he unto them, Render therefore *unto*
> Caesar the things which are Caesar's; and *unto* God
> the things that are God's.
>
> (Matt. 22:15-21, italics mine)

After studying these verses in depth, the light went
on and I saw what the Holy Spirit was telling us. We are
going to have to render value judgments concerning the
issues of life. We are going to have to make a determination about everything that happens to us, by us, and
around us, and we are going to have to determine if these
things are Caesar's or God's.

The very fact that Jesus asked the people, "Whose image is this? Whose signature is this?" lets us know that everything is not God's. Some things belong to Caesar. What the Holy Spirit is telling us *not* to do is to give God credit for Caesar's things, and give Caesar credit for God's things. The key word is *unto*. Notice, **"Giving thanks always for all things *unto* God."**

I believe that Jesus was giving us a divine principle in this verse. And I believe that this statement concerning Caesar really is a statement concerning the things of Satan. Let us explore this principle in more depth, and then you can see what I am talking about.

In the thirteenth chapter of Romans, the Apostle Paul makes a statement that is very similar to what Jesus said in the twenty-second chapter of Matthew:

> **Render therefore to all their dues: tribute to whom tribute is due; custom to whom custom; fear [or reverence] to whom fear [or reverence]; honour to whom honour.**
>
> **(Rom. 13:7)**

What Paul is telling us here is to give to everyone what belongs to them, and not to give it to someone else. So again, it is going to be my responsibility to make a value judgment. But I am going to have to have some way of making a judgment, because being human I might make the wrong judgment and give credit to the wrong person. Therefore, I have to use some guidelines that will keep me on track so that my human intellect does not get in the way.

I believe this business about Caesar is really showing us the spiritual principle of the division between God and Satan. For everything that happens in this world, there are two agents behind each situation: either God or Satan. We, however, are the ones who allow either God or Satan to get involved in our circumstances.

The issues of life are between what is called good and evil; and good and evil are personified in God and Satan (or the devil).

Some people do not like to talk about the devil. In fact, some very smart, sophisticated, and erudite educators of certain kinds of religious persuasions would try to have us believe there is no such thing as a personal devil. But we know who is behind this game, do we not? If you remove the devil, there is no one else to blame but God. And that is exactly what folk have been doing — blaming God. Even the insurance companies call certain calamities "acts of God," and they will not provide coverage in most of those cases.

> **He that committeth sin is of the devil; for the devil sinneth from the beginning. For this purpose the Son of God was manifested that he might destroy the works of the devil.**
>
> **(1 John 3:8)**

Now the word *committeth*,[10] in the original Greek, carries with it the connotation, "practices sin as a way of life." It is not talking about a Christian who sins. The second chapter of 1 John talks about the fact that Christians have an Advocate with the Father (Jesus Christ, the righteous). In 1 John 1:9, we read, **"If we**

confess our sins, he is faithful and just to forgive us our sins, and to cleanse us from all unrighteousness." Christians do not practice sin as a way of life, but sinners do because that is their nature.

For this purpose the Son of God...

We know that the Son of God is Jesus Christ.

...was manifested...

It does not say "is manifested"; it does not say, "will be manifested" — it says, **"was manifested"** — past tense. Yes, Jesus lived in the earth-realm, He died at Calvary, He rose from the dead, and He ascended to the right hand of the Father. And, yes, He is coming back again. Since Jesus did all these things — He was manifested — then the works of the devil must be destroyed.

Words have different meanings in different languages. For example, in the English language, the word *destroy* implies annihilation or obliteration. In other words, it means that whatever had existed is not there anymore.

In the Greek language, the language in which most of the New Testament was originally written, the word *destroy*,[11] as used here, does not mean annihilation or obliteration. The Greek word that is used here is the word *luo*, and it means "to loose, to dissolve."

One of the works of the devil is to bind up humanity — to bind people up and restrict them in their ability to navigate through life. Satan binds mankind with sickness, disease, prejudice, fear, poverty, frustration, and all the other things that are hurtful and harmful to our well-being.

Jesus was manifested to loose those bonds of infirmity that are placed on mankind by the devil. That is what the word *destroy* means in that verse — a loosening, and a setting free from those things that hold mankind in bondage.

The next question that arises is, "What are the works of the devil?" This subject is so important that we cannot afford to speculate about it. We need to definitely determine what the works of Satan are so that we do not ascribe to God the works that are Satan's and vice versa.

In the tenth chapter of John's Gospel, we are given guidelines that will assist us in making this determination:

> Verily, verily, I say unto you, He that entereth not by the door into the sheepfold, but climbeth up some other way, the same is a thief and a robber. But he that entereth in by the door is the shepherd of the sheep. To him the porter openeth; and the sheep hear his voice: and he calleth his own sheep by name, and leadeth them out. And when he putteth forth his own sheep, he goeth before them, and the sheep follow him: for they know his voice. And a stranger will they not follow, but will flee from him: for they know not the voice of strangers. This parable spake Jesus unto them: but they understood not what things they were which he spake unto them. Then said Jesus unto them again, Verily, verily, I say unto you, I am the door of the sheep. All that ever came before me are thieves and robbers: but the sheep did

not hear them. I am the door: by me if any man enter in, he shall be saved, and shall go in and out, and find pasture. The thief cometh not, but for to steal, and to kill, and to destroy: I am come that they might have life, and that they might have it more abundantly. I am the good shepherd: the good shepherd giveth his life for the sheep. But he that is a hireling, and not the shepherd, whose own the sheep are not, seeth the wolf coming, and leaveth the sheep, and fleeth; and the wolf catcheth them, and scattereth the sheep.

(John 10:1-12)

I believe there is a spiritual truth here that Jesus is showing us. He is using the metaphors of shepherds, sheep, wolves, and thieves to do so. In this parable, Jesus likens himself to the good shepherd. The thief would be whoever is stealing the sheep. We can determine, then, that if Jesus is the Good Shepherd, the thief would have to be Satan, since he is the one who is trying to thwart the work and the Word of God. He is the one who is trying to destroy mankind.

These Scriptures give a very precise look at what the works are that were destroyed by Jesus, as they relate to our lives.

Placed in juxtaposition to each other are two issues: (1) stealing, killing, and destroying; and (2) abundant life. Stealing, killing, and destroying are enemies to abundant living! Anything that steals from you, that kills or destroys what is yours, is the work of the devil.

Sickness or disease do not enhance life or promote abundant living. In fact, they kill, steal, and destroy. I have known people who have lost everything they ever had because of sickness in their families. Sickness and disease are the works of the devil.

If someone should steal something from you — your car, for example — that would not promote abundant living. In fact, that would cause quite a problem for you. If someone should break into your home and steal all of your furniture and belongings, that is not abundant living. Such a devastation would not enhance your life. Therefore, theft has to be a work of the devil.

With these Scriptures in mind, it is easy now to make a determination as to what is Caesar's and what is God's. All we have to do is look at the situation and determine if it is promoting abundant living or if it is stealing, killing, and destroying. If it promotes abundant life, it is the work of the Lord. We give God thanks for everything that gives and promotes life. It is appropriate to do so.

Whatever it is that steals, kills, and destroys is the work of Satan, however, and it is appropriate to give him credit for it and not to blame God.

In 1 Thessalonians 5, we have another verse of Scripture that supports Ephesians 5:20:

In every thing give thanks: for this is the will of God in Christ Jesus concerning you.

(1 Thess. 5:18)

First, I want to tell you what this verse does *not* say. It does not say, "*For* everything give thanks!" This is a very important distinction, not simply a play on words.

When most people read this verse, they read it with the word *for* in mind. But the Bible does not say *for everything*, but *in everything*.

"In everything" means that in the midst of sickness, when it rears its ugly satanic head, we can give thanks. We can give thanks because of the Word. God expects us, as His children, to read all His Word. He expects us to use our faith, and He expects us to search the Scriptures to find out those things that concern our daily lives; He does not tell us everything about living in this earth-realm in one or two verses. We have to know the Word so that we can understand the overall idea of the abundant-living principles of God.

How can I give thanks in sickness? Well, if I know the Word, it is easy. In sickness, I can give thanks for the realization that I do not have to be sick. Satan is the author and agent who brings sickness. God has never made anyone sick, and He never will, because He does not have sickness in Him. You cannot give what you do not have.

One of God's seven redemptive names is Jehovah-Rapha, which means, "I am the Lord that healeth thee." God cannot be the "Lord that healeth thee," and the "Lord that maketh thee sick" at the same time. If that were the case, He would be working against himself. People, including preachers, have been blaming God for sickness and disease through the ages, but since God has no sickness in Him, there is no way He can give it to anyone else.

I hear some Christians saying, "Well, since we are supposed to give thanks in sickness, what are we supposed to give thanks in sickness for? We are supposed to give thanks for Matthew 8:17:

> **That it might be fulfilled which was spoken by Esaias the prophet, saying, Himself took our infirmities, and bare our sicknesses.**

That is what we give thanks for. We give thanks for the fact that we do not have to be sick. We give thanks because Jesus took our infirmities and bore our sicknesses so that when sickness rears its ugly head, we can treat it as a lying vanity that has no legal right to encroach upon our bodies. If we do not know that Jesus took our infirmities and that He bore our sicknesses, we might just lie down and accept the sickness and disease Satan is trying to force upon us, and there will not be a thing God can do about it. The choice is not God's; it is ours.

It is the believer's responsibility to find out what God wants us to give thanks for. From Matthew 8:17, we know He wants us to give thanks that He has made healing available to us. This is also proof that God does not want us to be sick, because if He wanted us to be sick, He would not have provided healing through Jesus Christ, because healing is working against sickness.

If sickness comes, I can give thanks. You can give thanks, thanks that we can kick sickness in its ugly head in the name of Jesus and run it out of our houses and out of our lives.

**Who his own self bare our sins in his own body
on the tree, that we, being dead to sins, should live
unto righteousness: by whose stripes ye were healed.**
(1 Pet. 2:24)

We're not going to be, but we *were* healed. Therefore,
when disease comes, I can say, "You might as well just
back out of here, whatever disease you are, because with
Jesus' stripes I was healed." *Was* is a past-tense designation indicating that the time of the action has already
transpired. It is not in the process of transpiring, it is not
going to transpire, it is already done! And if I was healed,
I am; and if I am, I *is*; and I declare that I *is* healed from
the top of my head to the soles of my feet! That may not
be good English, but it gets the point across.

Paul did not tell us what to give thanks for in 1
Thessalonians 5:18. We have to go through the Bible ourselves and look at the principles to find out in which circumstances we are supposed to give thanks.

One of the best things in the world is to know that
when sickness comes we do not have to receive it. I can
imagine the worst news anyone can hear is to walk into
a doctor's office to hear the doctor say, "I am sorry, there
is nothing we can do." But if you are a child of God who
knows his covenant rights and knows how to walk in line
with the Word, the devil may try to creep into your house
and place some symptoms of sickness on your body, and
then shoot a thought to your mind that you are termi-
nally ill, but you can turn and point the finger of God's
Word at those symptoms and say, "In the name of Jesus
Christ of Nazareth, I curse you — wither and die." And
in it you can give thanks, because you do not have to
accept what the devil is trying to do to you.

What about abilities? I have been challenged in my life and in my ministry with all kinds of things that have come against me. Challenges for which I personally, in the natural, did not have the expertise to handle. But then I found out that *in* everything I can give thanks. Thanks for what? Thanks for the fact that when it seems as if my own human abilities have failed me to be the pastor, leader, or husband I want to be, I can give thanks *in* my inabilities because of Phillipians 4:13, which states:

**I can do all things through Christ which stength-
eneth me.**

It is good news to find out that I can do all things through Christ. In other words, whatever I need to do as a pastor, a father, a husband, a counselor, an advisor, a leader, or whatever else I may be called to do, the Bible tells me, that in the midst of my inabilities, I can give thanks — thanks that the ability of God is my ability. I can say, **"Greater is he that is in you** [me], **than he that is in the world"** (1 John 4:4). And I can shift over from Fred Price's inability to the Greater One's ability, and the Greater One will put me over. That is the way it works.

I am not afraid to face any issue of life. It does not make any difference to me what it is, because I know God's ability is my ability. And whatever the challenge, I can give thanks *in* it, because I am an overcomer through Him.

What about poverty? We are faced on every side with the escalating costs of living. I do not know whether you know it or not, but it is later than we think financially and economically. Every nation in this world is experiencing a financial dilemma. I am not being pessimistic, I am merely being a realist. It does not bother me, though, because the world's system is not my source. I do not care if the interest rates go to 9,000,000 percent. I do not want them to, but I am not going to lose any sleep over interest rates. They are not my source.

No, in the midst of financial dilemmas, in the midst of escalating prices that are going completely out of sight, we can give thanks. Why? Because of Philippians 4:19:

> **But my God shall supply all** [not some, not a little, not a few] **your need** [not according to the bankruptcy of nations; but] **according to his riches in glory by Christ Jesus.**

The Lord is my source. When government leaders talked about raising prices, it used to frighten me, and I would say to my wife, "What are we going to do, honey? What are we going to do?" Since learning about faith, it does not make any difference what they do. Whatever they do will just give my heavenly Father a bigger opportunity to show me how big He really is. If He has to raise my weekly income to $100,000 a week, that is not a big problem for Him. After all, He owns the cattle on a thousand hills, and the hills on which the cattle graze. He owns the grass that grows on the hills that the cattle eat. He owns the worms that crawl under the ground that till the soil that makes the grass grow that the cattle eat on a thousand hills. God is rich, and God is my source!

In the midst of a financial recession, depression, or whatever they want to call it — right in the middle of it — I can give thanks. Thanks that I do not have to worry if the dollar goes out of existence. I do not have to worry if the coinage and the currency of the nations fail. My God does not fail, and He is my source!

What about temptations, trials, and tests that come against everyone on the face of planet Earth? No one is immune to temptations and tests. "Well, the Lord is testing me, Brother Price." What is He testing you for? "Well, I don't know." I know you do not know, because you did not read it in the Bible. You picked this idea up from hearing someone say something like that.

God is not testing you or anyone else. He already knows what you are going to do. So He is not going to waste His time or your time testing you about something that He already knows. The only person that is going to test you is the devil. And he is testing you in order to kill you and to break your back because he does not know what you are going to do.

How can we give thanks in temptations, trials, and tests?

> **There hath no temptation** [the word *temptation* literally means "trials or tests"] **taken you but such as is common to man: but God is faithful, who will not suffer** [the word *suffer* literally means "allow or permit"] **you to be tempted above that ye are able; but will with the temptation also make a way to escape, that ye may be able to bear it.**
>
> **(1 Cor. 10:13)**

...but such as is common to man...

That is an interesting statement. It tells us that Satan does not have anything new. He is working the same tricks on people that he has been using since the Garden of Eden. And, unfortunately, people have been falling for them. In every generation he uses the same tactics because he knows they have worked before.

Sometimes you may feel like the person who sang the song, "Nobody knows the trouble I've seen. Nobody knows but Jesus." Friend, there are many people who know, because they have been through the same things. There is nothing unique about temptations, trials, and tests. None of us is going through anything that someone else has not already gone through or is going through.

...but will with the temptation also make a way to escape...

It could not be God who is bringing you the trial, test, or temptation, and then giving you the way of escape at the same time. He knows human nature, and He knows that we are always going to take the path of least resistance. We are always going to get out of a burning building. We are always going to jump off of the sinking ship; we are always going to try and get away from the problem. God would be working against himself if He were the one who was putting the test or trial or temptation on us, and then at the same time, He was giving us a way of escape. It would not make sense for Him to do so.

It is not God who brings the temptation, trial, or test — it is Satan. In essence, God is saying in this verse: "You are my child, and I will not allow you to ever be tempted, tried, or tested above your ability to overcome. But with that temptation, test, or trial I will make a way for you to get out of it."

...above that ye are able...

What is our ability? Jesus is our ability. The Bible says: **"Christ in you, the hope of glory"** (Col. 1:27). The Holy Spirit is in us as Christ's representative. And Jesus has already defeated the devil in all the devil has to offer. Jesus is in us, and He has been **"made unto us wisdom, and righteousness, and sanctification"** (1 Cor. 1:30). He has been made unto us the very power of Almighty God. Therefore, there is nothing that Satan can bring against us that Jesus cannot handle, if we will only allow Him, by faith in and through the Word, to take care of it.

When temptations, tests, and trials come, can we give thanks in them? You'd better believe we can! In fact, what we should learn to do is to use these trials and tests as stepping-stones to step on up a little higher, instead of going under and being bombed out by the temptations that come to everyone of us. We can overcome and be overcomers in this world, because we have the power of God available to us in Jesus' name.

It is amazing, but you can watch one Christian go down, while another Christian, facing the same circumstances, stands strong, goes through the situation, and then comes out better than he or she was before. What is the difference? They are listening to the same words, they have the same Holy Spirit, they have the same gospel. Yet, one makes it through the test, and the other does not. What is the difference?

It is a matter of what you do with the situations and circumstances. The situations and circumstances, by and of themselves, are neutral. They only become destructive when you allow them to. You can take the very same destructive force that Satan tries to bring against you, put it under your feet, step on it, and it can be your escape route, right out of the situation. But it is up to you to make a stand, and in the midst of your stand, you can give thanks.

Every person who comes to me with a challenge, whether it is in his marriage, with his children, with his job, relatives, or friends — whatever the test or trial — the answer to it all is in the Word of God. It is knowing the Word that allows us to be able to make a stand against the devil's onslaught and give thanks all the while, knowing that we are overcomers through Jesus.

Nay, in all these things we are more than conquerors through him that loved us.

(Rom. 8:37)

What most people want is instant solutions and instant answers. They did not get into the situations they face instantly. They have been messing up in their marriages and in their finances and working on their problems for years.

"Tithing does not work for me, Brother Price," I have heard some Christians say. They have been tithing for fifteen minutes, and they want the windows of heaven to open and give them a blessing (Mal. 3:8-10) *now*. It does not work that way. Faith is a way of life.

Some people who come to me for counseling will tell me, "I have been tithing, but the windows-of-heaven blessing is not coming my way, and I don't understand why." Well, number one, their motives are wrong. If you are tithing just to get the windows-of-heaven blessing, you are not tithing out of obedience and love for God, and you will hinder your faith from operating effectively.

Paul says we are more than conquerors, and if you are not winning you need to find out what the problem is. It may be that you are a talker about the Word, and not a doer of it. As long as you just talk about it, and are not doing it, the Word will not work for you.

Let us go back now to the fifth chapter of Ephesians and continue our verse-by-verse study of this important epistle.

> **Submitting yourselves one to another in the fear** [or reverence] **of God.**
>
> **(Eph. 5:21)**

Many people do not really understand the meaning of the word *submit*. They think it means to lose face, or to show that you are weak or fearful, which is not the case at all. The best example I can give to explain what *submitting* or *submission* means is that of a roadway sign that is seen in certain areas indicating the word YIELD, which means to let the other car go first. This does not mean that one car is better than another car; it simply means that in order for traffic to flow as it ought to, a car that comes to an intersection that has the YIELD sign displayed should give way to another car crossing its path. In other words, let the other person go first. That is all *submitting* means in the Bible. If everyone practiced yielding, we would not have clashes with one another or problems in the handling of our interpersonal relationships.

> **Wives, submit yourselves unto your own husbands, as unto the Lord. For the husband is the head of the wife, even as Christ is the head of the church: and he is the saviour of the body.**
>
> **(Eph. 5:22-23)**

There is a truth here that has been grossly overlooked. Paul is not saying that just because Jesus Christ is the Head of the Church that the husband is the head of the wife. And whatever the husband tells the wife to do, she has to do. I do not believe that this is what this verse is implying at all.

What we have to do is to stop and find out how Jesus is toward the Church, in His role as the Head of the Church, and when we make this determination, we will be informed as to how the husband is to be in his relationship with his wife, so that she can be submissive to his authority in the home.

How is Jesus toward the Church? He is sweet and kind to the Church. He is not fault-finding; rather, He is forgiving and willing to make excuses for the Church. He is always looking out for the best interests of the Church, seeking how He may edify and build it up. He is the protector and provider of the Church and readily gives of himself for its benefit. When a husband starts acting like that toward his wife, then she can afford to yield and submit to him.

Personally, I think it is terrible the way some Christian men treat their wives under the guise of following the Word of God.

There is a system called rank ordering in a chain of command. We understand the concept of rank in the natural order of things: There is the general; below him are the officers; and then the enlisted personnel. Often, the general is no better morally than the private is. It is just that he has been in the military for many years, has been given specialized training, or perhaps he has distinguished himself in battle or somewhere else in the corps, and eventually he is elevated through the ranks to the position of a general. But just because he holds the position of general does not make him intrinsically better (character-wise or even intellectually) than the buck private. It is all a matter of rank.

Likewise, God has a system of rank. God, the Father, is the Head over all; Jesus Christ is under Him as the Head of the Church. The Holy Spirit is under Jesus, giving direction to the Church, the Body of Christ; and then there is man. That is the spiritual rank.

In the domestic realm, the ranking system is first the husband, then the wife, then the children, in subjection to the wife and husband. However, this does not mean that because the husband is the head of the family, he is to dominate and lord it over his wife and his children. Jesus does not dominate and lord it over us. He treats us with tender, loving care. He is long-suffering with us, and not like some husbands, who, the minute the wife forgets to make the bed or something, is ready to divorce her.

The husband is the head from the standpoint of rank. He is not the head from the standpoint that he is supposed to give his wife orders and tell her what to do, especially when it comes to spiritual matters. When it comes to spiritual things, the husband is not the head of the wife, Jesus is!

A husband does not have any business telling his wife when she can read the Bible and when she cannot, when she can go to church and when she cannot, or how many times she can go to church and how many times she cannot. That is not his business. The Bible says, **"Not forsaking the assembling of ourselves together"** (Heb. 10:25). When it comes to domestic activity, God looks to the husband to take care of his wife and family; but when it comes to spiritual things, Jesus is in charge.

However, if the wife is not discharging her duties and is allowing other things, such as spiritual matters, to come in to keep her from carrying out her domestic chores, then the husband has the right to tell her what he expects of her with regard to taking care of the family.

There are some women who go to the extreme, running around all day long to every prayer meeting, home Bible study, and casting-out-demons session, leaving their household duties neglected. The woman's ministry is first to her family. God would not call any wife out into a field ministry to the neglect of her husband and her children. There is nothing in the Bible to support this practice.

However, when the wife's domestic activities have been taken care of, if there is some time left over, and she has the ability and God-given talent to operate in spiritual matters, then she can utilize her spiritual gifts.

God never, but never, take sides or gets into agreement with the husband because he is the husband or the wife because she is the wife. God gets into agreement with and sides with the party who is right!

In the Book of Genesis we see this principle in God's dealing with Abraham and his wife, Sarah. God did not side with Abraham in a particular situation. In fact, God told Abraham to do what his wife told him to do. Sarah had told Abraham to tell the servant girl Hagar and her child by Abraham to leave the family dwelling. Abraham got a little upset about it. God told Abraham to do exactly as his wife said, because the child, Ishmael, could not be an heir with the true son, Isaac. Sarah had implied the same thing to Abraham, and God sided with her because she was right in this situation. (See Gen. 21:12).

Therefore as the church is subject unto Christ, so let the wives be to their own husbands in every thing.
(Eph. 5:24)

As I said before, when the husband treats his wife like Jesus treats the Church, she can afford to submit to him, because she knows he will not take advantage of her.

> **Husbands, love your wives, even as Christ also loved the church, and gave himself for it.**
>
> **(Eph. 5:25)**

Jesus never lies to the Church, and the husband should not lie to his wife. Sometimes, husbands are not truthful with their wives. I do not mean they are necessarily mean about it or that they practice overt, deliberate deception. Everyone is aware of that kind of lie. I am talking about the subtle kind of lie in which a husband does not treat his wife in the way she really should be treated.

For example, when he was dating her, she was a petite size 8 or 9. Now she is a size 18, and he does not really like that. That was not what attracted his attention fifteen years ago. He goes along and acts as if it is all right for her to be five sizes too big, but then he recklessly eyeballs all the other little size 9's that walk by. That is not right. Or, there is the husband who mistreats his wife because deep down he is really angry at her for letting herself get out of shape, but he will not tell her that he does not like her at her present size.

The husband in such a situation needs to think about the fact that he shares a part of the fault. After all, he did not help his wife to keep in shape. She bore him four children, stretched herself all out of shape, and then she did not get any help or encouragement from him to get back into shape. It is a lot easier to gain weight than it is to lose it. The husband can help his wife, and do not tell me he cannot, because I have done it.

My wife was a size 14 when we got married. Since our marriage, she has had five children and is now a size

8/10. If I had not given her encouragement, she would be bigger than a size 8/10. She will tell you, if you talk to her in private, that she is glad that I stayed on her about it. She is glad that I helped her, because she likes nice clothes, and prettier clothes usually come in smaller sizes.

There are many things a husband can do to help his wife keep her appearance up. For example I do not like to come home for dinner and see my wife with rollers in her hair. There are other husbands who feel the same way, but they will not tell their wives how they feel. If the wife does not know how he feels, she will continue to wear rollers at the dinner table. It takes effort to keep one's self up. However, when you are inspired and encouraged by the person who loves you, then it makes it a lot easier to maintain a good appearance.

This is an area where the husband should exercise his domestic leadership, but then he has to keep himself in line, too. He cannot tell his wife to become a size 10 while his waist is 46. It works both ways.

...even as Christ also loved the church...

Notice the **"even as."** Paul is giving us a parallel here.

Some husbands do not give time to their wives, claiming they have something else to do or some other place to go. They act as though they do not want to be at home. They run in, eat, and then leave. Either that, or they run in, eat, and then go sit in front of the television the rest of the evening and do not spend any time with either their wives or their children.

Many husbands do not take time to go shopping with their wives, and then when the wives bring dresses home, the husbands do not like them. They should have gone with their wives in the first place to help them pick out something they both would like. "Well, you do not know my wife. She spends all day in the store," is a comment I hear from many husbands. Maybe she does so because she never had anyone who was interested enough to help her decide on an outfit that suits her.

Often, on my day off I will go shopping with my wife. I know how I want her to look, I know what looks good on her. She is my helpmeet; she is my queen. Consequently, I take time to go shopping with her. I pick out dresses, and she goes and tries them on, and then comes out and models them for me, and then we decide on what suits her best.

Every man needs to take time with his wife and with his children. I do everything in my power to get together with my family and do things with them. You cannot get too busy saving the world and let your own family go down the tube. That is what many ministers have done. They do not realize that they have a mission field right in their own homes.

Since I have come into the knowledge of the Word and found out how to be a real man in Christ, I have never told my wife, "I am the head of the house." I do not have to, because she knows I am. I carry myself like the head. If a man wants to be respected as the head, he has to carry himself in a respectful way, and people will respect him. You carry yourself in a loving way, and people will love you.

> **That he might sanctify and cleanse it** [that is the Church] **with the washing of water by the word.**
>
> **(Eph. 5:26)**

There is much misunderstanding among people about how God teaches and trains His children. Some people think that God teaches, trains, and/or chastises His children by putting afflictions on them. Unfortunately, that is a common concept that is promulgated from pulpit to pulpit around the world. God uses His Word to train us. He uses His Word to perfect (or spiritually mature) us. He does not use the pressures of life to get us to do what He wants us to do. He does not use fear and intimidation, and He does not use the devil to chastise us. If we will obey the Word, we can avoid a multitude of bad experiences that are waiting out there in the world to tear us down.

Yes, we can learn some things from experience. There is no question about that. But that is not the best way to learn. For example, it is never the best way for a woman or girl to learn that fooling around with sex prior to marriage is to get pregnant out of wedlock and then have an abortion. The best way to learn is to learn from others' experiences. That may sound callous, but think of all those babies that have been destroyed because some foolish female allowed her emotions to take control of her instead of common sense. You keep on playing around with sex, and you are going to get burned. You keep on playing around with drugs, and you are going to get hooked and your life will get messed up. You keep on playing around with alcohol, and you are going to have some serious problems!

When you keep on mixing gasoline and alcohol together, you will learn some lessons, but that is not God's way for you to learn. He does not want you to take a chance on killing your wife, your children, and some other innocent people in the process.

God teaches us by His Word. But when we fail or refuse to acknowledge His Word, we do not have any other way to learn but through experience. Experiences will always work against you because Satan operates in the experiences of life. If it were left up to him, he would tie a rope around our necks and kill us with experiences. And there would be nothing God could do about it because He has given us His Word to direct our lives.

Jesus is cleaning the Church up with His Word, but Christians are not taking the admonition of the Word of God and cleaning themselves up. When your clothes are dirty, you wash them. Very seldom do you ever use washing powders or other kinds of detergents without water. Water is a cleansing agent.

..cleanse it with the washing of water by the word.

God's detergent is the Word. And the active enzyme in God's detergent is the Holy Spirit. When the Holy Spirit works in you with the Word like the enzymes do in washing powder, you have the cleaning agent that can clean up your life. That is why the Word is so important. That is why, when there is an absence of the Word, there is usually much dirt.

If you will let the Word work on you, it will clean you up. If you are having problems with bad habits or other ungodly situations, you have to let the Word do its job. It will wash you clean.

Look at what Jesus says in John 15:3:

> **Now ye are clean through the word which I have spoken unto you.**

And John 17:17:

> **Sanctify them through thy truth: thy *word* is truth.**

That is how God sanctifies us and makes us holy — it is through His Word!

Put the Word up against your life to determine your level of spiritual development and your moral life-style. Never measure yourself by someone else's life-style — not your husband's, not your wife's, not your boss's, or even your pastor's — but by the Word. Because that person may be off-center, and if he or she is off, it can make you off, too.

I never look at other Christians to determine my manner of living. It does not bother me in the least what they do, or how they live. Of course, I want my brothers and sisters in Christ to live properly. And I appreciate those who are consistent in living godly lives, but it does not disturb me whether someone lives right or not as far as my living right is concerned. God has given me a guide to follow and that is what He is going to hold me accountable to. He is not going to ask me how well did so-and-so live, or did I compare my life with so-and-so's life. No, He is going to ask me about Jesus and about His Word.

That he might sanctify and cleanse it...

Drop the word *it* and substitute the words *the Church*, making verse 26 read this way: "That He might sanctify and cleanse THE CHURCH with the washing of water by THE WORD."

I had someone say of me one time concerning my ministry: "The only thing wrong with that Fred Price is he quotes too much Scripture!" Can you believe that? Too much Scripture, too much Word! In some churches, if you read three passages, it would be too much Scripture, because they are not used to using the Bible. The preacher might read one verse of Scripture and close his Bible and then go off on a tangent. But I am going to preach the uncompromising Word, and I do not care what anyone says or thinks. It is the Word that has set me free. I would quote more of it if I could get it all into my head and into my spirit, because it is the Word that has straightened me out.

That he might present it [the Church] to himself a glorious church, not having spot, or wrinkle, or any such thing; but that it should be holy and without blemish.

(Eph. 5:27)

...without blemish.

That is a tall order. Sometimes I look at the Church and it looks like the impossible dream to believe that it will ever be without spot, wrinkle, or blemish. I ask myself, "How in the world will Jesus ever do that?" "How will the Holy Spirit ever do it?"

A **"church, not having spot, or wrinkle."** Before the Church can be like that, every member in the Church has to be like that. It is the parts that make up the whole, and if the parts are defective, the whole will break down.

One time I took my family on a vacation. (This was before we had gotten into the Word and knew how to believe God.) We were living on a shoestring, and even the shoestring was borrowed. We had been traveling all day and had stopped to spend the night in a motel in New Mexico. I had just bought the car we were driving in; therefore, I was not totally familiar with its operation.

We got up the next morning, got dressed, packed the car and were ready to start on the next leg of our journey, but the car would not start. A great-big, brand-new automobile — I owed my soul to the company store for that car — and it would not work! I tried everything I knew to get the car started, and the thing still would not go!

Across the street from the motel there was a service station. I went over there and told the mechanic the symptoms of my non-working automobile. He said, "Oh, I think I can fix it." He walked across the street, opened the hood, took a ballpoint pen out, took the air breather off the top of the carburetor, set it aside, took his pen and stuck it down into the carburetor, clicked some-thing and said, "Start it up." The car started up and worked perfectly until the day I got rid of it.

It was one simple thing in the carburetor — a little float valve that had gotten stuck and all it needed was to be pushed back into its proper place. Here we were, my whole family, with all of our personal items in the trunk of the car in another state far away from home, and that one small part stopped us from moving. Good tires on the ground, and they would not roll because of one small part. We had an excellent air-conditioner in the car, but it would not work because of one small part.

It is much the same with the Church. We are all parts. You are one of those parts. Are you working right? You can hinder and foul up the whole mechanism. If you are not working right, you can keep all the rest of us from going on our trip. Just think about it, one little part stopped the car, the whole family, the luggage, everything from taking off. That car would not move because of one little part. Jesus is not coming back for a faulty automobile!

He is coming back for a Church that has no spot or wrinkle, or any such thing. He is coming back for a holy Church — a Church without blemish. Are you holy? If you are not, just know that Jesus cannot come back until you get holy.

> So ought men to love their wives as their own bodies. He that loveth his wife loveth himself.
>
> (Eph. 5:28)

Perhaps the reason why some men have such a problem with loving their wives is because they do not like themselves. There are many people who do not like themselves, and this makes it hard for them to love others, including their spouses, their children, and the other people around them.

Some Christians have been led to believe that we should not love ourselves; however, the Bible tells us that we should love one another as well as ourselves. The Bible teaches that we should not idolize ourselves. In fact, Jesus said in Matthew 19:19, **"...Thou shalt love thy neighbour as thyself."** How can I love you if I do not love me?

So ought men to love their wives as their own bodies...

The reason why Paul makes this statement is because the Bible teaches that husbands and wives are one. When a man leaves his mother and father and joins himself to his wife, they become one flesh in the sight of God. (See Gen. 2:24.) Even secular law recognizes the oneness of the marital union by the fact that the man's name becomes the wife's name.

He that loveth his wife loveth himself.

Notice again that in this verse, Paul is talking about love. He is not talking about idolizing your wife or your husband. He is talking about the God-kind of love.

> For no man ever yet hated his own flesh; but
> nourisheth it and cherisheth it, even as the Lord the
> church.
>
> (Eph. 5:29)

Notice how Paul keeps swinging like a pendulum on a grandfather clock, back and forth, between husbands and wives, and Jesus and the Church. The reason why is because people can relate to husbands and wives and the affection or love they have one for another. He is giving us a visible example of an invisible situation, the relationship between the Body of Christ and the Lord Jesus Christ.

> For we are members of his body, of his flesh, and
> of his bones.
>
> (Eph. 5:30)

When was Jesus Christ, the Son of God, ever sick in His body, in His flesh, and in His bones? The answer to this question is that He was never ill. If we are members of His body, of His flesh, and of His bones, then Jesus would not want any sickness in us either.

Jesus healed everyone who came to Him. There is not one Scripture in which we see an individual coming to Jesus to be healed only to hear the Master say, "No, it is not my will for you to be healed. No, you keep your sickness and your disease. God has a grand purpose in making you sick. Just grin and bear it, tiger. Just tough it out, and after a while, over there on the other side, it will be better."

Every person who ever came to Jesus, every person who ever appealed to Him, every person who cried out and said, "Thou Son of David, have mercy upon me," Jesus healed and made whole.

I do not care whether he or she was a Jew, or a Samaritan, or whomever. Not one single time did Jesus say, "No, I will not heal you."

Paul says, **"We are members of his body, of his flesh, and of his bones."** Since Jesus was never sick, He could not want sickness in the Body of Christ; we are His representatives in the earth-realm. Therefore, it is ridiculous for people to say that divine healing is not for Christians today.

> **For this cause shall a man leave his father and his mother, and shall be joined unto his wife, and they two shall be *one* flesh. This is a great mystery: but I speak concerning Christ and the church.**
> **(Eph. 5:31-32, italics mine)**

We have left our father and our mother. We have left the world, the flesh, and the devil, and we are now joined to Jesus, and we have become one with Him, just as a man does with his wife when he leaves his mother and father in order to be married.

This is a great mystery....

The Apostle Paul had been talking about the husband-and-wife relationship, yet he said this is a mystery. There is no real mystery concerning husbands and wives as such, but what he meant was that the mystery is how God sees the Church relative to Jesus Christ.

Jesus is referred to in the Scriptures as the "Groom," and the Church is referred to as the "bride." As in the natural, as a groom and bride are joined together to become one as husband and wife, so does the Church and Christ join together to become one. Paul uses the example of husband and wife to illustrate how close the relationship is between Jesus and His Church.

Unfortunately, there has been a vast disregard for the sanctity of marriage in recent years. Many couples actually join together and live as married people without really being married. They show a blatant disregard for the holiness of the relationship God instituted from the beginning of man's existence.

God sees the Church and Christ as one, just as He sees the husband and wife as one. Paul said this is a mystery because we cannot fully comprehend this spiritual relationship, but we can get an idea of its complexity and of its importance by looking at the husband-and-wife relationship.

It is understandable why some people have very little regard for the relationship of a Christian to Christ. It is because they do not have a real understanding of the husband-and-wife relationship (with which they are familiar) and, therefore, they can never fully appreciate the relationship of a believer to Christ. That is why they live such shoddy lives. It is easy for them to live together and perform all the acts of marriage without having the spiritual and legal ties of the marriage vows. It is only when one has an accurate understanding and appreciation and commitment to the marriage relationship that one has the capacity to truly understand his or her relationship to Christ Jesus.

> **For this cause shall a man leave his father and mother, and shall be joined unto his wife, and they two shall be one flesh.**
>
> **(Eph. 5:31)**

Spiritually speaking, when I left my father and my mother (the world, the flesh, and the devil), I became joined to my mate (Jesus Christ, the Groom).

For this cause shall a man leave...

The word *leave* means, "I am no longer over there; I am now over here." I left Mama and Papa over there, and I am now over here with my wife.

...shall be joined unto his wife...

Notice that it does not say, "joined back to his mother and father," *but* **"joined unto his wife."** The Bible does not say that they, plus Mama and Papa, shall be one, it says, **"...they two shall be one...."**

As a Christian, when you left your mother and father (Satan, the world, and the flesh), you were joined to your spouse (Christ), and you and Christ now are one in the sight of God. Your interests, your commitment, your devotion must be to each other.

Jesus gave all that He had for us. He has given us His Holy Spirit and His Word. And for the past 2,000 years, He has been seated at the right hand of the Majesty on High, making intercession for you and me. In other words, He not only saved us, redeemed us, bought and paid for us, empowered us by His Spirit, gave us a New Covenant and called us His own, but He has spent the last 2,000 years interceding on our behalf. That is commitment. Can we be any less committed?

My wife and I give to each other. It is a give-and-take situation, which causes us to flow together as one. I find myself thinking all the time of how I can make my wife happy, and vice versa. That is the same kind of relationship we should have with Jesus. I am always thinking, "What can I do for the Lord? What can I do that will please Him? What can I do that will show my love for Him?"

Do you think about how you can please your Lord? Do you think about what will make Him happy?

> **Nevertheless let every one of you in particular so love his wife even as himself; and the wife see that she reverence her husband.**
>
> **(Eph. 5:33)**

...and the wife see that she reverence her husband.

The verse does not tell the wife to idolize or worship her husband, but to *reverence* him. Proverbs 1:7 says, **"The fear of the Lord is the beginning of knowledge."**

The word *fear,* as it is used here, does not mean the scared kind of fear. It means reverential fear. This is the same meaning Paul is using in Ephesians 5:33. But one cannot, with any degree of sincerity or vitality, reverence an irreverent husband. People sometimes try to make the Bible fit those who do not fit within the framework of the Bible. They do not understand that the Bible is written to God's children. Consequently, biblical rules apply only to those who are in Christ. Those who are outside of Christ have no rules. It is the same with trade unions. If you are not in the union, you do not have any right to the benefits of being in the union. You have to be in Christ in order for the words of Christ to have any relevancy to your life.

The Bible is not for sinners. Sinners have no rules at all — not God's rules, anyway. The only thing sinners have from God is salvation, and until they accept Christ as their personal Savior and Lord, the Bible means absolutely nothing to them.

We can reverence our heavenly Father because He carries himself with dignity and respect. He carries himself in such a way that it is our desire to worship Him and to hold Him in the highest esteem. A wife can reverence a husband who is carrying himself like Jesus carries himself in relationship to the Church.

The Church can give love and adoration to Jesus because He carries himself in such a way that we can do no less than show Him the highest respect.

My wife reverences me. She loves me and cherishes me because I carry myself in a way that makes it easy for her to do so. I never said that I was perfect, and, thank God, the Bible does not say you have to be perfect. If that were true, none of us would make it. Yes, the Bible does say, **"Be ye therefore perfect"** (Matt. 5:48), but what that means is that we are to strive for perfection. And as we continue to strive for it, we will rise higher than we were before. No one will ever be perfectly perfect in this life because we live in an imperfect environment and in an imperfect body. There is no way you can be perfect in an imperfect world.

All of these Scriptures that compare the husband-and-wife relationship to Christ's relationship to the Church are illustrations indicating that we as husbands are to carry ourselves and act like Jesus does toward the Church. If we carry ourselves toward our wives as Jesus does toward the Church, then our wives can afford to reverence us just as we can afford to serve the Lord.

Jesus never takes unfair advantage of the Church. He is always seeking the best for the Church. He is always looking out for our welfare. He has made provision for us to be well cared for and loved. That is exactly what the husband ought to do for his wife.

I realize, of course, that we live in a different society than we did fifty years ago, and I do not mean to meddle in anyone's business, but, personally, I never wanted my wife to work. That is just my opinion, so do not get upset with what I am about to say.

There was a time when my wife insisted on working, so I let her get a job. What could I do? I could not chain her up in the house while I went to work, so I consented. I did not want her to work because I felt it was my duty, my responsibility to take care of her and to take care of her in the style in which she wanted to be taken care of. At this particular time in our marriage, things were very bad financially, even though I was doing the best I could. Betty decided she wanted to help out, so she insisted on getting a job. We went around and around about it, but in the end I consented, even though I was against it.

I told her that she could go to work on one condition. I said, "When I come home from work, my dinner is to be on the table just like it has been on the table while you were at home. I want the house cleaned just like it is now. I want the laundry done just as it was always done. I want the kids taken care of just the way they were being taken care of before, and I expect you to be the same in bed as you have always been. I do not want to hear anything about your being tired or anything like that." Then I continued, "If you can do all of that and work, too, go to it!"

She thought she could do it. She worked about a year and a half, and the poor girl could not make it. No one could, but she tried. Finally, she said, "I am going to quit, and I am never going to go to work again!" That has been many, many years ago, and now she would not go to work for anything, even though she voluntarily helps out at the ministry. I deliberately made it hard for her.

You may say that was selfish and unfeeling. But it was not. It would have been unfeeling for me to ask her to go to work to help out, and then to make those demands on her. That would have been totally unfeeling and wrong. I did not want her to go to work, and I told her so. She insisted on going because she is an adult, and she has a right to exercise her free will.

I think it is terrible the way some men treat their wives, and personally I would not put up with their attitude for five minutes. Some men beg their wives to go to work to help out financially so they can buy their fancy sports cars, and all the other little goodies they want. Then the fat, lazy, pot-bellied, beer-drinking rascal comes home and sits in front of the television all evening, while his wife, who also works all day, has to go and get the children from the day-care center, come home, cook the dinner, feed the family, clean the kitchen, help the children with their homework, get them ready for bed, and get their clothes ready for the next day. That is not right!

If a husband requires his wife to go to work to help him out financially, then he ought to help her out domestically. If he is having his wife bring home her paycheck and give it to him, or put it into the common pot, or split half of what she earns, then he ought to split half of the household chores. He ought to help his wife with the housework; he ought to help her with the shopping, and with everything else that needs to be done on behalf of the family. If a husband wants his wife to work outside the home, he ought to help her inside the home.

5

The Warfare of the Believer (Ephesians 6)

Part 1 — Ephesians 6:1-10

> **Children, obey your parents in the Lord: for this is right.**
>
> **(Eph. 6:1)**

I believe that Paul uses the term, *in the Lord,* because some times there is a problem with obedience when the children are saved, and the parents are not. Again, we have to take note that these Scriptures are written to Christians, not to sinners. Consequently, we are talking about Christian children and Christian parents.

> **Honour thy father and mother; (which is the first commandment with promise); That it may be well with thee, and thou mayest live long on the earth.**
>
> **(Eph. 6:2-3)**

To honor one's father and mother is one of the Ten Commandments, and, although Christians are not under the Ten Commandments as such, we are always under the principles of God's Word.

For example, even though we are not under the Law, per se, it is still wrong to steal. Ask any police officer, and he will tell you that it is wrong. If you do not believe it, try stealing something with a policeman in your presence, and he will put you in jail swiftly. There are certain moral principles that exist whether they are under the Old Covenant or the New Covenant.

...which is the first commandment with promise...

What is the promise? **"That it may be well with thee, and thou mayest live long on the earth."**

This clearly lets us know that God is not our enemy and that He is not the one who kills people at age twenty-five, or twenty-two, or seventeen, or ten. If God were the one who killed them,what would we say about a man who has been honoring his father and his mother all of his life and who is struck down in the prime of life, at twenty-five years, or thirty years, or even forty years? God said, "Honour thy father and mother so that you may live long on the earth." This is a promise carried over from the Old Covenant to the New Covenant.

Notice that it did not say, "Obey your father and mother that it may be well with thee, that thy days may be long" — because there are some parents who are not to be obeyed. There have been some parents who have placed their children in prostitution in order to bring money into the family. There are some parents who make their children steal and kill. Children cannot always obey their parents. It depends on who the parents are. It depends upon the parents' relationship with God. There are some strange folk walking around in this world. Just because you become a parent does not make you normal and right.

> **And, ye fathers, provoke not your children to wrath: but bring them up in the nurture and admonition of the Lord.**
>
> **(Eph. 6:4)**

It is interesting to note that it does not say, "Ye *mothers* provoke not your children." The reason why Paul makes this statement to fathers is because the man, the husband, is supposed to be the domestic head of the home, and he is supposed to be the one who gives the orders and direction to the rest of the family. It should be the wife who sees that the orders and directions are carried out.

Nurture means the training of the Lord. You can easily see that these Scriptures are directed specifically to Christians — an unsaved man could never bring his children up in the admonition of the Lord. He does not know anything about the Lord, so how is he going to train up a child in the ways of God?

...provoke not your children to wrath...

This admonition means that we are not to put pressure on our children to such an extent that we break their spirits. In other words, parents should not destroy their children's enthusiasm and desire to perform by making the standards and goals so unreasonable that the kids become discouraged, give up, and actually end up doing nothing.

After all, getting A's in school is not the most important thing in the world. Some parents show off their children like trophies and put extreme pressures on them to bring nothing but A's home. If the child has the mental capacity to do it, fine. But not all children have this capacity. You can beat them with a lead pipe, but they are not going to do it. If they are capable, then they ought to perform. Some children are mentally faster than others. This does not mean there is something wrong with them; it is just their makeup.

There are a lot of people who got A's in school, but their lives are absolute disasters. I am not against A's, I am simply saying that there is a balance that parents ought to have in order to help keep their children on an even keel.

...bring them up in the nurture and admonition of the Lord.

Proverbs 22:6 says, **"Train up a child in the way he should go: and when he is old, he will not depart from it."** The reason we have so many problems with children in schools today is because we have no discipline in the home. There is no training in the home and there is no training in the schools. One of the worst things that ever happened was when they took physical discipline out of the schools. Now children are running wild in the schools and the teachers cannot control them.

The thing is, though, if you were to talk with these children on a one-on-one basis, you will find out that they really want to be trained. They do not receive training at home, so they go out and do all kinds of things, hoping that someone will help them get on the right road.

There is an old saying that pastors' kids (PK's) are usually the worst children of all. In such cases, the PK's fathers are spending all their time trying to save the world, while their children are left to their own devices. And many of these children end up in a bad way.

Then there are other Christians, lovely people who love the Lord, who are heard to say: "I just do not understand my son, Johnny. We trained him, and I don't know why he is fooling around with drugs. I cannot understand why he likes associating with that bad element."

I ask them, "Well, did you ever make him go to church?"

Their answer is always just about the same, "No. We asked him if he wanted to go and he fell on the floor and had a fit. So we did not want to force him to do something that he did not want to do." Yes, you do want to force him. You had better do so!

I know there are people who will disagree with me about this. I know there are people who have gone to college and have taken some courses in child psychology that theorize that it is wrong to physically discipline a child. Almighty God knows more about how to raise children than you or me or some psychology professor will ever know. And He says to "use the rod of correction" on children. (See Prov. 22:15.) The administration of the rod of discipline should always be tempered with love for the child.

Many parents miss it with their children by asking them if they *want* to do something, and because the children usually do not, the parents do not make them. They do not understand what training means. A trainer makes the trainee do what is necessary to accomplish a goal. Training up children in the way they should go means to make them do whatever they need to do, even though they are unwilling to do so. You make them go to church; you make them do their household chores, such as cleaning their rooms and taking out the trash. And do not tell me it is wrong to make them do these things, because it works. God said it would, and it does!

With my children, I insisted that they attend church on Sundays — both morning and evening services. I told them, "As long as you live in my house, you are going to church whether you want to or not. When you get on your own, you can do whatever you want, but in my house we go to church as a family." While they were living under my roof, using my electricity, burning my gas, and eating my food, they were going to do as I said.

My eldest daughter, Angela, got to a point in her teen years when she did not want to go to church on Sunday evenings. I told her in no uncertain terms, "You are going to church!"

She kept telling me, "I don't want to go to church."

I reiterated, "I do not care what you don't want to do, you are going to church!"

Before I go any further, let me explain this, lest some people will think I am being too harsh. Think back. When you were a child, like most children, you probably had to be made to brush your teeth, wash behind your ears, and wash your neck. Most of the time, you probably had to be made to take a bath, if you were like the average child. You were also made to go to school, whether you wanted to or not. If you can make a child brush his teeth, clean up his room, take a bath, take out the trash, you can make him go to church. The same principle applies in each case.

The little church where I began pastoring had only eight rows of seats from the front to the back. From the pulpit, it was very easy to see what was going on in the whole church. Angela would come in and sit in the last seat in the last row. She would not participate in the singing, or in any of the congregational activities. She would just sit there with a frown on her face, and her mouth stuck out. I said to myself, "That is all right, at least you are here. Now whether you get anything out of the service or not is your problem. My problem is that I place you in a position as a child to receive spiritual things; if you do not, there is nothing I can do about it."

Week after week, she would come in, puffed up like a frog, and just sit there and not take part in the service at all. It would not really bother me. I said, "That is all right. The Lord told me to train you. I have a responsibility, and I am going to train you. I am going to expose you to the things of God, and I am going to teach you. What you do with it is your red wagon. But you will never be able to say that your father did not teach you or show you the right way."

God's Word is true. I made her go to church, and kept her going. Finally, when we moved from that little church to a larger facility, which was quite a distance from our home, she came on her own without anyone making her.

She got a job working a few hours after school and she wanted to come to church, but she could not get home in time to leave with the family, so she would catch the bus. It probably took her over an hour to get from her job to the new church, and she willingly did it, because she had committed herself to work at our little book table. She was not on salary, and I did not ask her to do it. She volunteered to do it and rode the bus every week to do it. Now, I cannot keep my children away from church, because this is the way I trained them. They have seen what God has done for our family. They have seen what God has done in my life, and they appreciate it.

Everyone of my children has received Christ as his or her personal Savior and Lord. Every one of them is filled with the Spirit and speaks with tongues, according to Acts 2:4. And every one of them joined the church on his or her own.

The easiest thing in the world is to give in and let your children have their way. It is less traumatic for everyone. It is less frustrating, because children can drive you up a wall, and through the ceiling, if you let them. But God expects us as Christian parents to train up our children in His ways.

Children need to be trained. What people do not realize is that there is a rebellious spirit running rampant among our kids today. It is an untamed, untrained, unsaved spirit, and that spirit is prompted by and motivated by Satan. That is why children are destructive and have no concern for the property of others.

Children need to be trained when they are young for their own good, not only for the rest of us. Because later on, it is going to be a terrible thing for them to have to deal with themselves. If they are not trained by parental authority, when they are grown and out there in the work-a-day world, they will not be able to cope because they have never learned discipline and self-control.

Christian parents have a responsibility to bring their children up by the Word of God. But how are you going to teach the Word to your child if you do not know it yourself? If you have a child that says, "I never heard of Jesus. I never went to church." That is the parents' fault. My children have watched my wife and me come out of poverty and lack through the Word of God. They have learned through watching our circumstances change right before their eyes.

There were times when we did not buy anything we did not need or could not afford. We just did not have the extra money to do it. There was a time when we did not even buy a Christmas tree, because we could not afford one. We did that for two years in a row, because we were working toward a goal to get out of that bottomless pit of debt. We could not afford to spend twenty dollars on something that would end up in the trash bin just a few days later. I know some people think that when I talk about this period in our lives that I am exaggerating, but am not; I am telling the truth. The only reason I tell about these bad times is to illustrate that the Word works, so that others can be inspired to put the Word to work for them. You cannot see Jesus, but you can see someone who claims to be connected to Him winning, and that is important. You cannot see the Holy Spirit, but you can see others who claim to know Him and you can see them winning. You can see them go from poverty to wealth; you can see them go from sickness to health, and it ought to be an inspiration to you. It was for my children.

When I tell you we could not pay our bills, I mean *we could not pay our bills!* When I tell you we did not have anything, we did not have *anything!* There was a time when we had holes in our carpet; we had to arrange the furniture to cover the holes. It was embarrassing to us when people came to our house. We had draperies at our windows that had become so threadbare that they had large holes in them and were falling off the rods. Financially, we were unable to do anything about it. Our children went through these things with us and they have learned what God will do when one is faithful to His Word.

Whenever God blesses me financially, I bring the check or money home and show it to my children and tell them, "This is what God does." They have seen the reality of the Word in operation; they know it works.

I have taught my children consistency. What my congregation sees on Sunday is the way I am on Monday, Tuesday, Wednesday, Thursday, Friday, and Saturday. I do not have a "preacher role" that I play so that when I go home I become someone else. I am the same all the time, because God is the same all the time. **"Jesus Christ the same yesterday, and to day, and for ever"** (Heb. 13:8).

Many people have had to use their faith to deal with some things in their lives because no one took the time to help them deal with their personality flaws when they were children. I had to deal with a temper and getting upset all the time when I could not get my way. After I became an adult, it was hard for me to discipline myself in those areas and, without the Word to direct me, I really do not believe I could have done it.

Often, I would embarrass myself and embarrass my wife, all because I had not learned how to control my temper. When I was growing up, I was left, for the most part, to do what I wanted to do. It was extremely difficult after I became an adult to control my temper, because I had become conditioned to doing certain things and acting in a certain way. I had to go through hell itself to straighten myself out as an adult, when the slack should have been taken out of me when I was a youth.

My children have never thrown a fit and fallen on the floor. I have gone into stores and seen children throw a literal tantrum because their parents would not buy a particular item for them. If my children had acted like that, I would have been on them like white on rice, like a streak of lightning and a bolt of heat. My children have never thrown a tantrum. They were trained not to. God has given the man — the husband, the father — the authority in the home, and that authority is needed in training children.

God's order is: The Father, the Son, the Holy Spirit, the husband, the wife, and then the children. God has built into the male an authority that the female does not have. God never meant for the mother to raise the child. Thank God for mothers and wives who *have* raised their children by themselves, because the scoundrel fathers ran off and left the family members to fend for themselves, but that is not God's plan. Thank God that these women did not go off and abandon the children like the fathers did, but it is not God's design for a woman to be the authority figure in the home. That does not put the woman down anymore than it would put the man down to acknowledge that he cannot get pregnant and have a baby. That is just the way God designed the system to work.

Men are given a quality from God to be the authority figure in the home, and when the man abdicates his responsibility for whatever reason and makes the woman do it, the child will not be all that the child ought to be. That does not mean children cannot turn out well and become successful in life. But if you examine these children carefully, there are some traits in them that would have not been there if the father had taken his rightful place.

There are people in our society who are functioning, but they are running on six cylinders when they ought to be running on eight. There are some people who have had accidents in life and have lost a finger or a limb. Do not tell me they can do as well with three fingers and a thumb on their left hand as they could with four fingers and a thumb. People adapt and they survive, and thank God for that.

It is a tremendous responsibility to raise children and to raise them in line with God's Word. They are going to rebel until they are born again and dedicated and committed to the Word. Until they respond in these spiritual ways, the father has the responsibility to lay down the law and then to see to it that the mother carries the law out when he is away from home.

> **Servants, be obedient to them that are your masters according to the flesh, with fear and trembling [or reverence and trembling], in singleness of your heart, as unto Christ.**
>
> **(Eph. 6:5)**

You can take the Bible and support anything you want to by taking paragraphs out of their setting and putting them together. This is usually done to support some kind of doctrine or some kind of purpose that an individual has in his or her mind that is different from the biblical norm.

We have to realize that when we read the New Testament, we are reading about Christianity in its infancy. It had no previous background to draw from in that God was doing a new thing with the Church.

The Old Testament saints did not understand what the Church would be, or that there was going to be any such entity as the Church.

When Christianity was first brought into the open by the apostles on the Day of Pentecost, it was like a pebble in the midst of a desert of polytheism — the worship of all kinds of gods, even some made by men's hands. Christianity not only continued the worship of one God that the Jews had inaugurated, but it also brought into the open a consciousness of sin in a way that nothing else had ever done before.

As Christianity began to make inroads into the societies of the world, it came upon conditions and situations that had been in operation since the beginning of time, such as slavery. Consequently, many people who came into a knowledge of Christ during the Church's infancy were people in servitude. Some were slaves or servants, others were slaveholders or slave owners.

Certainly God has much more sense than we do. Therefore, I am sure that He recognizes that certain dramatic changes in society or in an individual's life could be so traumatic that it could have a devastating effect. For example, missionaries in foreign countries, traveling from place to place where the gospel had never been preached, often went into areas where polygamy (a system where a man can have as many wives as he can afford) was acceptable. A man might have not only several wives, but also children by all of his wives. Of course, the Gospel of Christ fosters monogamy (one wife or husband at a time).

When a man in one of these polygamous situations heard the gospel (perhaps the chief of the tribe or village) and got saved and oriented to the things of God, what was he to do if he had ten wives and forty-five children? Was he to drop nine of his wives and leave them without a husband, or forty children without a father? Would the missionary have to say to him, "Well, God says only one husband to one woman and one wife to one man. That is it; turn the rest loose and let them make their own way!" What good would that do? What happened was that the missionaries would teach the people from that point in time what God expected of them.

Thank God that He does not require us to go back over our lives and undo all the messes we have made. We all would be up the creek in a boat with no oars. When we accept Christ as our Savior and Lord, God treats the old life as though it were dead, because it is! Even in a polygamous society, from the moment a man or a woman gets saved, he or she cannot marry any more spouses.

God is merciful. He is not trying to make our lives *hard*; He is trying to make our lives *right*. What these people had to do from the time of their salvation is to discontinue their polygamous activities and turn into a monogamous society, and through this process, polygamy would end in that particular area.

Using that same analogy, we see a similar situation in the early stages of Christianity. Let's read Ephesians 6:5 again:

> **Servants, be obedient to them that are your masters according to the flesh, with fear [reverence] and trembling, in singleness of your heart, as unto Christ.**
>
> **(Eph. 6:5)**

Some people have taken this Scripture to justify slavery. They say that since the Bible says "servant," it is all right for men to have slaves and hold people in bondage against their wills.

In ancient times, a man may have had twenty-five servants. Many of these servants may have come from a long line of servants who were brought up in the man's home. They did not know anything else or how to do anything else. The same principle that I covered concerning polygamy applies here as well.

Imagine if you had twenty-five servants who were born in your home, who had never been to school, who did not know how to do anything but wait on you, and you turned them out into the world, what would happen to them? They would not know how to take care of themselves.

What had to happen was that the slave owner who got saved, and the slave or servant who got saved, would stay in the same condition until they died. After their deaths, there would not be the perpetuation of slavery. Eventually, the slave's children would start out free. They would have been instructed, taught, trained, and prepared for the time when they would be free and released into society on their own. When we read Ephesians 6:5, we have to understand that the master/servant situation was not to continue on as before once the people came into a knowledge of the Word. The Bible does not justify slavery or holding people in bondage. You have to read analytically, and find out what situation is being addressed and what the reasoning is behind it.

God is not interested in tearing up families and breaking up homes or putting people out into the streets with no one to care for them. Paul is telling these Christians how to function and operate in the situations they were in at the time when they got saved.

There are some things you do not have to tell people when you are dealing with the Spirit of God. Some Christians tell people that in order to get saved they have to change their life-styles. "Brother, you have to stop drinking and stop smoking. You have to stop womanizing or God is not going to save you. But if you will stop doing all those things, the Lord will have mercy on you and save you." The Bible does not say that. You get a man saved, you get him born of the Spirit of God, and then instructed in the Word, he will change.

I am not talking about the majority of churches where people go to after they get saved. They will not learn anything there. Most of the time, these people will keep on drinking and chasing women or running men and doing all the other things they used to do because there is nothing to teach them why they should not do those things anymore. But where people are being taught the Word of God and being exposed to the full counsel of God, they will get to the point where they will not want to drink, smoke, gamble, or chase women or men anymore. They will not need to do these things because there will be something higher to achieve that will give them a greater satisfaction than the things they used to do that lasted only for a moment.

People argue all the time, "Well, I don't see anything wrong with this, that, or the other." Fine, go ahead. If you and the Holy Ghost can get drunk on Saturday night, fine. If you and the Holy Ghost can smoke together, fine. But I am sure we all know that God will not go along with anything that is not morally right.

I remember that at the time when I first got saved I had a record collection that was second to none. (I am just sharing something concerning me, so do not get in bondage over this.) I wanted to be a musician — a jazz saxophonist. So I spent most of my free time listening to jazz. When I became born again, no one said anything to me about my records, but I had no more desire to listen to jazz. I wanted to listen only to those things that exalted the Lord. I wanted to listen to things that would cause me to become heavenly minded rather than earthly minded. I did not read any place in the Bible where it said it was wrong to listen to jazz, but the new man on the inside needed something else. Eventually, I gave all my jazz records away and never bought another one.

The point I am making is that people have to grow up into the knowledge of God. These verses in Ephesians 6 are not justifying slavery. What they are emphasizing is that a man can and will react to his environment until that environment is changed.

At one time or another, there has been some form of slavery in every part of the world. People say, "But a lot of the slaveholders were Christians." Were they? There might have been many slave owners who were baptized and belonged to a church, but that does not mean they were Christians. There is no way in the world that these slave masters could have been saved and born of the Spirit of God and instructed in the Word of God and continued to have slaves.

People join churches in the same way they join the local social organization or country clubs. They sit in church and call themselves Christians, but that does not mean that their hearts have been changed. That does not mean that the love of God has been shed abroad in their hearts. If the love of God was in their hearts, they could not hold another man in bondage nor perpetuate slavery in any form.

Servants, be obedient to them....as unto Christ.

Paul is talking about servants and masters, but I believe we can get an analogy from this concerning employers and employees. The principle is the same.

I do not believe that an employee ought to treat his employer with any less fidelity and with any less commitment than a slave would treat his slave master. Today, there are many people who do not give an honest day's work for an honest day's pay. They think, "Well, it is all right to give the company seven hours and fifty-three minutes and get paid for eight hours. After all, the company has plenty of money and they can afford it." That is not right!

That is not the way you are supposed to treat the Lord. You should treat your job and employer as though you were working for the Lord. Coming back late from lunch or breaks, taking a little extra time — if the company were to dock your paycheck, you would get upset and want to holler, "Discrimination!"

Not with eyeservice, as menpleasers; but as the servants of Christ, doing the will of God from the heart.

(Eph. 6:6)

As Christians, we ought to be the best workers in our workplace. Instead of going around with bumper stickers on our cars that say, "Honk If You Love Jesus," and bugging everyone all day long, we need to act right on the job. Some Christians are slothful. They're late all the time, and generally dishonest. I would not even tell anybody I was a Christian if I were like that. The Christian should be the best employee the company has. He ought to be on time; in fact, the Christian should be the one who comes early and has the work of the highest caliber and of the highest quality. Some Christians even spend the company's time preaching. They were hired to work, not to preach. Now if they want to preach on their own time (lunchtime, breaks, before or after work, that is different), but not on the company's time. They are robbing their employer because they are not putting in a full day's work.

With good will doing service, as to the Lord, and not to men.

(Eph. 6:7)

Notice how Paul keeps saying, **"as to the Lord."**
How would you work for the Lord? That is why some
Christians have such sorry lives; they are treating Jesus
and the heavenly Father just like they treat their
employers.

Jesus made a statement one time that deals with an
important principle of living: **"He that is faithful in
that which is least is faithful also in much"** (Luke
16:10). If I cannot trust you with five dollars, do you
think I am going to trust you with $500? You show me
that you can handle five dollars, and I may give you
$100. The circumstances are not going to change what
you are on the inside. If you are a spendthrift and blow
five dollars, you would do the same with $5,000.
Because some Christians do not handle the things of
God correctly, they become slothful on their jobs. They
are late to church; they are late on the job. People who
are diligent about being on time are on time for everything. If you have a habit of being late, you are late all
the time.

> **Knowing that whatsoever good thing any man
> doeth, the same shall he receive of the Lord, whether
> he be bond or free.**
>
> **(Eph. 6:8)**

Paul is talking to the Body of Christ, and he is
saying if we do good, even if we do it to the slave master
or the employer, the Lord will see to it that we are
rewarded.

I realize that there are some bad employers, but
usually, if you can help it in any way, you will not work

for him or her too long. If you work for a crooked company, and the boss is cheating you all the time, you are not going to hang around there for any length of time.

> And, ye masters, do the same things unto them, forbearing threatening: knowing that your Master also is in heaven; neither is there respect of persons with him.
>
> (Eph. 6:9)

Paul addresses both the servant and the slave master. He tells the slave master to treat his slaves as though he were dealing with the Lord. That ought to be our constant attitude. Sometimes people will not understand their employer and they will accuse him or her of mistreating them. That is a risk factor involved in being the master or employer.

There are some people who are servants, even in our day, who are servants voluntarily. Oftentimes, these servants go to their employers' homes and take care of their children. Some even live in the home with the employers' families. There are people who hire themselves out for life to be a servant, maid, or a butler. That is fine, if that is what they want to do. The main thing for the Christian to keep in mind is that whatever he or she does ought to always be as unto the Lord.

I know of some ministers (and, of course, they will have to answer to the Lord, so I am not judging them) who are not doing their job. I am only sharing this to give an illustration. The Lord hired them, and He can fire them, and He surely is going to be the one who will pay them.

These ministers waste their time and do nothing really constructive for the sheep. Most churches do not have Bible studies during the week. The preacher comes in and preaches a fifteen-minute sermon on Sunday mornings, and the rest of the time he is living it up by going to ministerial conferences, seminars, and meetings, which, for the most part, are not worthwhile.

When I was in one particular denomination, I used to go with the head pastor to different meetings. It was a pitiful experience. They would talk about people like they were dogs. Some of the phraseology would actually be embarrassing.

It is a great responsibility when you are your own boss. It demands tremendous discipline. I am a pastor, but I am also an employer. I have quite a few people who work in my ministry. But who is really my boss? The Lord is my employer. I have to answer to Him. And I will have to give an account of my time to Him. The Bible tells me to redeem the time (Eph. 5:16), and this means I must make good use of my time.

No, I do not have an earthly boss, per se. But in respect to the Lord being my employer, I am careful to hold sway over me harder than I would any employee. I demand of myself that I do certain things. I talk to myself just like I talk to my congregation or employees. I tell me to get in line, to shape up, or to ship out. You ought to hear me talking to me sometimes.

If I do something dumb, I call myself dumb. Folk are always getting upset when I use terminology like that. I do so because I talk to myself that way. I do some dumb things sometimes — not intentionally, but because I am human. And when I do, I tell myself, "Get in line, boy, straighten up. You blew it again." I penalize myself because that is a part of training and discipline. You need to be that way as a Christian.

Many Christians have problems because they are undisciplined as employees, as servants, as employers, and they are undisciplined in their regular lives. They do not read the Bible on a regular basis or even pray consistently because there is no one who makes them do it. As a Christian, you have to be your own enforcer, and that is where discipline and training come in. That is where commitment comes in, and the rewards are marvelous.

> **Finally, my brethren, be strong in the Lord, and in the power of his might.**
>
> **(Eph. 6:10)**

Thank God, Paul says we are to **"be strong in the Lord."** Thank God, I do not have to be strong in myself. Thank God, I do not have to be strong in you, and you do not have to be strong in me. Do you know how to be strong in the Lord? We become strong in the Lord by being strong in faith! Faith is a divine law, and everything in the Kingdom of God works by faith. Most people who are weak in the Lord are weak in faith.

Finally, my brethren, be strong...

Notice the little word *be*. "Yes, but I don't feel very strong." Paul did not say anything about feel. He said, "Be." He did not even say, "Pray strong." He did not say, "Fast strong." He simply said, **"Be strong."** All you have to do is to ask yourself this question, "How do strong men act or react to certain situations in their lives?" As you determine the answer, that is the way you act.

Faith is acting on the Word. If God told us to be something that we are incapable of being, He would be unjust and unkind. In other words, if He tells us to be strong, we can be strong.

I have listened to people, including some ministers, talking about how hard things are. I hear them talking about how many defeats they have gone through, and how this is not working for them, and how that is not working for them. Every one of those things they complain about could be solved simply by their acting on God's Word, by faith.

I hear people talking about getting discouraged, "because life is so hard." Friend, I have news for you. Life in the natural may be hard, but the Christian life is *not* hard. Satan will attempt to make it difficult for you, but you must remember that we start out as Christians, **"more than conquerors"** (See Rom. 8:37). What you have to do is to act on the Word by calling those things which be not as though they were. (See Rom. 4:17.) You do this by finding out what God says about life and about your circumstances, and by finding out what God says about your physical body, your soul, and your spirit. You do this by finding out what the Word says about disease, sickness, and prosperity, and what the Word says about fear, victory, and being a winner in life.

When we find out what the Word says about us and we begin to confess what it says, it is then that we begin to call those things which be not as though they were, and then we will have what the Word says. This is faith in operation.

If you are sick, and the doctors say that you are going to die, and you start saying, "I believe I am healed," but you die anyway, you still did not lose anything. You had more to gain than to lose by confessing you believed you were healed. One thing is for sure, if you say you are going to die, you do not have a chance at all. I would rather say I am going to live and then die, saying I am going to live, rather than say I am going to die, because the latter choice is a guarantee that I am going to die.

The point I am making is that even if confessing the Word did not work, what would you have to lose? If you died, you would still win because you would be in heaven with Jesus, and all your problems would be over. This is the kind of attitude you must have. When you have this kind of attitude, the devil cannot frighten you into circumventing your faith.

God's Word works. If you do not believe anything else I ever tell you, believe me when I tell you that the Word of God works! You have to stay with it, just like you have to stay with anything at which you want to be successful. You do not always see instant results, and this is what has discouraged some people. Usually, when they come and find out about God's provisions, they are already in desperate situations. They are already at the ends of their ropes: their bills cannot be paid, they are sick, or they are already in divorce court, or the kids are already running wild.

Unfortunately, most churches have not told the average Christian how to walk in victory. All they have told him or her was how to "hold on, and hang on, and after a while, by and by, over there on the other side, it will all be worth it." The average believer has not been told how to be victorious, *now*, in this life. We need to know how to live *now*!

Many years ago, my wife and I were at the bottom of the barrel. In fact, the barrel was sitting on top of us. We could not pay our bills, or enjoy any of life's luxuries. But I began to say, "Praise God, every need is met, every bill is paid." I started envisioning our bills as being paid, ourselves as being dressed well and eating well, and all of our needs as being met. I started seeing myself as being able to give what I would like to give to the Kingdom of God. I started saying and confessing everything the Lord's Word said was rightfully ours.

I started being strong in the Lord, and in the power of His might! I was fully persuaded that what the Word said was true. I started saying it, and saying it, and saying it, and God started confirming His Word with signs following.

My whole ministry is an affirmation of that fact. God is our source. And He can be counted on to honor His Word. It is so exciting to be free! It is the biggest joy and the biggest thrill to be able to give. But you cannot give what you do not have, and the way you get something to give is by being strong in the Lord. And the way you do that is to be thoroughly convinced that what God said He will do, He will do.

Start living the Word, thinking it, dreaming it, and speaking it. Start forming mental pictures deep down inside of you. Start seeing in your mind whatever you are believing God for. Start seeing yourself as being successful; start seeing yourself as being strong in the Lord and in the power of His might. The Word works, but you have to work it.

...be strong in the Lord...

It is important to understand that for those of us who are in the family of God, it is the will of our Father for us to be strong. This bursts a big hole in the bubble of traditional religion. What is important to understand is that Christianity is not a religion. Christianity is a man — the man Jesus Christ! Jesus did not come to bring us religion. He came to bring us **"life, and that... more abundantly"** (John 10:10).

For the greater part, Christianity has presented a very weak picture to the world. It is almost universally believed that to be a Christian you have to be a weakling. However, Ephesians 6:10 contradicts this belief, because it tells us to be strong, not weak.

Notice where the responsibility for being strong is placed. The Apostle Paul is talking to the Body of Christ, so this is actually a commandment from the throne of God. The Father would be unjust and unkind to require us to be something we were incapable of being, and then hold us accountable for not being what He required us to be.

Because God tells me to be strong, I know I can be. Whatever is necessary to make me strong has to be made available to me and it has to be accessible to me.

Most people want to feel strong first, then based upon feeling strong, they will act accordingly. Such an approach would not be faith. Faith tells us to be strong even when we feel weak. "Yes, but that does not make sense." I know it!

The Bible never said that we were to walk by our senses. It says, **"We walk by faith..."** (2 Cor. 5:7). The Bible does not say, "Without the senses it is impossible to please God." It says, **"Without faith it is impossible to please him** [God]" (Heb. 11:6). The Bible does not say, "The just shall live by the senses." The Bible says, **"The just shall live by faith"** (Rom. 1:17).

Paul tells us that we are to be strong in the Lord. Where many folk miss it is that they are trying to be strong in themselves. You cannot be strong in you and I cannot be strong in me, because there is nothing in us that is strong. I am so glad that I do not have to rely on my own abilities. I would strike out before I ever came to the plate if I had to rely on my own strength. We need to find out how this strength works, because living the God-kind of life ought to be primary for every believer, and everything else ought to be a part-time endeavor.

Most of the time, Christians treat Jesus like they do a spare tire. They only bring Him into operation when everything else has failed. They do not realize that they are missing out on the best part of living. If you get the God-kind of life right, the other parts of life will flow more smoothly. Jesus said, **"But seek ye first the kingdom of God, and his righteousness; and all these things shall be added unto you"** (Matt. 6:33). That means everything else has to be secondary.

319

Nothing in your life is going to work as it should until you get things in their right order. Some people are beating their brains out trying to make their businesses work. The best business partner they can have is the Lord. Jesus knows more about business than any partner they will ever know. If they would put Him in charge of their businesses, they would find out that all that they do will be so much easier.

We have a good illustration of how faith is to be put into operation in the fourth chapter of Romans. Paul is taking a situation from the Old Covenant and putting it into a New Testament framework in order to give us an illustration of how we are to be strong in the Lord and in the power of His might.

> **(As it is written,** [this is God speaking to the patriarch Abraham] **I have made thee a father of many nations,) before him whom he believed, even God, who quickeneth** [or makes alive] **the dead, and calleth those things which be not as though they were.**
>
> **(Rom. 4:17)**

It is the calling of those things which be not as though they were that causes them to come into manifestation. God said to Abraham, **"As it is written, I have made thee...."** The term *made thee* is in the past tense. God did not say, "I am *making* thee" (present tense), nor did He say, "I will *make* thee" (future tense).

In fact, when God said that to Abraham, Abraham did not even have any children. We see God calling those things which be not as though they were. You may say, "Well, that is telling a lie." It could not be telling a lie, because the Bible says (in Hebrews 6:18) that it is impossible for God to lie.

God is a faith God. That is what faith does: **Faith calls those things which be not as though they were.** And that is what makes them come to pass.

Several years ago, when we first started Crenshaw Christian Center, I would stand in the pulpit and say, "The day will come when people will stand in line to get into this church." I used to say it all the time because I believed it. I saw the church filled up with people. I saw so many people that we could not get them all in. And that is exactly what happened. We had so many people coming to the church that we could not get them all in — even when we went to three services. Eventually, we had to build a 10,000-seat sanctuary to get our total congregation in at one time.

I encourage you to start calling those things which be not as though they were. You might say, "Well, I don't know if that will work or not." It does not make any difference. Look at it this way, if you said it and it did not come to pass, you could not be any worse off than you already are. What do you have to lose? You might as well start thinking big, talking big, and when what you are believing and confessing becomes *rhema* (alive) in your spirit, it will come to pass.

Then you can be a channel of blessing to others. The whole point is not just to get something for yourself to squander — that is an infantile approach — but so that you can be a blessing to others. And then as you are a blessing, you get blessed yourself.

(As it is written, I have made thee a father of many nations,)...

By this time, Abraham has become an old man. Sarah, at about ninety years of age, is far past the age of reproduction. Sarah had always been barren, and now God was telling them that in the next year they would have a child (Gen. 17:16). God was calling those things which be not as though they were. If you examine the Bible very carefully, you will find that Almighty God has always operated on that premise. Where we have missed it is that we thought we were supposed to wait to see it, then we would call it. No, you call it before you see it, and that is what will cause you to see it! To give you an example of what I am talking about concerning how God operates, consider the following Scriptures:

> **In the beginning God created the heaven and the earth. And the earth was without form, and void; and darkness was upon the face of the deep. And the Spirit of God moved upon the face of the waters. And God said, Let there be light: and there was light.**
>
> **(Gen. 1:1-3)**

God said, "Let there be light," when it was dark. He was using the calling-those-things-which-be-not-as-though-they-were principle. And He used the same principle when He told Abraham and Sarah that they were going to have a son. It was medically impossible for Sarah to have a child. All the circumstances were stacked against their having a child, but the Bible says that Abraham believed God, and because he did so, they had a son just as God had predicted.

We operate in the Kingdom of God through the Word of God. You have to start calling those things which be not as though they were. If there is a sickness in your body, start saying to your body, "Body, you are healed. With Jesus' stripes you were healed" (1 Pet. 2:24). **"Himself took our infirmities"** (Matt. 8:17). Talk to your finances, and say that all of your needs are met (Phil. 4:19), no matter what you see or feel. Remember, it is your believing and confessing that ultimately brings possession.

I started talking to my body, telling it to get in line with the Word of God. I started talking to my finances. Then, of course, I also started doing what the Bible said to do. I started bringing my tithes and offerings into God's storehouse, and then I believed God for the return on my giving. The principle works the same. It does not matter what it is. It works by calling those things which be not as though they were.

> **Who against hope believed in hope, that he might become the father of many nations; according to that which was spoken, So shall thy seed be.**
>
> **(Rom. 4:18)**

"Who against natural human hope believed in supernatural hope" is the meaning of this verse. Where did this supernatural hope come from? It came from the Word of God, when God said, **"I have made thee a father of many nations."**

When God deals with something, He will take the impossible situation and make it possible. And when He gets through with it, there is nothing anyone can say, except "Praise the Lord!"

> **And being not weak in faith, he considered not his own body now dead, when he was about an hundred years old, neither yet the deadness of Sarah's womb. He staggered not at the promise of God through unbelief; but was strong in faith, giving glory to God.**
>
> **(Rom. 4:19-20)**

Abraham did not feel strong. It said Sarah's womb was dead, so there was nothing there to cause him to feel strong. Apparently, he must have acted like he was strong in the face of being weak in the natural. He was strong in faith! And that was what caused him to act strong.

> **And being fully persuaded that, what he had promised, he was able also to perform.**
>
> **(Rom. 4:21)**

How did Abraham know what God promised? God spoke it to him. In other words, God gave Abraham what He has given us. In fact, God has given us more than He gave Abraham. All Abraham had were God's oral words. We have His oral words and His written Word!

The very fact that it says, "being not weak" means that weakness was available to Abraham. He had the option of being weak or strong. We have that same option.

And being fully persuaded...

You have to be fully persuaded by what God has promised. It does not matter what anyone else says, *you* have to be fully persuaded. That is why it is so very important to have an accurate knowledge of God's Word. There is no way you can be strong in the Lord without being fully persuaded, and you cannot be fully persuaded without knowing what God has promised.

You probably have heard some people ask, "How do you know that the Bible is really the Word of God?" There is only one way to find out whether it is or not. Arguing about it, discussing it, having dissertations on it, and writing up treatises on it will not do it. You are going to have to start doing what the Bible says. Then if it does not work, you can say that it is not the Word of God. But you have to work it according to the rules. I am here to tell you that it works. I have heard some people say, "Well, I've tried that and it did not work." That is why it did not work. It does not say a thing about *trying*, it says to *do* it. It does not say, "Try to be a doer of the Word" — it commands, **"Be ye doers of the Word, and not hearers only, deceiving your own selves"** (James 1:22).

Ephesians 6:10 says, **"Finally, my brethren, be strong...."** It does not tell us to *try* to be strong — but to *be* strong. The key to it all is being fully persuaded. Being fully persuaded that the Bible is God's Word will make you strong when you start acting on it.

In developing your "Word knowledge," there are several things you need to be aware of as you start studying the Bible. Number one, you need to be aware of the tense of the verb that is used in any given Scripture. In other words, you need to know whether something is in the past, present, or future tense. Take the subject of healing, for example. Matthew 8:17 says that Jesus **"Himself took our infirmities, and bare our sicknesses."** The words *took* and *bare* are in the past tense.

In 1 Peter 2:24, we read that it is with Jesus' stripes that **"ye *were* healed."** *"Were"* is in the past tense — the action has already taken place. So you can see how important it is to know what tense a verb is when you read the Bible.

Another thing you need to be aware of is who is responsible for doing what the verse says. There are some things that God is responsible for doing, and there are some things that the believer is responsible for doing. Take salvation, for example. Jesus said, **"Go ye into all the world, and preach the gospel to every crea-ture. He that believeth and is baptized shall be saved"** (Mark 16:15-16).

Our responsibility as born-again believers is to share the gospel. That is as far as we can go. We cannot make anyone believe the gospel, and God does not require us to make anyone do so. We do not have to argue with anyone or to try to browbeat or con them into believing the Bible.

The Bible says that faith comes by hearing, and hearing by the Word of God. (See Rom. 10:17.) Therefore, faith cannot come if people do not hear the gospel, and people will not hear it if we do not preach it. So the preaching of the Word of God has to be the starting point in order for people to have faith.

I found out early in the game that you cannot convince anyone if he does not want to be convinced. All we have to do is to plant the seed, and that is where our responsibility ends. The Holy Spirit has the responsibility of bringing conviction to the hearts of the people. All that most traditional churches preach today is a salvation message, week after week. Salvation is all the people get. The minister may start out in one place, but he will end up in the same place every time. The whole messsage really is a salvation-oriented sermon. Most preachers try to preach their people into a state of conviction to make them feel a sense of sin-consciousness. Consequently, the people, who have already been saved, stay under condemnation because every week they are told what sinners they are. They can hardly lift their eyes up to God because they feel so unclean and unworthy.

It is not the minister's responsibility to put people under conviction. His responsibility is to preach the Word. It is up to the Spirit of the living God to bring conviction into a person's heart. The reason there is not more honest conviction brought to the hearts of many people is because they do not hear the Word, and the Holy Ghost does not have anything to work with. That is why it is so important to understand what the Bible is saying in order to know who is responsible for doing what.

If we try to do the Holy Spirit's job, it will not work. We need to find out what God wants us to do and then make sure we are doing it. To be effective for the Lord, we need to be strong in faith. And to be strong in faith, we need to be **strong in the Lord, and in the power of His might** (Eph. 6:10).

Part 2 — Ephesians 6:11-12

Put on the whole armour of God, that ye may be able to stand against the wiles of the devil.

(Eph. 6:11)

We are told to put this armor on. That means that the responsibility for the armor being in place is ours. Notice that it does not say that God will put the armor on for you. Neither does it say that the Holy Ghost will do this for you. Paul clearly lets us know that it is the Christian's responsibility to put the armor of God on.

The word *whole* implies that this armor must be in pieces, or there would be no need to talk about the **"whole armour."** Paul also lets us know that this armor is immediately and readily available to us. If it were not, God would be unkind and unjust in requiring us to do something we could not do.

...that ye may be able to stand...

Paul did not say that you *would* stand, but rather that you *would be able* to stand, which implies that if we do not put the armor on, we will not be able to stand.

The question is, "Will you stand, or not?" You may have all the ingredients you need to bake a cake, but do you know how to bake one? There are some people who cannot follow a recipe and put a cake together. Therefore, it is not just having the necessary ingredients available to you, but are you able to put them together in proper proportion and produce the end results?

May is a word of permission. It indicates you have the permission to stand, which also means that God wants you to stand. He does not want you on your back; He wants you on your feet.

Someone will always try to cop out by saying, "Well, if it were not for my wife, or my husband, or my parents, or the white folk or the black folk, or inflation, or this, that or the other, I would be successful, I would be a winner in life." Let me tell you something. You do not have anyone to blame but yourself. God has made success available to us through His Word, and it is up to us to get it.

I know there are some people who will say, "Yes, but what about all those people who have been poor all of their lives, who live in certain parts of the world where they do not have anything?" I am sorry about that, and I am doing all I can to get the message of God to them so that they can come out of their unfortunate circumstances. But we should not go down the tubes because they are going down the tubes, when we have the knowledge of the Word of God. It could be that God has given us the ability and opportunity to help them to get spiritual knowledge. Just because they do not have it is no reason for me to fall down and be whipped, defeated, and bombed out by the devil. If someone does not take the good news and help these people get out of their circumstances, they never will get out. I am not going to be intimidated by some person telling me, "Well, what about those poor people in such-and-such a place?" I am responsible for the knowledge God has given to me, and He expects me to do something with it.

There are Christians who have been exposed to the Word for quite some time, and they still do not have victory in their lives. Is it the Word's fault? No, it is the people's fault. If I fail, it is my fault that I do. God has made everything available that you and I need to win, but it is up to us to do the winning.

Notice again what this eleventh verse says: **"Put on the whole armour of God."** Paul is talking to us, not to God. He is not saying, "Lord, clothe them with your armor." He says, "*You* put it on!"

...against the wiles of the devil.

The word *wiles*[12] comes from the Greek word *methodia*, and it means "deceits" or "deceptions." Satan will try to deceive you and trick you in any way he can. He will try to get your attention on the things around you so that he can then govern your life. Most people operate by the circumstances of life, even some

Christians, unfortunately. It is a big temptation to be governed by the circumstances, but the Bible tells us not to yield to temptation.

I do not deny the existence of the circumstances, but what I do is deny their right to rule my life. Jesus Christ told me that whatever I desire in my heart and believe that I have received when I pray, I will have. (See Mark 11:24.) He told me that if I would say to the mountain to be removed and cast into the sea, and not doubt in my heart, but believe that those things which I say would come to pass, I would have whatsoever I say. (See Mark 11:23.) I know that being victorious over the circumstances is within the perfect will of God for my life, because the Bible lets me know that God wants me to be a winner.

Paul tells us to put on the whole armor of God so that we can stand against the deceptions of the devil, which implies that the devil exists. There are many academicians — even some Christians — who believe there is no such thing as a personal devil. God believes in the devil. It would seem that these people ought to have enough sense to know that if God believes in Satan, then they surely ought to believe in him also.

> **For [or because] we wrestle not against flesh and blood, but against principalities, against powers, against the rulers of the darkness of this world, against spiritual wickedness in high places.**
>
> **(Eph. 6:12)**

The word *wrestle* implies a struggle, contention, and hostilities. It also implies that there is an opponent.

As I have traveled through different parts of the world, I have discovered that people are basically the same everywhere. I have found prejudiced white folk, prejudiced black folk, prejudiced brown, red, and yellow folk. I have found white folk who steal, black folk who steal, red folk who steal, brown folk, and yellow folk who take what is not theirs. People are the same everywhere. They are the same, because it is the same devil who is causing the world's turmoils. However, he cannot do his dirty work without the cooperation of a person. By the same token, God cannot do His good work without the cooperation of a person. That is the way God has designed the system to operate, and He cannot violate His own creation.

Do you think that God would depend upon us to get the gospel out — we who are sometimes on and sometimes off, petty, jealous, and strifeful — if He did not have to? But He has designed the system that way, and He cannot do His work in the earth-realm, except through yielded vessels. Satan cannot do his evil works either, except through yielded vessels, whether knowingly or unknowingly. He cannot do what he wants to do without men, because if he could, he would not depend upon us either. We are the determiners of whether good or evil prevails. We have the choice to either side with evil or to side with good. But here, in this twelfth verse, we are told that we **"wrestle not against flesh and blood."**

There are four classes of spiritual creatures that mankind must wrestle with. As in the military, these creatures have rank. There are privates, lieutenants, captains, and generals. As in the military, these creatures do not all have the same authority. This is also true in the ranks of the angels of God. There are seraphims, cherubims, and archangels. An archangel is a top angel.

The four basic ranks in Satan's kingdom are: principalities, powers, the rulers of the darkness of this world, and wicked spirits in high (or heavenly) places.

The most important and powerful of these four classes are the wicked spirits in high (or heavenly) places. The second highest group is the rulers of the darkness of this world. After these two groups are the powers and principalities.

Some of these spirits, such as the principalities, do not have much thinking ability and they do whatever they are told by the higher ranks. The other spirits are the ones who actually are involved in planning the activities for the kingdom of darkness.

This whole world has been mapped out by Satan, and he has certain detachments of demon spirits stationed in different parts of the world to do different things. Over every government of the world there is a demon spirit that influences the top man in every nation. The man does not even know it, but he is being manipulated and influenced by these evil spirits. To the extent that the man knows about Jesus Christ, he can resist the influence of these evil forces. They cannot lord their evilness over him. If you have wondered why some leaders in the world have done, or are doing, the kind of things they have done, or are doing, it is because these evil spirits are driving them.

There are certain kinds of spirits that inhabit certain parts of this world system. There are sex-perversion spirits, alcohol spirits, drug spirits, tobacco spirits, etc. I am not saying that everyone who smokes a cigarette is possessed by a tobacco spirit, but people who smoke are influenced by these spirits. I know of instances where people have become so addicted to tobacco that they become controlled by it. It is the same with alcohol. Some people actually believe they cannot function without having a drink of alcohol.

There are even religious spirits. These spirits work through religion to bring men into bondage to religion. These spirits operate in certain places. They act in certain ways. There are certain spirits that occupy certain territories in an effort to bring destruction, such as poverty. That is why some nations of the world are so poor, because they are being controlled by these poverty spirits. And until the salvation of Jesus Christ and the Word of God are allowed to permeate these areas to break the hold of these spirits, the territories or countries will remain in poverty.

In the fifth chapter of Mark, verses 1-20, a story is told concerning Jesus and the Gadarene demoniac. Jesus was going through a place called Gadara. When He arrived on the scene, a man who was possessed of the devil met him. This man had been living in the cemetery. He was stark naked, dirty, and wild-looking. He had been cutting and torturing himself and was generally in a tormented state.

Jesus discerned the evil spirit that was possessing the man because discerning of spirits operated in His ministry. The Bible does not record all the things Jesus said to these evil spirits, but Jesus and the spirits held a conversation. Finally, Jesus asked the spirit, "What is your name?" (If you read the four gospels, you will notice that Jesus did not always do that with spirits. Sometimes He would just speak and command the spirits to leave. But there are certain kinds of spirits that have to be identified by name and you must know how many are present before you can cast them out.)

The man answered and said, **"My name is Legion: for we are many"** (Mark 5:9). Only one spirit had actually possessed the man, but that spirit had opened the door and let other spirits come in. And they had driven this poor man insane and were literally torturing him.

Jesus commanded the spirits to leave. And they said to Him, "Don't send us away out of this country. There is a herd of swine feeding over there by the mountainside, let us go into the swine." Jesus told them to go. The spirits left the man and he was instantly restored. The spirits went into the swine, and even pigs have enough sense not to be demon-possessed. They ran down the hill and over the cliff and drowned in the water below. It was not the demons that caused the pigs to drown themselves. If it were the spirits that were drowning the swine, they would have had no place to inhabit.

Spirits have to have a physical vessel by which they can manifest themselves in this physical world. That is why they desire to possess people. That is how they can do their greatest degree of harm. However, if they cannot get to their primary target (a flesh-and-blood, human body), they will take a secondary target, which is an animal of some kind. Failing to get control of an animal, they will go into a house, a building, or a particular geographical area and inhabit it so that they can in some way manifest themselves. Their highest goal, however, is to possess a human being, because then they can do their greatest degree of damage in the earth-realm in their malicious efforts to thwart the work of God.

The point of the story is that the spirits asked Jesus not to send them out of that country because that was where they had been assigned to work by Satan. You might wonder where these spirits went after they left the swine. They probably went and tried to find someone else to inhabit. That is all they could do.

Perhaps they did find someone else. We don't know, because the Bible does not say. Personally, I believe they did, because there is always someone who is willing (whether they know it or not) to open the door and let Satan have control.

You might also wonder why we Christians cannot cast these spirits into hell where they belong. If this could be done, Jesus would have gotten rid of all of them for us. Notice that when Jesus sent them out of the man, He did not tell them to go into hell, because it was not time for this to happen. In Matthew's record of this incident (Matt. 8:29) we find that the demons said to Jesus: **"What have we to do with thee, Jesus, thou Son of God? art thou come hither to torment us before the time?"** These evil spirits know that there is a time that God has set for them to be cast into the pit.

There was another time recorded in the Bible when Jesus had contact with another demon-possessed man. When Jesus walked into the synagogue, the man cried out in a loud voice, **"What have we to do with thee, thou Jesus of Nazareth? art thou come to destroy us?**

I know thee who thou art, the Holy One of God"
(Mark 1:23-24). Demons know Jesus, and they know
the children of God.

They know who we are, and they are actually
afraid of us, especially when we come into a knowledge
of the Word. If they can keep you ignorant of spiritual
things, they will manipulate you, influence you, and
control you in very subtle ways.

God's clock is ticking away, and the demons know
it. Satan knows he has but a short time left. That is why
he is accelerating his work to do everything he can to
drag as many people to hell with him as he can. He
wants to make people as miserable as he can and to
thwart in any way the work of Almighty God in this
earth-realm.

These spirits inhabit the whole world, just like
angels are all over the world. There have to be angels all
over the world because every single person on the face
of planet Earth has a guardian angel, and we never lose
our angels until we leave this physical world. God
sends these angels to try to keep people alive long
enough to find out about Jesus so that they can get
saved.

That is why sometimes people have narrow
escapes. Later, you hear them say: "I sure was lucky."
They were not *lucky*; that was their angel keeping them
alive so that they could get saved. However, these
angels can only do what we let them. Even though they
are here, they have no power to make us do anything; if
they could, they would make everyone get saved.

When you learn that as a Christian you have angels here to work on your behalf and you start putting them to work, they will assist you in all kinds of ways that will help to make your life more comfortable.

Satan also has angels assigned to you, only their job is to break your head. These evil angels will do anything they can to stop you from progressing in the things of God, and that is why people have so many problems.

For instance, perhaps there was a time when you did not go to church too often, even though you were a Christian and had been saved since childhood. Perhaps, you got away from church. Then some time later, you decided to rededicate yourself to the Lord. You were filled with the Spirit, spoke with other tongues, and began to grow in the knowledge of faith. All of a sudden, it seems that all hell broke out against you. It seems like mama, papa, the cat, the dog, the neighbors — everybody — was on your case.

But, if you will think back, you will notice that things did not start to go wrong until you started getting into the Word and confessing the Word over the circumstances of your life. That pressure started coming on you because you had now become a threat to the kingdom of darkness. Satan has to stop you if he can. You are a person who can cause an epidemic if you ever get loose in society. The Word is contagious, and when you begin spreading the good Word of God, it has the effect of getting to other people. The Christian life is a warfare, especially when you get into the knowledge of the Word.

When you learn that as a Christian you have angels here to work on your behalf and you start putting them to work, they will assist you in all kinds of ways that will help to make your life more comfortable.

Satan also has angels assigned to you, only their job is to break your head. These evil angels will do anything they can to stop you from progressing in the things of God, and that is why people have so many problems.

For instance, perhaps there was a time when you did not go to church too often, even though you were a Christian and had been saved since childhood. Perhaps, you got away from church. Then some time later, you decided to rededicate yourself to the Lord. You were filled with the Spirit, spoke with other tongues, and began to grow in the knowledge of faith. All of a sudden, it seems that all hell broke out against you. It seems like mama, papa, the cat, the dog, the neighbors — everybody — was on your case.

But, if you will think back, you will notice that things did not start to go wrong until you started getting into the Word and confessing the Word over the circumstances of your life. That pressure started coming on you because you had now become a threat to the kingdom of darkness. Satan has to stop you if he can. You are a person who can cause an epidemic if you ever get loose in society. The Word is contagious, and when you begin spreading the good Word of God, it has the effect of getting to other people. The Christian life is a warfare, especially when you get into the knowledge of the Word.

No one has more authority or power than Almighty God. But He has designed human life, the planets, and the laws of nature to function in certain ways. Once God has put it all into operation, it is up to us to operate within the framework of these laws — both naturally and spiritually. For example, if you were to go up to the tallest building in the world, the New York Trade Center, 110 stories above the pavement, and jump off, you would come in contact with the law of gravity. The concrete would suck you down so fast that I guarantee you would make a smash hit on Broadway! You have violated a natural law, the law of gravity. There is a law of electricity. Electricity can work for you or against you. It will light your house, keep you warm, and cook your food. But if you touch the wrong wires, that electricity can kill you.

God has set certain laws into operation, and it is up to mankind to operate within those laws. If we do not, there is nothing God can do about it. God has a spiritual law that can override everything the devil does. What we have to do is to get in line with the laws of God or they will not work on our behalf.

This world is all messed up because Satan is running the world system. Some people who are ignorant of the Bible will say that I have just made a false statement. In fact, I have heard people say, "Well, the Lord has everything under control." Friend, if this world is an example of how God has things under control, I do not want to go to heaven. But since this world is in the condition it is in, it is clear that God must not be the one ordering the events of man. Yes, in the overall scheme of things, God is in control, in that nothing can happen without His allowing it to happen. That is the way He has designed the system to work. But at this present time, Satan is the one who is controlling the world system, and he will do so until Jesus returns to set up God's kingdom and make things the way God intended them to be before Adam's fall. Second Corinthians 4:1-4 bears out the fact that Satan is in control:

> Therefore seeing we have this ministry, as we have received mercy, we faint not; But have renounced the hidden things of dishonesty, not walking in craftiness, nor handling the word of God deceitfully; but by manifestation of the truth commending ourselves to every man's conscience in the sight of God. But if our gospel be hid, it is hid to them that are lost: In whom *the god of this world* hath blinded the minds of them which believe not, lest [or unless] the light of the glorious gospel of Christ, who is the image of god, should shine unto them.
>
> (Italics mine)

Paul says that **"the god of this world"** blinds the minds of people who do not believe so that they will never be able to believe. That cannot be Almighty God! The Bible says it is not God's will that any should perish, but that all should come to repentance. (See 2 Pet. 3:9.) Satan is the god of this world, and he has everything all messed up. In fact, Jesus called him the "prince of this world."

> [Jesus is speaking] Peace I leave with you, my peace I give unto you: not as the world giveth, give I unto you. Let not your heart be troubled, neither let it be afraid.
>
> (John 14:27)

> ye might believe. **Hereafter I will not talk much with you: for** *the prince of this world* **cometh, and hath nothing in me.**
>
> **(John 14:28-30, italics mine)**

The word *prince* in the Greek is the word *archon*, which means "ruler"[13]. It goes right along with the Scripture we just read in 2 Corinthians, **"the god of this world."**

Many times people do not understand what is going on around them. Behind the scene of every event in this world are evil spirits. In fact, good and evil spirits are engaged in a titanic struggle in the spirit-realm. When people involved in certain situations are not Christians and are not open to the Spirit of God, they throw the game to the evil spirits, and the evil spirits then have the advantage.

When the people involved are Christians who are operating in the Word of God, they throw the game to the angels of God who can then overcome these evil spirits.

There are many things that happen in societies that are quite tragic. They happen because these demons are constantly working to bring about conditions that will put people in bondage, poverty, sickness, and disease.

For example, there really is more than enough food in this world to feed everyone, and yet a great part of the world is hungry. Actually, most of the world's hungry could be fed on the food that Americans throw away. It is truly sad, but that is the way the world system operates. Just about everything in this world is done for **"the love of money... the root of all evil"** (1 Tim. 6:10). There is a lot of money in starvation, and evil spirits are behind it all. They play upon the greed that is in men.

To illustrate how these wicked spirits operate, let's take a look at Daniel 10:1-11:

> In the third year of Cyrus king of Persia a thing was revealed unto Daniel, whose name was called Belteshazzar; and the thing was true, but the time appointed was long: and he understood the thing, and had understanding of the vision. In those days I Daniel was mourning three full weeks. I ate no pleasant bread, neither came flesh nor wine in my mouth, neither did I anoint myself at all, till three whole weeks were fulfilled. And in the four and twentieth day of the first month, as I was by the side of the great river, which is Hiddekel; Then I lifted up mine eyes, and looked, and behold, a certain man clothed in linen, whose loins were girded with fine gold of Uphaz: His body also was like the beryl, and his face as the appearance of lightning, and his eyes as lamps of fire, and his arms and his feet like in colour to polished brass, and the voice of his words like the voice of a multitude. And I Daniel alone saw the vision: for the men that were with me saw not the vision; but a great quaking fell upon them, so that they fled to hide themselves. Therefore I was left alone, and saw this great vision, and there remained no strength in me: for my comeliness was turned in me into corruption, and I retained no strength. Yet heard I the voice of his words: and when I heard the voice of his words, then was I in a deep sleep on my face, and my face toward the ground. And, behold, an hand touched me, which set me upon my knees and upon the palms of my hands. And he said unto

> me, O Daniel, a man greatly beloved, understand the
> words that I speak unto thee, and stand upright: for
> unto thee am I now sent. And when he had spoken
> this word unto me, I stood trembling.

Daniel had prayed. There were some things he did
not understand, and he had set his heart to discipline
himself so as to put himself in a frame of mind where he
could hear from God. While he was waiting to hear
from the Lord, some things were happening in the
spirit-world that were the results of Daniel's prayer.

> Then he said unto me, Fear not, Daniel: for from
> the first day that thou didst set thine heart to under-
> stand, and to chasten [or discipline] thyself before thy
> God, thy words were heard, and I am come for thy
> words.
>
> (Dan. 10:12)

The angel told Daniel that from the very first day,
his words were heard, but twenty-one days (three
weeks) had passed before this angel could come to
Daniel.

> But the prince of the kingdom of Persia with-
> stood me one and twenty days: but, lo, Michael, one
> of the chief princes, came to help me; and I remained
> there with the kings of Persia.
>
> (Dan. 10:13)

We found out that the word *prince* means "ruler."
The angel was not talking about Cyrus, the physical

king on the throne of Persia. He was talking about one of those wicked spirits in heavenly places who was influencing King Cyrus. There was a warfare going on in the spirit-world. It was not until the angel Michael came and began to do battle with that evil spirit over the kingdom of Persia that the angel Gabriel was able to get through and bring Daniel the message.

There is a warfare going on in the spirit-world all the time. That is why so many times when we make our claim by faith, the answer does not come right away. And the only thing that causes the angels of God to be able to get through with the answer is our steadfastness in making our confession of faith. That is why you have to continue to make your confession of faith on a daily basis, based on whatever it is that you claim from God.

I have heard some Christians say, "Well, it is not God's time." It does not have anything to do with God's timing. It is a matter of faith and the warfare going on in the spirit-world.

God is not some kind of sadist who holds healing over the heads of His children while they are suffering and bleeding and in pain, waiting for thirty-five days to pass before He heals them. He is capable of doing it the minute the prayer is prayed. It is a matter of us keeping our faith on the line to such an extent that the angels who are working on our behalf in the spirit-realm are able to overcome the wicked spirits of Satan and bring the answers through. I want to emphasize that the thing that makes it work, is our continual, steadfast confession of faith. If we do not maintain our confession, Satan's host will overcome the angels of God, and the answers we may be waiting for will never come.

When you make your confession, "I believe I have received," it is your faith that is talking, and that gives the angels something to work with against the wicked spirits, the princes of Persia, and the princes of the United States, the princes of Los Angeles, the princes of India and England, and all those other princes out there in the spirit-world who are causing all the confusion and trouble in the earth-realm.

It is the power of God that overcomes these evil spirits, but it is our faith that makes that power work. That is why Jesus would say over and over again to people who came to Him for healing: "Thy faith has made thee whole." He did not say God did it. He did not say the power did it, yet it was God and it was the power. But it was the people's faith that released that power.

All you have to do is to stay with it. Christians need to have as much confidence in their faith as the farmer does in his planting. A farmer goes out and plows some ground. He plants seed in the ground, and then covers up the seed. He cannot see the seed nor know for a fact what it is doing. He does not know if the seed is growing, but he believes that it is. He is exercising faith.

Even while the seed is still in the ground, unseen, the farmer begins making plans for a harvest. He calculates the number of workers he will need to help him harvest his crop when it comes in, the type of equipment he will use and how big the harvest will be. He even determines where he will take the crop once it has been harvested. He makes all these preparations and plans, and he has not seen anything yet telling him that he will even get a harvest because the seed is working underground. During the time that the seed is developing, the farmer never runs out to the field to dig the seed up to see if it is growing.

There is no book that I know of, no publication that I have ever heard of, no law that I have ever seen engraved in stone that says, "Thus saith God to the farmer, if you will plant on Monday, I will guarantee you a harvest." There is no written record anywhere that I know of that tells the farmer to plant something, and he will get a crop.

How then can a farmer plant a seed and expect a harvest? He must exercise faith. Human, natural faith! He planted the seed, covered it up, then the next day, and days afterward, he watered the seed, even though he could not see anything but water and dirt. Underneath the ground, unseen by human eyes, germination is taking place. When the little green sprout starts coming out of the ground, that is not when the plant started growing, that is just when the farmer sees what was taking place under the ground. The seed had to be growing all the time.

Why can't Christians have that much faith in the Word of their heavenly Father? He said, "Believe, and you shall receive." Why can't believers have as much faith to wait for the harvest to come in like the farmer does? This is where people are missing it. They are operating on a double standard. When it comes to the natural world, they are operating on one standard, and they will accept anything and everything that nature tells them. But when it comes to Almighty God, who hung the stars, moons, and sun in the heavens and causes all of them to work like they ought to, people want a sign. If we can have faith in planting a seed, then why can't we have faith in the Word of God and have the patience to wait for the manifestation of it?

There is a warfare going on out there in the spirit-world, and Satan is trying to keep your blessings from you. You have to maintain the tenacity of a lion. You have to make up your mind that, sink or swim, live or die, come hell or high water, here I stand, and I will stand until I get what I want!

If you do not have an attitude like that, the devil will put symptoms on you, thoughts in your mind, and try to frighten you off. He will have you thinking you are going to die the next day, but you are going to have to maintain confidence in the Word of God. You have to make up your mind that you are going to stand on God's Word and work the Word in your life. When you do that, God will back you up. The angels are out there working on your behalf, but it takes faith to keep the channels open for them to bring the blessings of God to pass.

Many years ago, I determined that I was going to be a winner. When I made that decision, I did not have a dime to my name. I was poverty going somewhere to happen. But I saw how I could be a success in the Kingdom of God. I saw that my heavenly Father wanted me to be a winner. I saw that He had made provisions for me to win in every area of life — physically, mentally, spiritually, and financially.

For seventeen years, I had been a minister of the gospel, going nowhere fast, whipped in everything I did. Every week, every year the same thing — defeat, sickness, and deprivation. There was never enough money to take care of my family. I was sincere, I meant well, I was living as well as I knew how to live, and I was going nowhere, but to the bottom of the barrel. Thank God, I found out that the Word of God was true! Before I found that out, I was out there hoping and praying that something would work. Hoping and praying will get you zero, followed by another zero, multiplied by a million other zeros. You will get nothing by "hoping and praying." It is faith that moves the hand of God. So I started putting the Word to work. I sounded like an idiot. People looked at me as if they thought I had lost my mind. I was going around saying, "Praise the Lord, all my needs are met. Praise God, I am wealthy. Praise the Lord, I am healed from the top of my head to the soles of my feet." When I was saying these things, I was in pain and could hardly stand up.

I would be sick with something all the time. Month after month, something was always wrong with me. Of course, I expected it, I prepared for it, I said it, I believed it, so I had it. I did not know that I was operating under a spiritual law. Ignorance of the law will still work against you. I did not know that spiritual power is released by the words of your mouth, either positive or negative. (See Prov. 18:21.) When you release negative words, you permit Satan to get involved in your circumstances. When you release positive words that are consistent with the Word of Almighty God, you release the power of God into your life.

When I learned about faith, I began to say what the Word said about my health. I began to say, "I believe I am healed." I began to make that confession over and over again. I would say it all day long, whenever I thought about it. The devil began to put pressure on me. I felt he was hitting me with everything in his grab bag. I thought I was going to die in the natural. But I knew by the Spirit of God that I was going to live.

One time I had all the symptoms of the flu for ninety days straight. I coughed, I wheezed, I had a sore throat, and I had a runny nose. I would go to the pulpit with a handkerchief in one hand and my Bible in the other. I remember one of my church members felt so sorry for me that he pulled me aside one Sunday and began to tell me about the virtues of Vitamin C, and other vitamins and medicines he felt would help me. I was determined that I would either stand and be healed or I would die, one of the two. It did not make any difference to me at that point, because I was tired of being a loser.

One night after Bible study, I was standing and talking to two of my members, when all of a sudden I felt a pain so sharp in my back that I doubled over and would have fallen if one of the men had not caught me. I had never in my life experienced anything so painful; I could feel the pain in my legs, and my right leg began to get numb. I did not know what was happening to me, I was hurting so badly. I went home, still confessing, "I believe I am healed; I believe I am healed." I could hardly walk. The next morning I could not get out of bed. I had to roll out onto the floor. My wife was alarmed and did not know what to do.

One of my members worked at Orthopaedic Hospital and she made an appointment for me to see a doctor. I could not drive or even sit straight in the car seat. My wife drove me to the hospital, where they took X-rays and had a couple of doctors check me over. They could find nothing wrong. They suggested that I stay in the hospital for a day or two so they could run more intensive tests.

I said, "No thanks. I am going home." I had made up my mind right then that I was going all the way with God's Word. I went back home, determined to win.

Sometimes my leg and back would hurt me so badly that I would stand in the shower and scream. Still, I was determined that I was not going to stay in bed, because I believed I was well. A well person is not supposed to be in bed, so I went about my normal duties as best I could. I would drive myself to work, gritting my teeth and biting my tongue to keep from crying out from the pain. It went on like this for about a year. One day the pain just completely disappeared. I had won the victory.

I realized that I had been wrestling against spiritual forces, and they were trying to stop me by putting pressure on me. That is why I am not intimidated by people when they say faith does not work, because I know it does. Now I am not telling anyone to do what I did. You have to know your own threshold and your commitment. I am not against doctors and hospitals. Thank God for them. But I just want to show you to what extent the devil will go when he wants to stop you from progressing in the Word of God.

I had another situation in my body. I had a tumor in my chest, right under the mammary gland. The first one started growing when I was in junior high school. It started out as a little knot about the size of a green pea. Over a period of years, it grew and developed to be as large as a silver dollar. It became extremely painful, so much so that just having my shirt touch it was excruciating. Of course, at that time I did not know about faith and healing, and you cannot use what you do not know.

I was going to churches and they did not know anymore than I knew. They told me nothing about divine healing. They just told me to, "Hold on, tiger. Just hang in there. God knows how much you can bear, and He will not put on you any more than you can bear." It is a slap in God's face to accuse Him of putting sickness and pain on His children. How we have hurt our heavenly Father with such unscriptural accusations.

Thank God for doctors. The fact that I believe in divine healing does not mean that I do not believe in doctors. I believe in doctors, nurses, hospitals, medical plans, medicine, and dentists. I believe in anyone who can do anything to help people get well and have good health. If your faith is not sufficiently developed, you had better have a good doctor, or Satan will take you out.

At any rate, I went to the doctor about the tumor in my chest. The doctor examined me and told me that he would have to operate and remove the tumor to determine if it was malignant. Thank God, it was not cancerous. Following surgery, the doctor assured me that I would be all right. However, he did warn me that tumors of this nature would sometimes reoccur on the opposite side of the chest cavity.

Sure enough after a period of time, one day as I was showering, I noticed a little growth under my mammary gland about the size of the other one. This time the tumor grew like wildfire. Before I knew it, it was up to the size of a silver dollar, and the pain was excruciating. By this time, I had heard about divine healing, and I took a stand on the Word.

Even though I was hurting most of the time, the people in the congregation did not know what I was going through. I was determined to win, because I knew if I could not get faith to work for me, I could not promote it to anyone else.

One day, I stood in my room and I said, "Heavenly Father, in the name of Jesus, I take my stand on the Word. Your Word says in Matthew 8:17, **'Himself took our infirmities and bare our sicknesses.'** First Peter 2:24 says, **'Who his own self bare our sins in his own body on the tree, that we, being dead to sins, should live unto righteousness, by whose stripes ye were healed.'** Now if I was, I am; and if I am, I is (present tense). I believe I *is* healed. [That may not be good grammar, but I believe you get the point.]

"You said, in Mark 11:24, **'What things soever ye desire, when ye pray, believe that ye receive them.'** Father, I desire this tumor to disappear out of my body. I desire that this pain stop. That is my desire, and I am now praying. I believe right now that I receive healing for this tumor condition. In the name of Jesus, tumor, I curse you, I command you to wither and die, and to cease to exist. Father, you said if I believe I receive; I will have it. So I thank you, Father. I believe I have it; I believe I am healed."

Every day in my prayer time, I would say, "Father, I want to thank you. I believe I am healed." I kept saying it, and saying it, and saying it. Three months passed. The tumor grew larger and the pain got worse. The devil would say, "You are going to die, fool. And then what will all those people think? You have been talking about healing and saying the Lord wants you well. What are people going to think when you die?"

Let me tell you, that will rattle your cage. And that is what Satan wants to do. He wants to scare you off the Word. I said, "Devil, according to the Word of God, I am healed, and I believe I am." Six months later, the growth grew larger and the pain got worse. And the devil kept telling me that I was going to die. All this time I was preaching on faith, trusting in God, and believing in divine healing.

My confession concerning the tumor was that I believed I was healed. I never said I *felt* like it, because I didn't. If you get into the sense-realm of *feeling*, you will miss it. Satan operates in the sense-realm, and that is where he wants to keep you. I never said the pain was not there. The pain was there. The tumor was there. But I never gave it any credit for having any authority in my body. I talked about the cure instead of the problem.

Nine months came and went, the tumor was still there, the pain was still there, and I was still preaching and confessing God's Word. The devil was still telling me I was going to die. He would say, "You are not healed; if you were healed, you would not have any pain. Do you have pain? If you were healed, you would not have a growth there. Is there a growth there?" I could not deny that the growth was there. I could not deny that I had pain. But I would say, "Devil, I never said I *felt* like I was healed. I never said that I *looked* like I was healed. I never said there was no pain. I never said that the tumor was not there. I said, I *believe*, according to the Word of God, that I am healed. And I believe I received my healing over nine months ago when I first prayed."

For over 300 days, I waged this warfare in my body without letup. The Bible tells us that, **"We wrestle not against flesh and blood, but against principalities, against powers, against the rulers of the darkness of this world, against spiritual wickedness in high [or heavenly] places"** (Eph. 6:12).

Out there in the spirit-world, those demons were exerting their influence upon my physical body. At the same time, my confession of faith allowed the angels of God to see to it that the power of God was brought to bear upon that tumorous condition.

For eleven months I kept saying every day, "Father, I thank you. I believe I am healed from the top of my head to the soles of my feet. I believe this tumor has disappeared, that it is cursed, that it is dead, in the name of Jesus!" One day, I was taking my shower. I had my washcloth and soap, and I got over there to the right side of my chest, and I did not feel the extreme pain I usually felt when I would touch that area. I dropped the cloth, grabbed my chest, and the thing had disappeared — it was completely gone! I do not know when it left, and I do not care. It was gone, and it shall never return, in the name of Jesus!

During all those eleven months, the pain became more excruciating and the tumor got bigger. In the natural, some folks would say I was a fool. But you have to make up your mind that you are going to stand, no matter what. Many times, the reason the Word does not work is because most Christians are not willing to take a stand. Yes, you are going to have opposition. Demons are real, and they will come against you with all they have, but we have to remember that we have victory over them in the name of Jesus.

Some people have said, "Well, it just worked for you because you are a preacher." I wish these same people could tell me why for seventeen years, before I came into the knowledge of the Word, I was a minister, and nothing worked for me. You do not get anything from God because you are a preacher or a non-preacher. You receive because you operate in the power of God, through the word of faith.

I started planting seed. I tithed and I gave offerings. I started confessing that every need was met. I could not pay my bills when I said that, but I was putting spiritual law into operation. I was causing the angels of God to have ascendancy over the demon power of Satan who was trying to hinder my money from coming to me. I began tithing 10 percent, then 12½ percent, then 15 percent, then 20 percent, and then 25 percent, and God has opened the windows-of-heaven blessing, as it says in Malachi 3:8-10. He has done exceedingly abundantly above all that we could have ever asked or thought.

I encourage you to start utilizing the Word of God, wherever you are and God will promote you. He will promote you in your business; He will promote you in your profession; He will promote you as a husband, a wife, a parent, a student, and an employee. He will promote you in whatever you put your hands to do.

Part 3 — Ephesians 6:13-24

> **Wherefore take unto you the whole armour of God, that ye may be able to withstand in the evil day, and having done all, to stand.**
>
> **(Eph. 6:13)**

Every day is the evil day! The devil is out there doing evil every day. He takes no vacations or rest periods. Therefore, you have to be on your toes each and every day.

> **...and having done all, to stand.**

The **"having done all"** that Paul is talking about here has to do with putting on the whole armor of God. Your being able to stand is predicated on your putting on this entire armor. The good thing about this armor is that there are instructions that come with it that tell us how to use it successfully.

> **Stand therefore, having your loins girt about with truth, and having on the breastplate of right-eousness.**
>
> **(Eph. 6:14)**

Four times the Holy Spirit, through the Apostle Paul, repeats the word *stand:* (1) In verse 11b, **"That ye may be able to STAND...** (emphasis mine); (2) in verse 13a, **"That ye may be able to WITHSTAND"** (emphasis mine); (3) in verse 13b, **"and having done all, to STAND** (emphasis mine); and (4) in verse 14, **"STAND therefore..."** (emphasis mine). This means that God wants us **STANDING,** not lying down.

In verse 14, Paul begins to describe each piece of armor. He is using an analogy to compare our armor to the Roman soldier's military uniform. The then-known civilized world was under the dominion of Rome, and the Roman soldier could be seen everywhere throughout the conquered kingdoms. There was a particular way in which this soldier was attired for battle. Paul knew that the people to whom he was writing at Ephesus would understand his analogy.

The battle that every Christian must wage is first fought in the spiritual realm. It is, however, also manifested in the physical world. This armor that Paul describes is obviously not for the physical body. Think of your spirit-man, the real you, as the engine on the inside of your physical body. If Satan can cause a breakdown in your inner man, he has you where he wants you. However, his control of the inner man will ultimately manifest itself in the physical realm.

...having your loins girt about with truth,...

Think of the physical body and physical armor to get a picture of the spirit-man. In other words, in order to understand this spiritual armor, you have to understand the makeup of the human being.

Man is a tripartite creature. The word *tripartite* is a theological term which simply means, "three parts."

For example, a tricycle has three wheels; a bicycle has two wheels, and a unicycle has only one wheel. Man is a tri-part creature.

You are a spirit. You do not *have* a spirit; you *are* one. You have a soul, and you live inside of a physical body. People are made in the image of God. The Bible says: **"In the beginning was the Word** [or the *Logos*, and that Logos was Jesus Christ], **and the Word was with God"** (John 1:1). Since Jesus is the Word, and the Word was with God, then if anyone ought to know what God is, Jesus ought to know.

In the fourth chapter of John's Gospel, Jesus was conversing with a woman at Jacob's well near the city of Sychar, in Samaria. After talking about places of worship and things of that nature, Jesus finally said to the woman: **"God is a Spirit"** (John 4:24). The reason Jesus said that was to distinguish God from other spirits. Angels are spirits, demons are spirits, and man is a spirit. Genesis 1:26 says that man is made in the image of God. If God is a Spirit, then man would have to be a spirit, too.

Not only are you a spirit, but you will never cease to conciously exist. You will be alive as long as God is alive. There is no such thing as the cessation of existence. There is, however, such a thing as transference of existence. You may transfer out of this physical, three-dimensional world by what we refer to as physical death. However, physical death is not the end of anything but physical existence. The real you that is on the inside will never cease to exist. Physical death is the separation of the spirit and the soul from the body.

I like to think of it this way: Think of a glass of water as being the physical body. Think of the spirit and the soul as the water and the wet inside of the glass. You cannot separate the water from the wet. Neither can you separate the soul from the spirit. The soul part of you is what makes up your personality. It contains your desires, your will, your emotions, and your intellect.

Through your body, with its five senses, you operate in the physical, three-dimensional world. With your spirit you contact God who is a Spirit. You cannot contact God with your body, and you cannot contact God with your soul. That is what has been wrong with the Christian world for too long. We have been trying to operate in the realm of the soul instead of the realm of the spirit. We have gone to two extremes: either we have gone completely intellectual with the mind, or we have gone wild with the emotions, thinking we are moving by the Spirit.

Jesus Christ said God is a Spirit, and **"they that worship him must worship him in spirit and in truth"** (John 4:24) — not in the flesh and in the emotions. That means we are to worship God out of our spirit-man and bring our souls and our bodies along for the ride.

The Bible does not tell us exactly what our spirits look like. But I have a suspicion that the spirit-man is shaped the same way the body is shaped, except it is probably not overweight.

If we reason from the known to the unknown, we can get some idea of what our spirits are like. Since God is a Spirit and He made us in His image, He more than likely would have made us after His own pattern.

We know that God has hands, eyes, and ears. We know this, because the Bible says that **"The eyes of the Lord are upon the righteous, and his ears are open unto their cry** [prayers] (Ps. 34:15). The Bible says, **"The eyes of the Lord are in every place beholding the evil and the good"** (Prov. 15:3).

The Word of God tells us, in the Book of the Revelation, that after the Apostle John was caught up to heaven, he made this statement: **"He that was seated upon the throne had a book with seven seals in his right hand"** (Rev. 5:1). You do not have to use the term *right hand,* unless there is a left hand. So I believe we look very much on the inside like we look on the outside, in terms of shape.

...having your loins girt about with truth...
(Eph. 6:14)

The loins are the part of the body that begins just above the kidneys. In the seventh chapter of John's Gospel, Jesus, addressing His disciples, said, **"If any man thirst, let him come unto me, and drink. He that believeth on me, as the scripture hath said, out of his belly shall flow rivers of living water"** (John 7:37-38). Jesus was not talking about man's physical stomach or bowels, but rather He was making reference spiritually to the loins, the innermost being of man — his spirit.

In John 17:17, Jesus said that God's Word is truth. If your loins (spirit-man) are girt about with truth, that means your spirit-man is supposed to be filled with the Word of God. The Christian should be so strong in the

Word that the Word should come up out of his spirit at a moment's notice and be spoken out of his mouth, releasing God's power on the Christian's behalf.

...and having on the breastplate of righteousness...

The breastplate is the part of the physical armor that covers and protects the vital organs, such as the lungs and the heart, which are the seat of physical life. Paul is talking about protecting yourself in the spirit-realm, and the way you do that is with the breastplate of righteousness. How do you put the breastplate on? You put it on by recognizing what God says about you and your relationship with Him through Jesus Christ. He says that you are the **"righteousness of God in him [Christ]"** (2 Cor. 5:21).

> **And your feet shod with the preparation of the gospel of peace.**
> **(Eph. 6:15)**

So this spirit-man must have feet. That is why I believe the spirit-man looks like the physical man, because Paul is describing spiritually what we are familiar with in the nautral.

> **Above all...**
> **(Eph. 6:16)**

Whatever Paul is getting ready to say now is very important. He has already told us to be strong, to put the armor on, to have our loins girt about with truth, to have on the breastplate of righteousness, to have our feet shod with the preparation of the gospel, and now he says: "Above all this, do this!" In other words, if somehow you miss the other admonishments or forget to do them, do not forget this!

...taking the shield of faith...

A shield is a covering that protects you from the flak coming against you from the enemy. There was a type of shield that the Roman soldier used that had a point at the end of it. The point was there so that the soldier could stick the shield deeply enough into the ground so that it would not move. It provided a block of protection for the soldier to hide behind. He could look out through slits in the shield to see what was going on. In this way he was protected from the spears and arrows of his enemy until he saw that it was clear to move. Then he would pull the shield up, rise, and advance forward. There were, of course, smaller shields that were used in hand-to-hand combat. But whatever the size and type of shield, its primary purpose was to provide a covering for protection.

...wherewith ye shall be able to quench all the fiery darts of the wicked.

The word *darts*, in the Greek, is a very interesting word. It means *missiles*.[14] A missile is something that is coming at you. Paul tells us that with the "shield of faith" we are able to quench all the enemy's darts. If we are able to quench all the darts, that means none are going to get through to hurt us.

Quench means to "put out." This term is often used relative to quenching thirst. Water can be used to "quench" or to put out a person's thirst.

If you want to put a fire out, you normally would pour water over the fire, or smother it in some way. When you do that, you are quenching the fire, or putting it out. Likewise, the "shield of faith" will put out the fiery attack of the devil when he comes against you. Notice, however, that Paul says, **"ye shall be able to quench."** He did not say you would. This means then, it is up to you to use the shield. If you do not know how to use the shield, you are going to be a victim instead of a victor. One Scripture that supports this principle is found in Luke 10:19.

> **Behold** [This is Jesus speaking to His disciples], **I give unto you power** [or authority] **to tread on serpents and scorpions, and over all the power** [or ability] **of the enemy: and nothing shall by any means hurt you.**

That means that if the fiery darts are getting through, and you are being hurt, you are missing something. It does not mean that you are a bad person or that you do not love the Lord. It does not mean that you are not saved and that your name is not written in the Lamb's Book of Life. What it does mean is that you need to get stronger in the Word.

If you are going to win with God, you are going to have to stand. It takes work to stand. Sometimes you can get so tired of standing that you wish you had never heard about the shield, or armor, or authority, or faith. Sometimes I want to throw my hands up and go on and die and go on to heaven. Then I will not have to put up with struggling against the enemy anymore.

Yes, it is work to stand, no doubt about it. But it is easy work. If it is not easy, then Jesus lied to us when He said, **"Come unto me, all ye that labour and are heavy laden, and I will give you rest. Take my yoke upon you, and learn of me; for I am meek and lowly in heart: and ye shall find rest unto your souls. For my yoke is easy, and my burden is light"** (Matt. 11:28-30).

Paul tells us in 1 Timothy 6:12, **"Fight the good fight of faith."** Fighting is work. But you have to make up your mind that you either want to win or just be mediocre. I do not want to be mediocre. I want to be on top of the heap, with the devil under my feet.

There are many people who have victory in the mind-realm. They listen to my teaching on how to be a winner in life, and they say: "Glory to God, Brother Price, I believe that and I agree." They have head knowledge, but they do not have victory experientially. If you ever get a taste of really defeating the devil and winning, you will not settle for anything less again.

There is a taste that goes with victory and there is nothing else like it. Just stand long enough to get the victory, friend. And if you get that thirst for victory, you will never be satisfied with anything less than total victory all the time.

**And take the helmet of salvation, and the sword
of the Spirit, which is the word of God.**

(Eph. 6:17)

A helmet is protection for your head. Both the
Hebrew and Greek words for *salvation* have the conno-
tative meaning of "deliverance, safety, preservation,
healing, and soundness." The Christian needs to
develop strength in knowing and using the Word in
these particular areas. When he does, he can rest
assured his helmet of salvation will stay firmly in place.

...and the sword of the Spirit which is the word of God.

The sword and the shield work hand in hand. If
you happen to be using a King James Version of the
Bible, you will notice that in the seventeenth verse the
word *Spirit* is capitalized. This leaves the impression
that it is talking about the Holy Spirit.

Many of the major ancient manuscripts, from
which the New Testament was translated, were written
in all capital letters, with no verse designations, no
chapter divisions, or punctuation marks. The transla-
tors divided the Bible into chapters and verses, and put
the capitalizations where they thought appropriate,
along with the punctuation marks. You can understand
why this was needed, because without these divisions
and designations, we would not have any reference
points, and it would be very difficult to find anything in
the Bible.

366

I personally believe that everyone, unfortunately, who worked on translating the Scriptures at different times throughout the history of the Bible, were not always Spirit-filled men. They may have been academically trained and very well educated in the Hebrew and Greek languages, but did not necessarily have the guidance of the Holy Spirit.

I believe that when they translated this seventeenth verse, they made a mistake, not in the words, but in the capitalization. I have enough sense to know that you do not add or take away from the Word of God, and I have no intentions of doing that. I believe that the words themselves are exactly as the Spirit of God gave them. However, depending upon the context in which they are used, the way they are punctuated, and the way they are either capitalized or not capitalized can change the entire meaning and emphasis of words.

As I said before, in verse 17, the word *Spirit* is capitalized, so it makes it appear that it is the sword of the Holy Spirit. However, the armor is for the benefit of Christians, and not for the Holy Ghost. The Holy Spirit is the interpreter of the Word. He is the Giver of the Word, but the Word is not given to Him; it is given to those of us who are in the family of God. So, then, if the helmet of salvation is for the believer, then the sword has to be also.

I submit that the word *Spirit* should have been left in the small-case designation, and that it is the sword of the re-created human spirit that is being talked about here.

If you look very carefully over the cataloguing of the armor, you will find that every piece of armor is for defensive purposes. It is not until you get to the sword of the spirit that you begin to deal with offensive weaponry. All the rest of the armor is to protect you from the onslaught of the enemy. But there are times when we need to be on the attack.

How do we go after the enemy? You cannot go out there with your fists and try to knock him down or stomp him in order to put him under your feet. You have to have a weapon. Thanks be unto God that He has made a weapon available to us. And what a weapon it is! The Spirit of God, through the Apostle Paul, tells us exactly what the sword of the spirit is so that we cannot mess it up with our theology and with our denominationalism.

...the sword of the Spirit, which is the word of God.

If we do not really understand what this verse means, we will not know how to use our sword — the Word of God. And because they do not know how to cut the devil down with their swords, many Christians are whipped and defeated in their spiritual lives.

The church for too long has been in a holding pattern. There was a song some time back that gave the idea that we were supposed to go up somewhere on a mountaintop and hold the fort. But that is not what Jesus said we are to do.

When He walked the Earth, Jesus said, **"Upon this rock I will build my church; and the gates of hell shall not prevail against it"** (Matt. 16:18). We have thought that we were supposed to stand somewhere in a location and Satan was going to come against us and that we would stand right there and never be moved.

When Jesus said **"upon this rock,"** He would establish His Church, that rock was the fact that He is the Son of God — that rock of truth, not on Peter. Gates are usually hung on walls, and are at a place where there is an opening or breach. Gates are usually kept closed so that the wall would be continuous all the way around; then, when there is a need for a break, the gates can be opened. Jesus was saying that the gates (or walls) of hell that imprison the unsaved world would not be able to stand against the invasion of His Church!

We are not supposed to be standing still, waiting for Satan to come and get us and gobble us up. We are supposed to take the sword of the spirit and go into the enemy's territory and run him out of the Kingdom of God.

Jesus did not say that the gates are going to come against the Church, but that the Church is going against the gates, and the gates will not be able to prevail against the attack.

When we go against these gates, they are going to open, and the walls are coming down just as they did around the city of Jericho. However, we need to learn and understand that we are not in a holding pattern. We are marching around the walls of hell and we are grinding the enemy under our feet as we go along — at least that is what we are supposed to be doing.

Of course, the enemy is going to be shooting at us all the time. But we have the armor of God to protect us from being destroyed. Armor, however, will not do you any good if you do not know how to use it. In the fourth chapter of the Gospel of Matthew, Jesus shows us very clearly how to use the sword of the spirit. All we need to do is follow His example:

> **Then was Jesus led up of the Spirit into the wilderness to be tempted of the devil.**
>
> **(Matt. 4:1)**

Notice who the tempter is. This verse tells us that the devil is the tempter, not God. God is not our problem; He is our solution, and He is not putting anything on us except blessings.

> **And when he had fasted forty days and forty nights, he was afterward an hungred. And when the tempter came to him, he said, If thou be the Son of God, command that these stones be made bread.**
>
> **(Matt. 4:2-3)**

The word *tempt*,[15] in the original Greek, is the word *peirazo*, and it means "temptations, tests, and trials." *Tempter* then means "one who tries, tests, and tempts." That is not God. He would not waste His time by testing you. He already knows what you are going to do.

The devil does not know. In fact, he has no way of knowing what you are going to do except by two methods: (1) Either he will program your mind to get you to act in a certain way, or (2) you let him know what you are going to do by the words of your mouth. What has happened is that Satan has deceived the world (even some Christians) into thinking that he is omnipotent, ominiscient, and omnipresent, when in actuality he is absolutely ignorant.

When he was originally created, he was referred to as the **"anointed cherub that covereth"** (Ezek. 28:14). But when he rebelled, he lost his anointing. He is a dumb spirit. That is obvious, because if he were a smart spirit, he would read the back of the book and find out that we win and he loses, and he would quit. That tells you that he does not know anything. He wants to fool mankind into thinking that he is in a class with Almighty God. There is no doubt that he is a powerful opponent. But, thanks be unto God, Jesus Christ is our Redeemer, our Savior, our Lord, our High Priest and Coming King, and He has defeated him on our behalf, and His victory is our victory!

We are told, in the fourth chapter of Hebrews, that Jesus was tempted with the same temptations we go through, but He came out victoriously against His enemy. And because He is our example, so can we.

> **For we have not a high priest which cannot be touched with the feeling of our infirmities; but was in all points tempted like as we are, yet without sin.**
>
> **(Heb. 4:15)**

Jesus had the opportunity to yield to sin, because if He did not, then He was not tempted as we are. I have said this before, but it bears repetition. I used to think of Jesus as being somewhere way up on a pedestal, that He was untouchable, and that He could do no wrong because He was the Son of God.

When I found out that He was tempted like any ordinary man, but never yielded to the temptation, it made my love for Him more realistic, more abiding, and more committed. He outwitted the devil and came out on top, "clean as a whistle." That gives me great encouragement, because I know that if He could do it, I can do it. That is why He came and subjected himself to the same temptations that mankind is subjected to.

Jesus did not have to come down from the royal heights of heaven, down to this cesspool of sin and damnation. He was the Son of God, and He did not have to prove anything to God, the Father, or to himself or to the Holy Spirit, or to anyone else for that matter. He did not have to come down to this world to prove that He was the Son of God. Why did He come? He came to show us how to win.

Jesus was the Master Teacher, and He came to show us how we are to live and how we are to defeat the devil and keep him under our feet. In fact, the whole Bible tells us that Jesus has left us a great legacy to follow. He was never defeated. He was never sick, and He never went with His needs unmet. He won and so can we, because the way He won was by operating by the Word of God and by the power of the Holy Spirit. It is a matter of commitment, it is a matter of dedication, it is a matter of making up your mind to go all the way with God.

...if thou be the son of God...

(Matt. 4:3)

That is always Satan's approach to the child of God, the creating of doubt as to who we are in God. He approached Jesus with the same method. It was this approach that he used on Eve when he said to her: **"Hath God said...?"** (Gen. 3:1). He knew exactly what God had said. But if he could get her to misrepresent what God had said, he would have her right where he wanted her.

God gave man dominion over this world. Satan, through his treacherous lies, actually stole this world. He tricked Adam and Eve into giving it away, and all they got for it was death.

If the devil can get you to question the veracity, the truthfulness, the accuracy of God's Word, he will wrap your own tongue around your neck and kill you with it.

The Bible says Eve looked at the tree, saw that it was good for food, partook of the fruit, and gave it to her husband (the dumbest man that ever lived) to eat. I would call him that to his face if he were here. He is the one who got us into all of this mess, following his wife instead of following God.

Hath God said...?

That is always the devil's approach: "If it really is God's will for you to be healed, you would not be in pain, would you?" That is his approach to you and to me today when we are believing for a healing in our bodies.

Satan cannot read your mind, because if he could, he would stop every move you intend to make on behalf of God and the Kingdom of God. Your mind is open to both God and Satan. They both work on the same premise and they both operate by way of influence. All God can do in your life is to use influence. Once you accept His influence, then His power comes into play on your behalf. When you accept the influence of the devil, then his power comes into play against you.

> ...command that these stones be made bread.
>
> **(Matt. 4:3)**

In essence, what Satan was saying to Jesus was: "If you are really the Son of God, use your power. You have been here forty days and forty nights. I know you are hungry because I can hear your stomach growling. Look at those loose rocks over there. You had better check it out and see if the power is still on. After all, there may have been a power failure in heaven, and yours may not work. **'If thou be the Son of God, command that these stones be made bread.'**"

Unlike Eve, Jesus did not fall for Satan's trickery. In fact, He took this opportunity to show us how to use the sword of the spirit.

> **But he answered and said, It is written, Man shall not live by bread alone, but by every word that proceedeth out of the mouth of God.**
>
> **(Matt. 4:4)**

In a sword fight or a fencing match, the duelists slash and point their swords at one another, trying to make physical contact with the blades. Jesus and Satan were dueling, so to speak, with words: the Word of God against the word of the devil.

In days of old, those who fought with swords carried their weapons at their sides, just as the modern-day policeman carries his weapon at his side. The swordsmen carried their swords in what is known as a scabbard. The scabbard was a hollow steel covering that they could put their blades into to keep the blades from cutting them. The scabbard fit on a belt, or a chain, around their waists, and when they got ready to fight or duel, they would grab the handle of the sword with one hand and hold the scabbard steady with the other hand, while pulling the sword from the scabbard and then they would begin to fight.

With the sword of the spirit, the principle is the same. Paul is telling us that when we use the spirit's sword, we use it exactly like a sword fighter uses his physical sword. The only difference is that our swords are made of words instead of steel.

When Jesus responded to Satan's goading, He reached, as it were, for the handle of His double-edged sword, which is the Word of God, and said:

...It is written....

He pulled that double-edged sword — that Word that is sharper than any two-edged sword — out of its spiritual scabbard, and said:

> **Man shall not live by bread alone, but by every word that proceedeth out of the mouth of God.**
>
> **(Matt. 4:4)**

And He rammed that doubled-edged blade right into the devil's belly.

> **Then the devil taketh him up into the holy city, and setteth him on a pinnacle of the temple.**
>
> **(Matt. 4:5)**

Notice how fast the devil got off of the rocks-and-bread business when Jesus put that blade into him. Notice that he did not hang around the rock pile, trying to convince Jesus to turn rocks into bread. No, he grabbed his belly and went on up to the Temple because Jesus had wounded him when He used the sword of the Spirit, and Satan did not want anymore of that.

The Bible clearly lets us know that Jesus won in life and so can we. The way He won was by operating in the Word, and in the power of the Holy Spirit. He was given the same Word — that is, the sword of the spirit — that we have been given. So that means we can win, too, if we want to. It is a matter of commitment, it is a matter of dedication, it is a matter of making up our minds that we are going to go all the way with God. And Jesus showed us how it was to be done.

A great part of living the successful Christian life is based on words. In fact, the whole universe started out with words. God spoke this Earth into existence with faith-filled words. Jesus Christ himself is called the Word of God because He is God's Word physically manifested to mankind.

John 1:1-5 states: **"In the beginning was the Word, and the Word was with God, and the Word was God. The same was in the beginning with God. All things were made by him; and without him was not anything made that was made. In him was life; and the life was the light of men. And the light shineth in darkness; and the darkness comprehended it not."**

In Rev. 19:13, when the Apostle John was caught up into the spirit-world, speaking about Jesus, he said: **"And he was clothed with a vesture dipped in blood: and his name is called The Word of God."**

Jesus came into this physical world, and His words, which are God's words, have been given to us in written form. The Bible contains God's words, direct to us. You do not need to hear a voice or have a dream or have an angel appear to you. You may have a dream, but let it happen when it happens. A voice may speak to you, but let it speak when it speaks. An angel may appear to you, but do not go out looking for angels or try to make something out of nothing. Let God do what HE wants to do. Other than that, you have no excuse for not taking advantage of the written Word.

Until the Word becomes a reality in your life, you will be a mediocre Christian. Once Jesus taught a spiritual truth illustrating that there are degrees to commitment and development. There are people who will be above-average Christians, average Christians, and below-average Christians. At the end of the parable Jesus said that some seeds **"brought forth fruit, some an hundredfold, some sixtyfold, some thirtyfold"** (Matt. 13:8).

It would seem that if the seed had the capacity to produce a hundredfold, it would do so all the way across the board. The reason Jesus said that some seeds would produce a hundredfold, sixtyfold or thirtyfold was because it is up to us. I plan to be in the hundredfold group myself. Why settle for thirty, when a hundred is available? What about you?

> **Study to shew thyself approved unto God, a workman that needeth not to be ashamed, rightly dividing the word of truth.**
>
> **(2 Tim. 2:15)**

You never use the word *rightly* unless it is in contradistinction to the word *wrongly*. In essence, what Paul is saying is that if you do not know how to read the Bible, you could misinterpret what you have read and think that the Scriptures sometime contradict one another. The Bible does not contradict itself. If it does, then God contradicts himself, because the Bible is His Word. It is simply that you have to understand what you are reading. Let me give you an example of what I am talking about.

> **For I say, through the grace given unto me, to every man that is among you, not to think of himself more highly than he ought to think; but to think soberly, according as God hath dealt to every man the measure of faith.**
>
> **(Rom. 12:3)**

Then look at 2 Thessalonians 3:2:

> **And that we may be delivered from unreason-
> able and wicked men: for all men have not faith.**

One verse says God has dealt to every man the measure of faith, then another verse says that all men do not have faith. If you do not know how to rightly divide the Word, you could get confused as to what each verse actually means.

There is no contradiction between these two verses. You have to determine what is being said by the context. Romans 12:3 is not saying that every man in the world has faith. Paul makes it quite plain in the first chapter of Romans to whom he is writing: **"To all that be in Rome, beloved of God, called to be saints...."** (verse 7). This Scripture is talking about saved people — Christians.

It is by faith that we are saved. So if we are in the Body of Christ, whether we are in Rome, or Corinth, or Thessalonica, or Los Angeles, or London, we are in the same Church, and we have the same Head over us, Jesus Christ, and the same heavenly Father. That means we must be given the same measure of faith the Lord dealt to those Christians in Rome. Otherwise, He becomes a respecter of persons.

In 2 Thessalonians, Paul is not talking about men in Christ, but about those in the world — the sinners. Unsaved people are not children of God. Therefore, they do not have God's nature or the God-kind of faith. They cannot be given the measure of faith.

What you have to do is to program the Word into your spirit so that it will come out of your mouth at a moment's recall. That is how to use the sword against Satan and against all of the other negative circumstances that come against you in this life. The devil is the one who is actually behind those circumstances, and his whole mode of operation is geared to wipe you out. The way you counteract his attacks is by speaking the Word of God aloud to the situations he brings. You have to have confidence in the words you speak, however, as well as confidence in the Lord. In 2 Timothy, Paul lets us know what the Word is for.

> **All scripture is given by inspiration of God, and is profitable** [number one] **for doctrine,** [number two] **for reproof,** [number three] **for correction,** [number four] **for instruction in righteousness.**
>
> **(2 Tim. 3:16)**

The word *righteousness* means right-standing with God. People need to be taught how to stand in their place in God. This does not just happen; people need instruction. That is where many churches, by and large, have failed. Instead of instructing the people, they have been emotionalizing and inspiring them. Inspiration is fine. But, friend, when I am hungry and it is time for dinner, I do not want any inspiration, I want some food! Inspiration is great, but you cannot live on it. You need the Word if you want to be an overcomer.

> **That the man of God may be perfect, throughly furnished unto all good works.**
>
> **(2 Tim. 3:17)**

The word *perfect* in this Scripture, does not mean flawless. It means "fully developed" or "full-grown" or "mature in the things of God." The sad thing about it is that there are too many baby Christians. I am not talking about folks who have just received Christ. I am talking about people who have been Christians for five, ten, twenty, twenty-five years or more. Yet, they are still just as much babies as they were the day they got saved. You hear them shouting the loudest in a church service, "Praise the Lord, I love Jesus." "Praise God, Hallelujah!" But they will be the first to cave in when the devil comes against them.

Friend, you had better know more than "I love the Lord" when Satan comes in like a flood. You had better know how to resist him with the Word of God. You had better know how to use the sword of the spirit.

The way you program the Word into your spirit is to memorize Scriptures that apply to you and keep those Scriptures ever before you by saying them or reading them. How do you memorize something? One way is by listening to it all the time. You can read it and you can hear it. Get a tape recorder and play the Word as often as you can. Once the Word gets into your spirit, and starts automatically coming out of your mouth, the devil will not be able to handle you anymore as he once did.

The Bible says, **"Submit yourselves therefore to God. Resist the devil, and he will flee from you"** (James 4:7).

The way to resist Satan is by speaking the Word. He does not mind you saying, "Glory, glory, glory,

glory!" Or, "Jesus, Jesus, Jesus!" But he does not want you to have anything to do with the Word, because it was the Word that bombed him out at Calvary.

The Bible says that the devil, as a roaring lion, walks about seeking whom he may devour. (See 1 Pet. 5:8.) It did not say that he was a lion, but he tries to act like one in order to frighten the child of God. He is nothing but a big, fat pussycat who does not even have any teeth in his mouth. Jesus pulled his teeth long ago, and left him without any gums to grow new teeth.

All you have to do is to put the Word on Satan, and he will turn tail and run. Take advantage of memorizing Scriptures while you can, and start talking the Word of God instead of all that garbage the world talks about.

If you go into a restaurant or somewhere else, and the people are sitting around making a lot of noise, just start talking the Word, and see the effect the Word will have in that atmosphere. When you get around people who are always talking sickness and disease and what bad things are going on in the world today, start talking the Word and see what light it will bring into the conversation.

> **Praying always with all prayer and supplication in the Spirit, and watching thereunto with all perseverance and supplication for all saints.**
>
> **(Eph. 6:18)**

The Bible also says, **"Pray without ceasing"** (1 Thess. 5:17). This does not mean that when you rise in the morning, you pray throughout the rest of the day on a non-stop basis. What this means is that we, as Christians, are not to give up on prayer as a way of communicating with the heavenly Father, as a way of making intercession, and as a way of making our petitions known to Him.

...with all prayer...

This statement immediately alerts us to the fact that there are different kinds of prayer. The prayer that most people know is "Lord, give me, give me, give me. My name is Jimmy and I'll take all you'll give me!" Technically, this type of praying is called the "prayer of petition." There are actually several ways of praying that Christians should be involved in. Each kind of prayer is governed by a specific spiritual rule or law. One reason why more people do not accomplish very much through prayer is because they are often using the wrong rules for the type of prayer they are praying.

No one has any problem with playing sports according to the rules established for a particular sport. Whether we realize it or not, the Christian life is also circumscribed by certain rules and regulations. Our heavenly Father is a God of precision, and everything functions according to a prescribed set of laws, and if we do not flow with these rules or laws, we will be penalized in life. Unfortunately, the devil is the referee, and he is looking for any infraction on our part so that he can enforce a penalty.

Since Satan is a legalist, any time we make a mistake, he is on us like white on rice in order to bomb us out. And there is nothing that God can do about it because He has already done all He intends to do for this present time. He has given us His rule book (the Bible) to follow, and we can keep the devil off our backs if we play according to the rules. Tragically, the majority of Christians do not take time to read the rule book, so they make mistakes in life. And some of us who read it, do not understand what we are reading. That is why God has placed teachers in the Body of Christ. If we could understand without a teacher, there would not be any need for teachers. The very fact that the Bible says that God has set **"...apostles; ...prophets;... evangelists;... pastors, and teachers..."** (Eph. 4:11) in the Church lets us know that the Church needs teachers.

The important thing to remember is that we have to listen to the teachers. This does not mean that the teacher knows everything, and that what he or she says is *always* the gospel truth. It simply means that there is such a thing as a teaching gift in the Body of Christ. If we do not follow the rules by allowing the teaching gift to work, we will end up missing something.

...all [manner of] prayer...

There are at least five different kinds of prayer, and each kind is circumscribed by a different set of rules. If you try to use prayer-number-one rule with prayer-number-three, your prayer will not work, even though you are as sincere as you can possibly be. We do not receive an answer to prayer because of sincerity. We receive an answer because we pray according to the rules established in God's Word.

384

The first kind of prayer we will discuss is the Prayer of Dedication and Consecration. We have a good illustration of this method of praying in the twenty-sixth chapter of Matthew's Gospel, beginning at verse 36:

> Then cometh Jesus with them unto a place called Gethsemane, and saith unto the disciples, Sit ye here, while I go and pray yonder. And he took with him Peter and the two sons of Zebedee, and began to be sorrowful and very heavy. Then saith he unto them, My soul is exceeding sorrowful, even unto death: tarry ye here, and watch with me. And he went a little farther, and fell on his face, and prayed, saying, O my Father, if it be possible, let this cup pass from me: nevertheless not as I will, but as thou wilt. And he cometh unto the disciples, and findeth them asleep, and saith unto Peter, What, could ye not watch with me one hour? Watch and pray, that ye enter not into temptation: the spirit indeed is willing, but the flesh is weak.

Let us stick a pin here. I believe one reason why some Christians are having prayer problems is because they are not doing what Jesus said — **"Watch and pray."** They may be watching, but they are watching the wrong thing in the wrong way. "Boy, she sure is pretty!" That kind of watching can get you into trouble. "Oh, isn't he handsome! Look at all that curly black hair. I would sure like to run my hands through his hair." That is not the kind of "watching" Jesus was talking about. Look at that verse again. He has given us a tremendous rule to follow here:

Watch and pray, that ye enter not into temptation...

Notice something very carefully. Jesus did not say, "Watch and pray, and ye will not be tempted." The very fact that he says, **"that ye enter not into temptation"** means that the temptation is there. However, the temptation is nothing until you enter into it. Could it be that the reason some believers are finding themselves embroiled in temptation, is because they are not watching and praying? No one is immune to temptation. Some people might think because I am the pastor of a church that there is some kind of exoneration for me. Friend, that means I have more opportunities to blow it, more opportunities to mess up. This is true of anyone who is in a leadership position. There are all kinds of temptations I could enter into, but I have been watching and praying. And, thank God, I have been, because it has kept me from messing up. If you think that you are ever going to get to a point in life where you are so spiritual that you are not going to be tempted, forget it! There is no such place. In fact, the higher you go in the things of the spirit, the greater the temptations.

Watch and pray....

The devil comes in very subtle ways, ways that seem so innocent. If you are not careful, before you realize it, you find yourself into something. You may not have meant to be, but that does not make any difference. If you mess up, you will be disqualified from the game, and you will be penalized. Satan will see to it that you are.

He went away again the second time, and prayed, saying, O my Father, if this cup may not pass away from me, except I drink it, thy will be done.

(Matt. 26:42)

This is the Prayer of Consecration and Dedication, and there is a particular rule that governs this kind of prayer. If you use that rule for any other kind of prayer, you will cancel or short-circuit your prayer.

The Prayer of Consecration and Dedication is the only prayer where we are to ever use the statement, "if it be thy will." To use this statement with any other prayer will cancel the prayer. People have used "if it be thy will" with almost every prayer they have prayed, thinking they were being humble: "Lord, heal me, if it be thy will." "Lord take this pain away from me, if it be thy will." These statements usually come from a false sense of humility which, in turn, comes from a feeling of not being worthy of God's healing. What people do not understand is that if they use statements like this in praying for healing, unless they have a good doctor, they may die. This, too, is why many believers who were prayed for that way died.

I prayed that way for years until I got wise to the Word. Every prayer I ever prayed ended with "if it be thy will." Perhaps you are still ending your prayers this way, and I do not say this to condemn you, but I want to clarify some things so you can understand why your prayers may not have worked.

If we say, "if it be thy will," we are saying that we do not know what God's will is. Because if we knew what His will was, why would we insult Him by saying, "if?" The word *if* is always the badge of doubt.

In illustrating Jesus' use of the statement, **"if it be thy will,"** we have to understand that Jesus was coming to that point in His life for which He had been born, which was to die and become the Lamb of God who takes away the sin of the world. We also have to understand that just as much as Jesus was the Son of God, He was also a man. He did not get His body from heaven. He received His flesh from Mary, His mother.

Jesus was a man who had desires like other men, which He suppressed for the greater desire to fulfill the will of His Father. He had to deny himself things in the earth-realm in order to please the Father. He said at one point in His ministry: **"I do always those things that please him** [the Father]" (John 8:29).

No one wants to die — people want to live. And Jesus wanted to live. But He knew that His purpose for coming to the Earth was to redeem the world; however, as He approached the hour when He had to become sin for us, the physical part of Him recoiled.

From the day of Adam and Eve, Jesus was the only man who walked the Earth in whom there was no sin. His flesh had never experienced the degradation of sin; therefore, His flesh recoiled at the thought of being made sin. Additionally, He had never been separated from God. He had known perfect fellowship with the

Father from time immemorial. Now that He was going to become sin for the sake of all mankind, He was going to have to experience what had never happened to Him before — separation from His Father.

Jesus did not want this separation, but He was obedient even unto death. So He said, in essence, "Father, if there is another way to redeem mankind without me having to become sin, let it be done. Let this cup pass from me. Not my will, but thy will be done." The cup represented what sin was, and Jesus was going to have to drink that cup, which meant He would become sin. The Bible says: **"For he hath made him to be sin for us, who knew no sin; that we might be made the righteousness of God in him"** (2 Cor. 5:21).

I used the Prayer of Consecration and Dedication in keeping with what Jesus showed us about this prayer format. Many years ago, when I started out in a little church located on the west side of Los Angeles, we were bursting at the seams. We were packing 300 people each week into a little building that seated only 158 people comfortably. Folks started arriving at 9:30 AM on Sunday mornings for Bible study so they could be in the building at 11:00, when worship services began.

I could see that we were well out of room and we had to do something. In addition, the denomination that I was in at that time did not look too kindly upon the gifts of the Spirit as we practiced them. So I knew we were going to have to make a clean break from this denomination.

As long as I remained in the denomination, I had full use of the church building and the church grounds. But if I ceased to be affiliated with this particular group, the property would revert to the parent organization. I did not know where to go, and I did not know what to do. I knew God was dealing with my spirit about starting a ministry that would be non-denominational and full-gospel in the truest sense of those words.

I laid my desire before the Lord (I thought about Jesus in the Garden, and I prayed as He did). I said: "Now, Lord, if it be thy will that I start a church in Los Angeles, I will do that. If it be thy will that I start a church in Inglewood, I will do that. And if it be thy will that I start a storefront church, I will do that, even though that is not my desire. I am willing to do whatever your will is for me to do."

Why did I pray such a prayer? Simply because I could not go to the Bible and find chapter and verse that said, "Fred Price, go to Inglewood, California, and start Crenshaw Christian Center." In essence, I was saying, "Lord, I am willing to do whatever you want me to do and go wherever you want me to go — not my will be done, but yours."

Later, the Lord showed me this church in Inglewood. We did not have any money, but the Lord said, *"This is it!"* I and some members of my staff walked around the building and the church grounds and said, "We declare this property to be ours, in the name of Jesus. And, Lord, just as you told Joshua to walk around the walls of Jericho and you would give him the city, we believe we now receive this property into the ministry and that Crenshaw Christian Center will be the result."

That is the Prayer of Consecration and Dedication. However, if I need some money to pay bills and I pray "if it be thy will," I am going to the poor farm. If I am sick, and the doctor tells me I am about to die and I pray, "Lord, if it be thy will, heal me," the doctor may as well go ahead and sign the death certificate.

I know of people who have prayed, "Lord, you know I need a new car and I would like (I am just using this as an example) the biggest Oldsmobile there is — a total luxury car, 'if it be thy will,'" and then suddenly someone comes to them with a Volkswagen at a good price. (Understand, now, I am not talking about the quality of cars, but there is an obvious difference between the size of an Oldsmobile and a Volkswagen.) They responded, "Well, the Lord knew it was better that I have a Volkswagen. Maybe the Lord knew that if I got that big Oldsmobile, I might become proud and might even stop going to church."

If you prayed for an Oldsmobile and you got a Volkswagen, God did not answer your prayer. God did not have a thing in the world to do with it, because it is not what you asked for. Why would you say that God gave you a Volkswagen when you had asked for an Oldsmobile? Are you saying that God's integrity is not worth anything?

Jesus said once, "What man of you, having a son, if he came to you and asked for bread would you give him a rock? Or, if he asked for a fish, would you give him a serpent?" Then He went on to say, "If you being evil know how to give good gifts unto your children, how much more shall your heavenly Father give good things to them that ask him?" (Matt. 7:9-11).

Christians have been tricked into accepting things that God did not have anything to do with — and, yet, people blame God for them. "Well, the Lord knew I should have this imbecile baby." That is not what you prayed for, therefore, it is not the work of God. Understand that the devil can answer prayers, too, in order to get you to accept something less than what you prayed for, and then blame God for it.

The second kind of prayer I want to talk about is the Prayer of Faith, which is a prayer of petition. It is found in Mark's Gospel, the eleventh chapter.

> **Therefore I say unto you, What things soever ye desire, when ye pray, believe that ye receive them, and ye shall have them. And when ye stand praying, forgive, if you have ought against any: that your Father also which is in heaven may forgive you your trespasses. But if you do not forgive, neither will your Father which is in heaven forgive you your trespasses.**
>
> **(Mark 11:24-25)**

Simply stated, this means that if you go to God to exercise the prayer of faith, and you have malice in your heart against your wife, your husband, your children, your boss, your pastor, or anyone else, and you do not forgive them, your faith is automatically short-circuited, and your prayer will not work.

The formula for petition prayer is when you pray — not after you pray, not six months later, not when you see something, but when you pray. When you pray would be N-O-W. That is what Hebrews 11:1 says: **"Now faith is...."** It does not say, "Tomorrow faith is...."

Or, "Yesterday faith was...." It says that faith is *now* — present tense. In other words, your desire is to be expressed when you pray, not after you pray.

Notice also that it does not say, "Feel like it," or "Understand it." It says, "Believe it." How do you believe something that you cannot see? This happens in the same way that you believe your employer is going to give you some money at the end of the forty hours of work, even though you have not seen his bank account or even know if he has money in it to pay you or not. No one has ever challenged his or her employer to show his checkbook, to see if he has enough money to pay him or her. They have more confidence in the word of a man — who may not even believe in God — than they do the Word of their heavenly Father.

In fact, they believe the employer's word so much that they go and spend the money before they receive it. They may even purchase a car, furniture, or clothes, based on the fact they *believe* they are going to receive money for the time they have worked.

However, when it comes to the things of God, we have to have a sign. Why not ask the employer for a sign? No, we willingly take him at his word. The principle is the same. The employer does not show us anything for us to believe him, but we do anyway. Why not do the same with God, the One who upholds the universe by His own power and might? Why not take Him at His Word? The Prayer of Faith requires you to believe you receive when you pray, and you have to pray in line with God's Word.

The third kind of prayer is the Prayer of Agreement. The very fact that I said "agreement" alerts us to what kind of praying this must be — you and other individuals are in one accord.

Again I say unto you, That if two of you shall agree on earth as touching any thing that they shall ask, it shall be done for them of my Father which is in heaven.

(Matt. 18:19)

It is not necessary to use the Prayer of Agreement in order to get an answer from God. However, the idea of this form of prayer is that if your faith is not sufficiently developed, or if you do not believe that your faith is strong enough to bring to pass the thing you desire, you can pool your faith together to get the job done.

The important thing is not the people who are involved; rather, the important thing is the level of faith generated by each of the agreeing parties. By the believers coming together in agreement, they can pray as one unit, and God can move on behalf of the prayer when the needed faith force is produced by the agreeing parties.

It is important to understand that faith is a spiritual force, and it can be operating at a greater or lesser degree of manifestation at any given time. Jesus made that very plain throughout the gospels when He referred to the faith of the people involved in the particular situation. He said on one occasion: "O thou of *little* faith, why did you doubt?" On another occasion, He said, "I have not found so *great* faith." Another time, He said, "According to your faith be it done unto you." So it shows that faith can be at a greater or lesser degree of manifestation.

For example, in the homes around our nation some houses are wired for 110 to 115 volts of AC electricity, and some homes are wired for 220 volts. If you have a home that is wired for 110 volts and buy an appliance that is designed to operate on 220 volts, nothing is going to happen when you plug it in, because there is not enough power being generated. What you would have to do is upgrade the electrical output from 110 to at least 220 volts.

Think of a problem in your life — perhaps a sickness or a disease in your body — that is like a 220-volt problem, but you only have 110 volts of faith operating. You need to step up your faith output to move that 220-volt problem. What you would have to do is to find a brother or a sister in Christ who has at least a 110-volt faith, and the two of you join your faith together. You now have 220-volts of faith, if both of you get into agreement on the same thing. In other words, the faith of the agreeing parties can work on behalf of the person who needs the prayer, and God can bring healing to pass.

The important thing to remember when using this prayer format is that there must be agreement. If not, your prayer will be nullified. If we do not operate in the appropriate spiritual laws, we will not get the desired results. That is why, when someone asks me to pray with him or her, I first locate where the person is faith-wise and what am I asked to agree to. I may not agree with what they are praying about. Personally, I lived too many years when prayer did not work, and since I found out how it does work, I am not going back to what I used to have. I am going to operate in what works now.

When people say to me, "Pray for me," I always ask, "Pray for what?" This sometimes throws them a curve, but you cannot intelligently pray about something if you do not know what it is they want. There must be agreement. If one party is praying to die, and the parties who have been asked to agree with the person are praying he lives, the prayer for life will not work because there is no agreement. Then when the person dies, people wonder why the prayer was not answered. They think that it is not God's will to heal everyone.

Another person's prayer cannot override the will of someone else. If a person wants to die, 5,000,000 people can pray for him or her to be healed, but their prayers will not work. God does not allow us to exercise faith over someone else's will. I am glad that He does not, because if He did, folks would be putting all kinds of things off on each other. No one can exercise his will over yours — unless you allow him to.

The Bible says that it is not God's will that any should perish, but that all should come to repentance (2 Pet. 3:9). Yet people die and go to hell all the time. If God was violating people's wills, He would make everyone get saved.

You have to find out, when you are praying for people, what they really want before you tell them that you agree. They may want you to agree for a $75,000 Mercedes-Benz or a $500,000 house. There is nothing wrong with these things, and God wants His children to have them. But do they have enough faith to maintain these expenses if they were to get them? Can they afford to keep the car tuned up, can they afford the yearly license fees, or taxes, or monthly notes? There is no point in going to all the trouble to believe for them to get the car or the house if they will not be able to keep them. So find out what the person wants, and then decide if you want to agree. If you do, both of you have to say the same thing and make the ongoing confession of faith over the situation. When that happens, God will move on behalf of the prayer when enough faith is being generated by the persons involved.

The best people to effect the Prayer of Agreement are a husband and wife. That is, if both are walking in the Word, and there is harmony between them. My wife and I pray in agreement on just about everything in our lives, from our children to the ministry, and God has never failed to answer our prayers. I encourage every Christian couple to learn to utilize this powerful form of prayer.

The fourth kind of prayer is the Prayer of Thanksgiving. Do you take time to thank the Lord? Do you thank Him that every one of your taste buds is working right, that your nose is smelling as it should, that you can taste an orange and smell its delightful aroma? Do you ever thank God for your eyes and the ability to see His great creation? Or do you take God's blessings for granted and not give a thought to what He has done and is doing in your life?

In the Prayer of Thanksgiving you are not asking God for anything, but rather you're telling Him, "Lord, I love you, I appreciate you, I thank you. I thank you for saving me. I thank you for adopting me into your family, I thank you for placing my name in the Lamb's Book of Life. I want to thank you for filling me with the Holy Spirit. I want to thank you for giving me a detachment of angels to walk with me. I want to thank you that you brought me out of darkness, into your marvelous light. I want to thank you, Father, for the covenant that I have with you. I want to thank you for the promises you have given to me. I want to thank you for blessing me — blessing me when I go out and when I come in. I want to thank you for blessing me in the city and blessing me on the beach and blessing me in the country. I want to thank you for making me the head and not the tail, and for placing me above and not beneath."

Do you ever thank the Lord? Or, is it constantly, "My name is Jimmy, so give me, give me, give me — I'll take all you'll give me!" That is the way most people pray. They never just thank God for His kindness, mercy, and His ever-flowing blessings. The Prayer of Thanksgiving is the simplest way of praying, but it is one of the most effective ways to pray.

The fifth kind of prayer is the Prayer of Intercession. Technically, intercession means to take the place of someone else. Intercessory prayer is when you are praying for someone else, not for yourself.

One of the reasons I believe God has given Christians the capacity to pray with other tongues (that is those who have been filled with the Holy Spirit) is because tongues is the most perfect way to pray, and it is especially beneficial when praying for other people. Nine times out of ten we do not know enough facts about a person or a particular situation in order to pray effectively. But the Holy Spirit does, which makes it a great benefit to pray with tongues. When we pray in the understanding, we end up praying based on our perceived knowledge, which means that our prayers will be limited to what we know about a particular person, place, or thing.

The Holy Spirit, the third person of the Godhead, knows everything, and praying in our heavenly language makes us much more effective because we are praying in accordance with His guidance. (See Rom. 8:26.)

When you pray in the spirit, you are praying by your spirit in a coded language to the heavenly Father. Two very important things happen at this time: Number one, your mind cannot get in the way to confuse the issues, and number two, neither can the devil.

By way of illustration: Have you ever been praying in your understanding, perhaps on your knees by your bed, when all of a sudden, out of the clear blue sky, the thought pops into your mind: "Did you lock the back door and put the dog out?" What does the door and dog have to do with your praying? But because praying occurs in the same arena as your thinking process, your prayer was interrupted.

I have heard some people talk about praying while they are driving. There is no way in the world you can drive and pray at the same time, unless you are praying in the spirit. You had better keep your mind on the road, or you may end up in a ditch, or worse. However, when you pray with other tongues, your mind is free, because the prayer is not coming out of your mind, but out of your spirit — out of your heart. Consequently, you can pray with other tongues and drive at the same time. Your mind is taking care of the driving, controlling your body in terms of what needs to be done at the time, while your spirit is talking to the Father God in a language that cannot be interrupted by your mind or the devil. It is the perfect way to pray.

Another benefit of praying with other tongues is that Satan does not know what you are saying or what you are praying about. Yes, he knows you are praying, but since you are speaking in a coded language, he does not know what is being said. However, when you are praying in your natural language, he does know what you are saying. Therefore, he can interject some thoughts into your mind while you are praying.

Another important thing to remember about prayer is that when you pray in the understanding, you should pray specific things. Some people pray unspecified prayers and leave themselves open to receive unspecified answers: "Lord, bless so-and-so." What does "bless him" or "bless her" mean? The Bible tells us we are already blessed (Eph. 1:3).

You would never send your child to the store with a ten-dollar bill and say, "Bring back some food" or "Bring back ten dollars worth of groceries." More than likely the child would ask, "What kind of groceries?" "What kind of food?" Even children know you cannot send them to the store without telling them specifically what you want. But that is what most people do when they tell God to bless someone without being specific as to what kind of blessing is needed. Is it a job that is needed, or healing for the body, or a broken marriage restored? What blessing?

It takes time to pray. Often, people just jump out of bed at the last minute and do not spend much time in prayer. They have been up most of the night, watching the late show on television. Then they get up in the morning and spend two minutes in prayer for their conscience's sake. The bless-so-and-so type of prayer becomes the catch-all prayer for everyone and everything. Prayer is like most everything else in life, you only get out of it what you put into it.

There is what is called a burden of prayer or a burden of intercession. It is not a "burden" in a negative sense. This terminology is used to describe an intense urge to pray about a specific person or a particular situation. It is true intercession when you pray in the spirit. In this kind of atmosphere, you pray until the burden lifts. It may be for fifteen minutes, or an hour, or it might be all day. The important thing is to pray until you receive a release in your spirit. You will know when this happens.

As I said before, it takes time to pray. I usually spend about an hour and a half during my prayer time each day: one hour praying with other tongues and one-half hour praying in the understanding. That is a lot of time out of the day, but the benefits are well worth the time spent.

Christians need to pray one for another. Satan is out to get us all, and we are all in the same family — the family of God. We need to rally around one another just as worldly families do when a member of the family gets hurt. Too often, we just walk by one another and never give one another a second thought. We are in the same family, and we are going to live together throughout eternity.

We ought to pray specifically for one another in a true spirit of intercession. We should pray every day for our national leaders and our governments, both nationally and locally. We should pray for the unsaved and that the Lord of the harvest will send the right laborer to the right people. (See Matt. 9:37-38.)

There is an old saying: "Prayer changes things." That is not quite true. It is not prayer that changes things, it is the exercising of faith on the part of the children of God that changes things through the vehicle of prayer. Faith is what causes the change!

Through prayer, you can change things in your own circumstances. If you do not like what is happening to you, start changing the circumstances by your praying, by your confessing, by your believing, and by your acting on the Word.

Christians are not victims of circumstances! That is glorious news. We are not out there like leaves blown from the trees by the mighty winds of time. We can change and alter our course. I have done it through the principles outlined in the Word of God. And I am not talking about any mind-over-matter business either. I am talking about taking the Word to deliberately bring about a change in your life through believing what God has said about you as His child. Satan will try to get involved and deceive you into thinking that a change is not possible. I am telling you that faith in the Bible and operating in the principles it outlines works. I have proved that faith works, and I know many, many others who have proven the same thing. God is no respecter of persons, so you can count on the Word working for you.

> And for me, that utterance may be given unto me, that I may open my mouth boldly, to make known the mystery of the gospel, For which I am an ambassador in bonds: that therein I may speak boldly, as I ought to speak. But that ye also may know my affairs, and how I do, Tychicus, a beloved brother and faithful minister in the Lord, shall make known to you all things: Whom I have sent unto you for the same purpose, that ye might know our affairs, and that he might comfort your hearts. Peace be to the brethren, and love with faith, from God the Father and the Lord Jesus Christ. Grace be with all them that love our Lord Jesus Christ in sincerity. Amen.
>
> **(Eph. 6:19-24)**

This is the conclusion of Ephesians. Of course, what I have said about this important New Testament book is not all there is to say and teach, but it is all that the Spirit of God has given me concerning it based on my level of faith, understanding, and spirituality at this time in my life.

I expect that as time goes on, I will know more about this book than I do now. The Word of God is pregnant in that it constantly gives birth to new facets of revelation as you apply yourself to it.

End Notes

1. James Strong, *The New Strong's Exhaustive Concordance of the Bible*, Greek Dictionary, #4841, Thomas Nelson Publishers, P. 68.

2. W.E. Vine, *An Expository Dictionary of New Testament Words*, Third printing, Thomas Nelson Publishers, P. 913.

3. *The New Strong's Exhaustive Concordance of the Bible*, #758, P. 16.

4. Ibid, #1847, P. 30.

5. *Vine's Expository Dictionary of Biblical Words*, P. 128, 1985, Thomas Nelson Publishers.

6. *Vine's Expository Dictionary of Biblical Words*, P. 50.

7. *The New Strong's Exhaustive Concordance of the Bible*, #391, P. 225.

8. *Vine's Expository Dictionary of Biblical Words*, P. 472.

9. *The New Strong's Concordance of the Bible*, #433, P. 12.

10. *Vine's Expository Dictionary of Biblical Words*, P. 113.

11. *Vine's Expository Dictionary of Biblical Words*, P. 164.

12. *Vine's Expository Dictionary of Biblical Words*, P. 676.

13. *Vine's Expository Dictionary of Biblical Words*, P. 540.

14. *The New Strong's Concordance of the Bible*, #956, P. 19.

15. *The New Strong's Concordance of the Bible*, #1598, P. 27.

For a complete list of books and tapes by Dr. Frederick K.C. Price, or to receive his publication, *Ever Increasing Faith Messenger*, write:

Dr. Fred Price
Crenshaw Christian Center
P. O. Box 90000
Los Angeles, CA 90009

Books by Frederick K. C. Price, Ph.D.

HIGH FINANCE
(God's Financial Plan: Tithes and Offerings)
HOW FAITH WORKS
(In English and Spanish)
IS HEALING FOR ALL?
HOW TO OBTAIN STRONG FAITH
(Six Principles)
NOW FAITH IS
THE HOLY SPIRIT —
The Missing Ingredient
FAITH, FOOLISHNESS, OR PRESUMPTION?
THANK GOD FOR EVERYTHING?
HOW TO BELIEVE GOD FOR A MATE
MARRIAGE AND THE FAMILY
LIVING IN THE REALM OF THE SPIRIT
THE ORIGIN OF SATAN
CONCERNING THEM WHICH ARE ASLEEP
HOMOSEXUALITY:
State of Birth or State of Mind?
PROSPERITY ON GOD'S TERMS
WALKING IN GOD'S WORD
(Through His Promises)
KEYS TO SUCCESSFUL MINISTRY
NAME IT AND CLAIM IT!
The Power of Positive Confession
THE VICTORIOUS, OVERCOMING LIFE
(A Verse-by-Verse Study of the Book of Colossians)
A NEW LAW FOR A NEW PEOPLE
THE FAITHFULNESS OF GOD
THE PROMISED LAND
(A New Era for the Body of Christ)
THREE KEYS TO POSITIVE CONFESSION
THE WAY, THE WALK, AND THE WARFARE
OF THE BELIEVER

Available from your local bookstore

About the Author

Frederick K.C. Price, Ph.D., founded Crenshaw Christian Center in Los Angeles, California, in 1973, with a congregation of some 300 people. Today, the church's membership numbers well over 14,000 members of various racial backgrounds.

Crenshaw Christian Center, home of the renowned 10,146-seat FaithDome, has a staff of more than 250 employees. Included on its thirty-acre grounds are a Ministry Training Institute, the Crenshaw Christian Center Correspondence School, the Frederick K.C. Price III Elementary and Junior High School, as well as a Child Care Center.

The "Ever Increasing Faith" television and radio broadcasts are outreaches of Crenshaw Christian Center. The television program is viewed on more than 100 stations throughout the United States and overseas. The radio program airs on approximately forty stations across the country.

Dr. Price travels extensively, teaching on the Word of Faith forcefully in the power of the Holy Spirit. He is the author of several books on faith and divine healing.

In 1990, Dr. Price founded the Fellowship of Inner-City Word of Faith Ministries (FICWFM) for the purpose of fostering and spreading the faith message among independent ministries located in the urban, metropolitan areas of the United States.